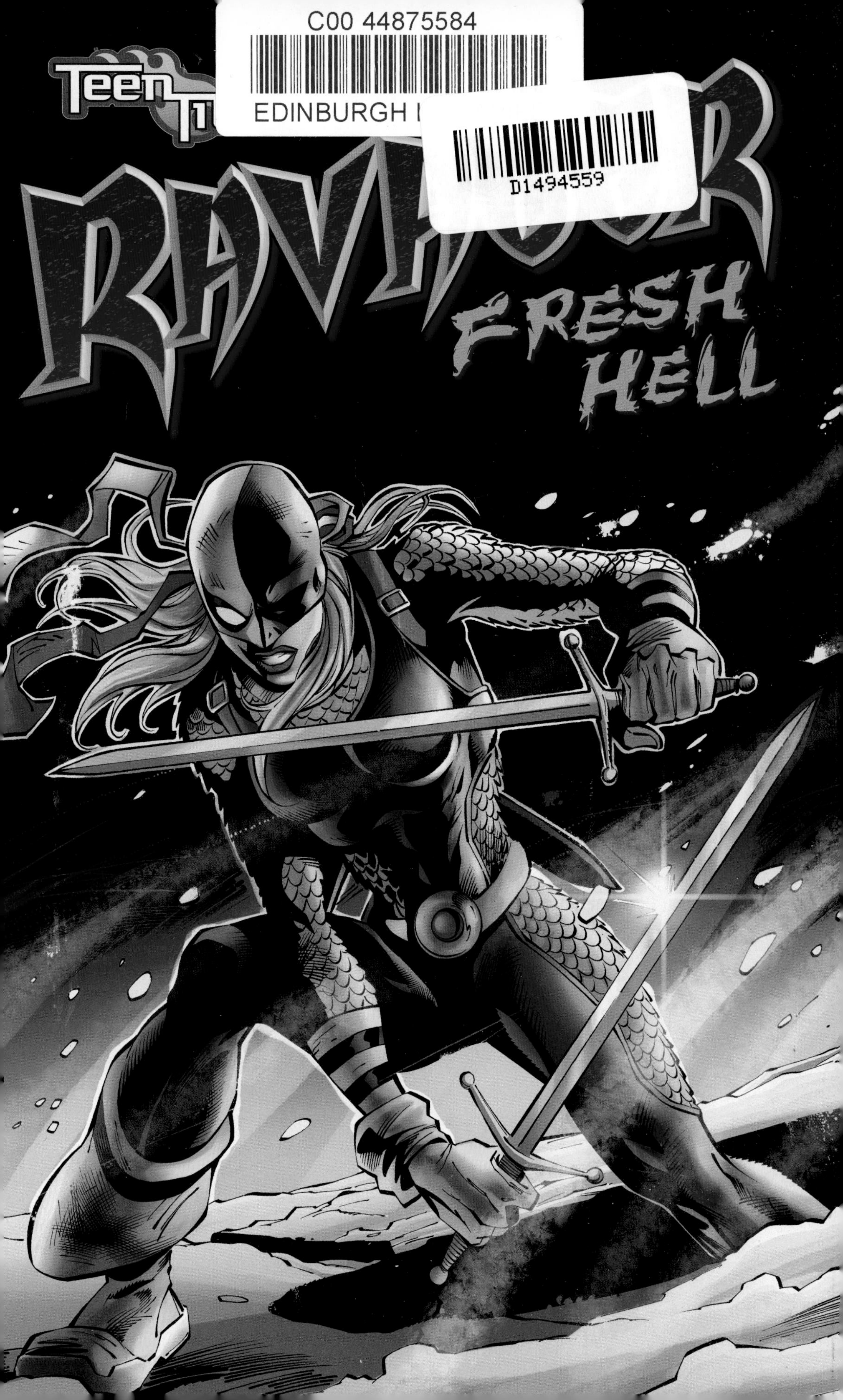
Teen
FRESH
HELL

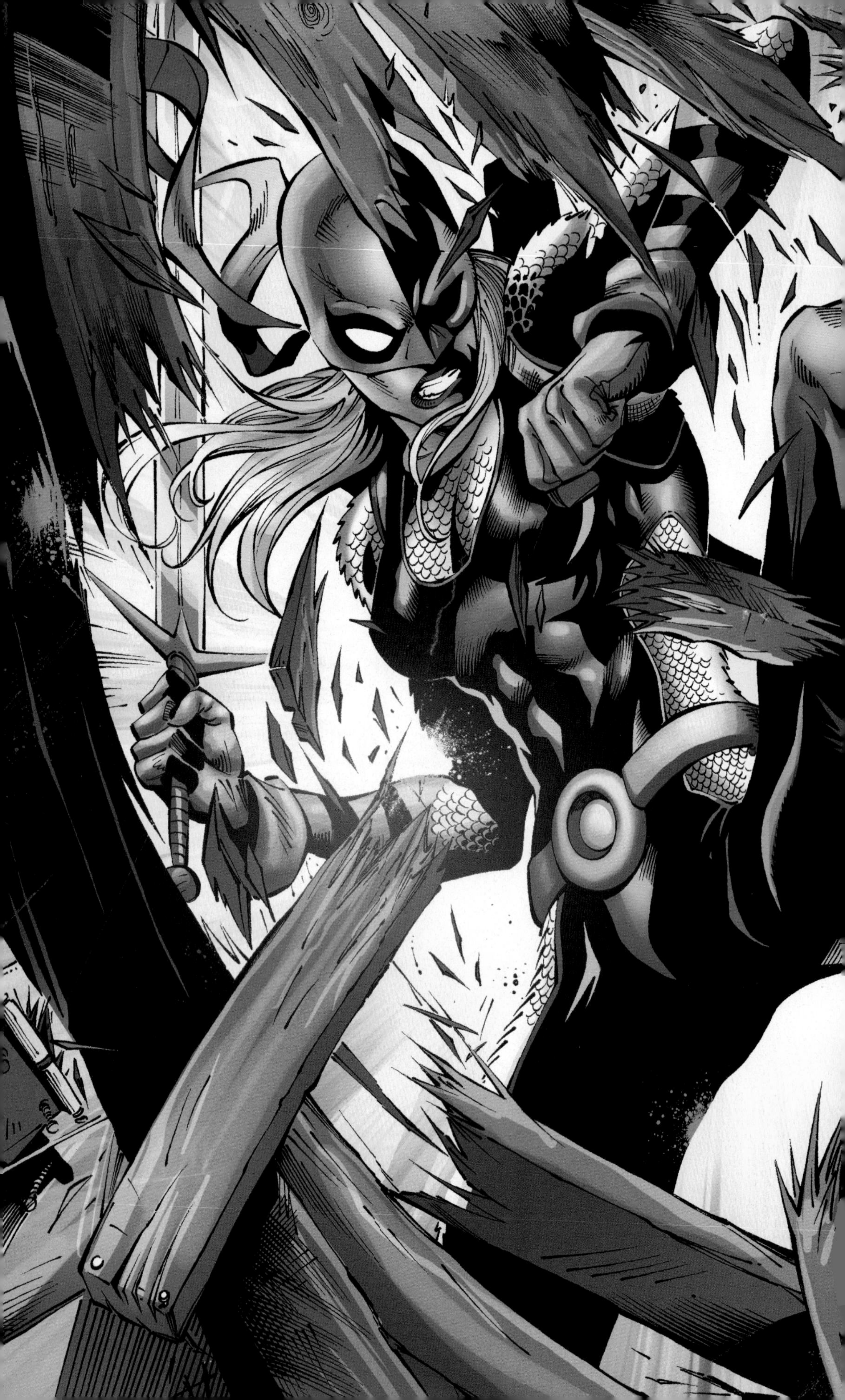

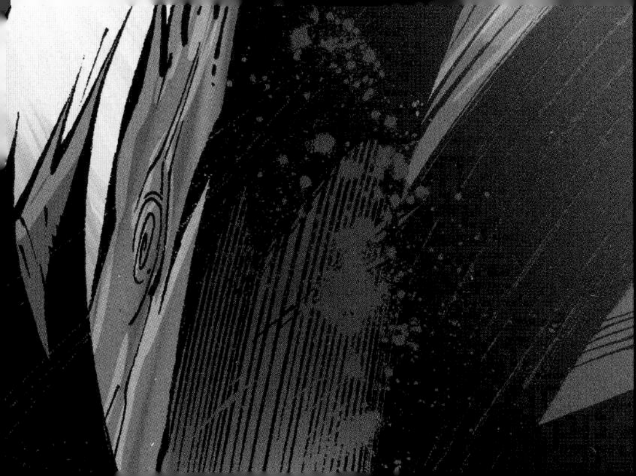

Colorists

Sal Cipriano
Pat Brosseau

Letterers

Yildiray Cinar

Collection cover

Deathstroke & Ravager created

Marv Wolfman & Georg

A Warner Bros. Entertainment Company
Printed by Quad/Graphics,
Dubuque, IA, USA. 11/24/10. First Printing.
ISBN: 978-1-4012-2919-1

SUSTAINABLE
FORESTRY
INITIATIVE

Certified Chain of Custody
Promoting Sustainable
Forest Management
www.sfiprogram.org

Fiber used in this product line meets the sourcing requirements
of the SFI program. www.sfiprogram.org PWC-SFICOC-260

Cover by Ladrönn

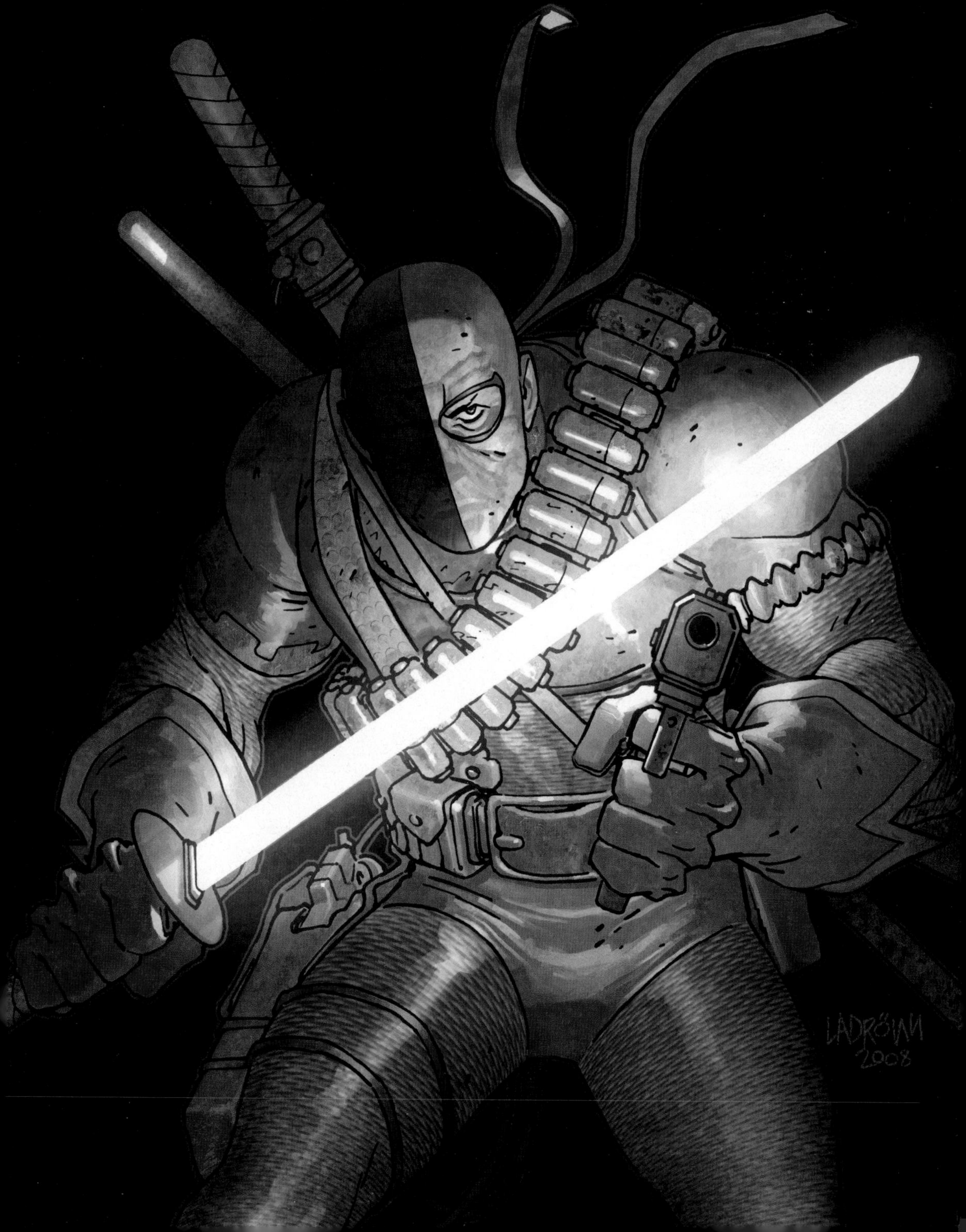
LADRÖNN
2008

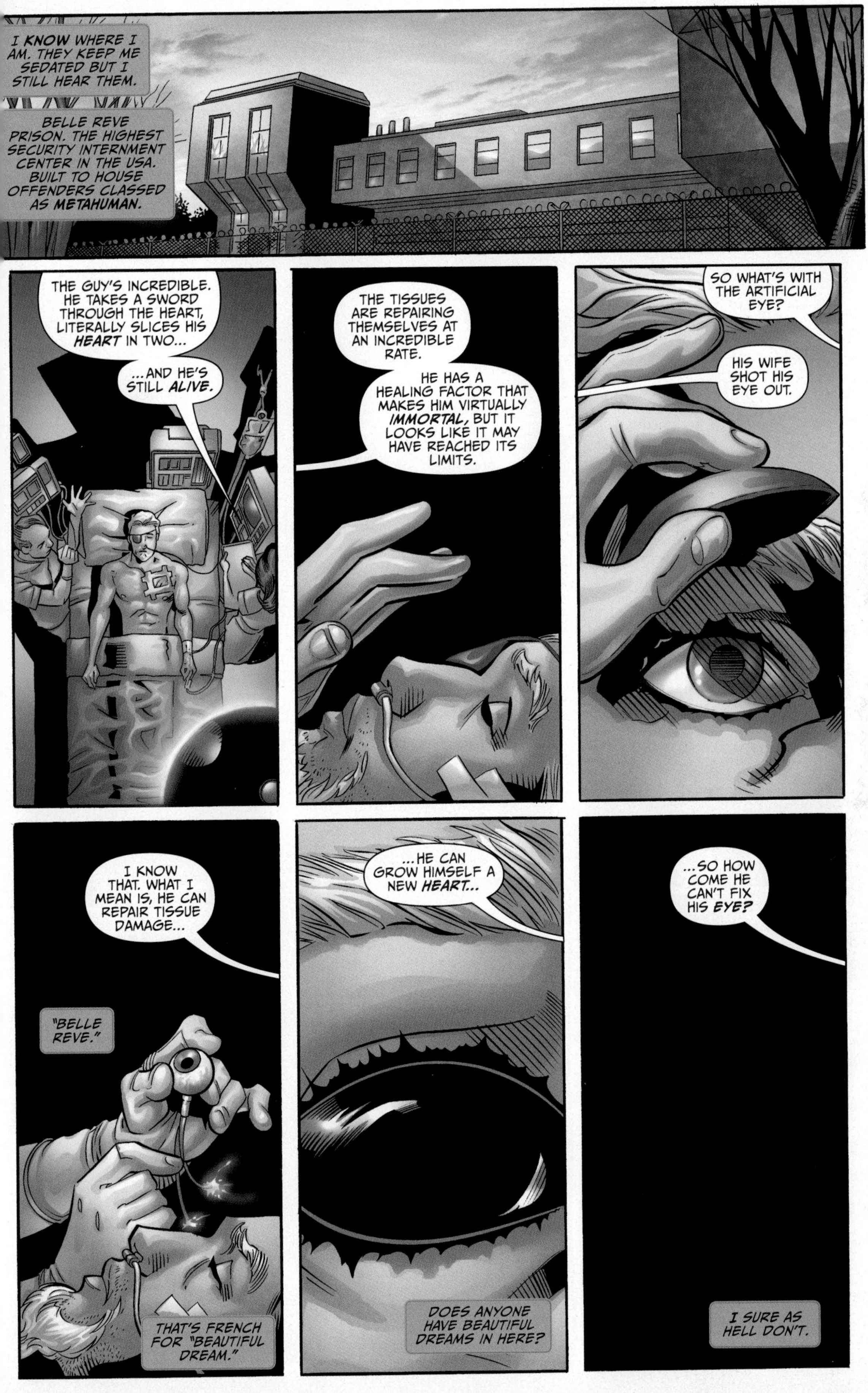
I KNOW WHERE I AM. THEY KEEP ME SEDATED BUT I STILL HEAR THEM.
BELLE REVE PRISON. THE HIGHEST SECURITY INTERNMENT CENTER IN THE USA. BUILT TO HOUSE OFFENDERS CLASSED AS METAHUMAN.
THE GUY'S INCREDIBLE. HE TAKES A SWORD THROUGH THE HEART, LITERALLY SLICES HIS HEART IN TWO...
...AND HE'S STILL ALIVE.
THE TISSUES ARE REPAIRING THEMSELVES AT AN INCREDIBLE RATE.
HE HAS A HEALING FACTOR THAT MAKES HIM VIRTUALLY IMMORTAL, BUT IT LOOKS LIKE IT MAY HAVE REACHED ITS LIMITS.
SO WHAT'S WITH THE ARTIFICIAL EYE?
HIS WIFE SHOT HIS EYE OUT.
I KNOW THAT. WHAT I MEAN IS, HE CAN REPAIR TISSUE DAMAGE...
"BELLE REVE."
THAT'S FRENCH FOR "BEAUTIFUL DREAM."
...HE CAN GROW HIMSELF A NEW HEART...
DOES ANYONE HAVE BEAUTIFUL DREAMS IN HERE?
...SO HOW COME HE CAN'T FIX HIS EYE?
I SURE AS HELL DON'T.

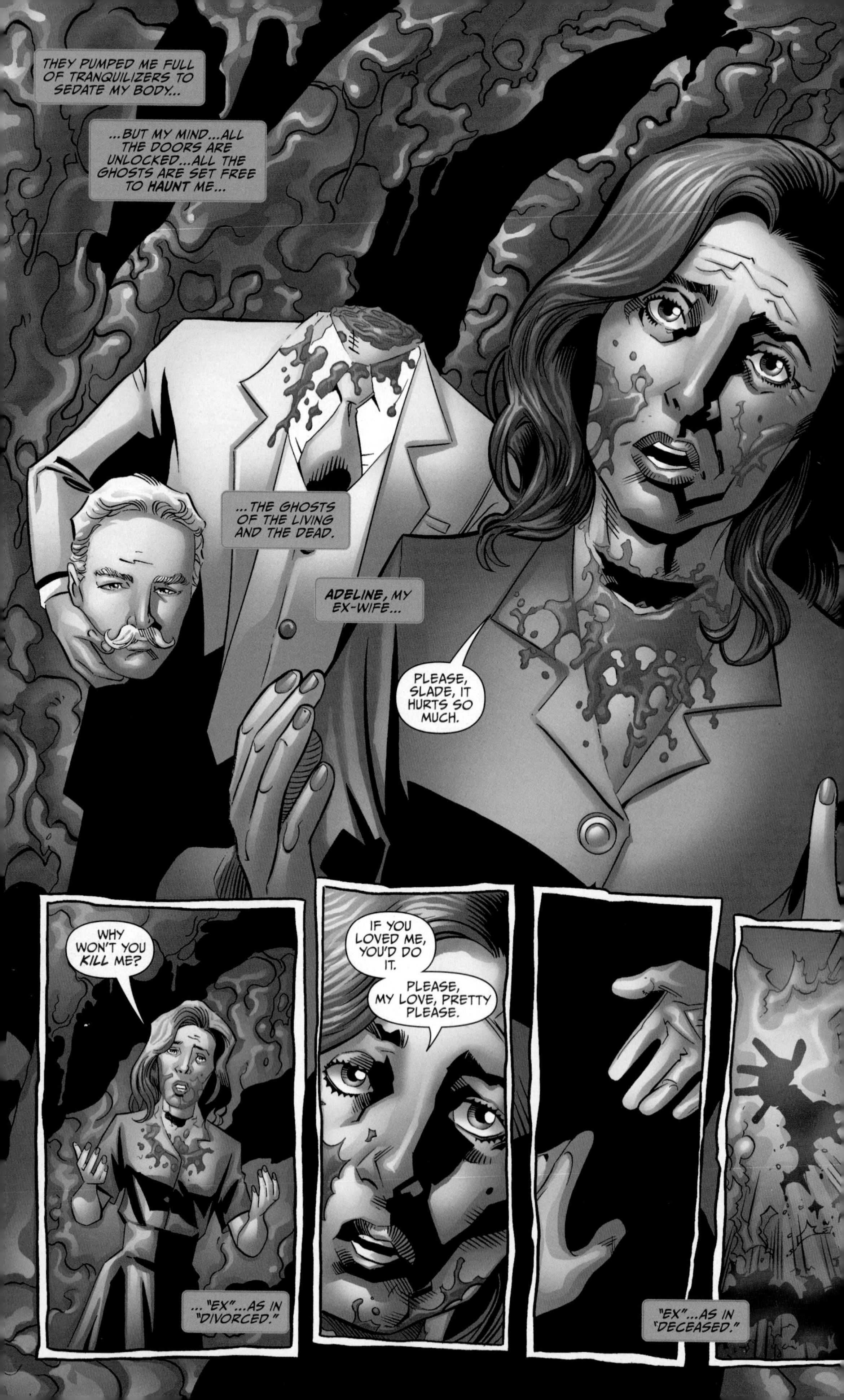
THEY PUMPED ME FULL OF TRANQUILIZERS TO SEDATE MY BODY...
...BUT MY MIND...ALL THE DOORS ARE UNLOCKED...ALL THE GHOSTS ARE SET FREE TO HAUNT ME...
...THE GHOSTS OF THE LIVING AND THE DEAD.
ADELINE, MY EX-WIFE...
PLEASE, SLADE, IT HURTS SO MUCH.
WHY WON'T YOU KILL ME?
..."EX"...AS IN "DIVORCED."
IF YOU LOVED ME, YOU'D DO IT.
PLEASE, MY LOVE, PRETTY PLEASE.
"EX"...AS IN "DECEASED."

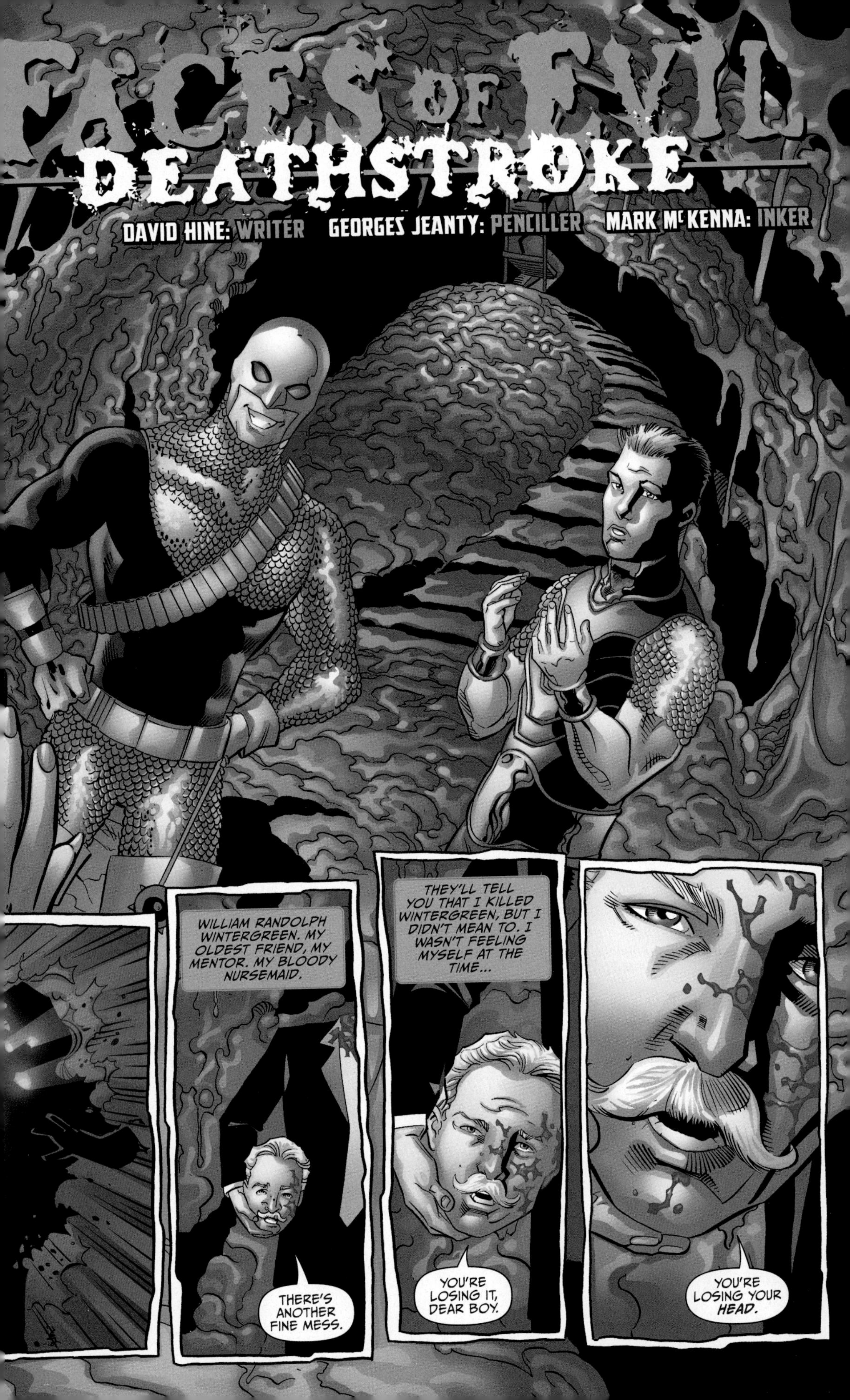
FACES OF EVIL
DEATHSTROKE
DAVID HINE: WRITER GEORGES JEANTY: PENCILLER MARK McKENNA: INKER
WILLIAM RANDOLPH WINTERGREEN. MY OLDEST FRIEND, MY MENTOR. MY BLOODY NURSEMAID.
THERE'S ANOTHER FINE MESS.
THEY'LL TELL YOU THAT I KILLED WINTERGREEN, BUT I DIDN'T MEAN TO. I WASN'T FEELING MYSELF AT THE TIME...
YOU'RE LOSING IT, DEAR BOY.
YOU'RE LOSING YOUR HEAD.

RAVAGER.

THE ORIGINAL AND THE BEST.

NO, SON. PLEASE DON'T TAKE THE MASK OFF.

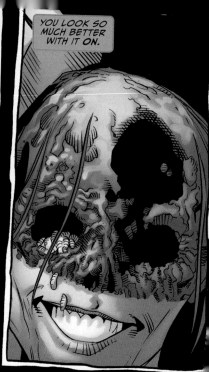

YOU LOOK SO MUCH BETTER WITH IT ON.

SSS-SS-SSS

AND THERE'S MY SECOND SON, JOSEPH. LITTLE JOE. THE QUIET ONE.

WHAT'S THAT, JOSEPH?

RRUSSUS

ROSE

SPEAK UP, I CAN'T HEAR YOU.

ROSE.

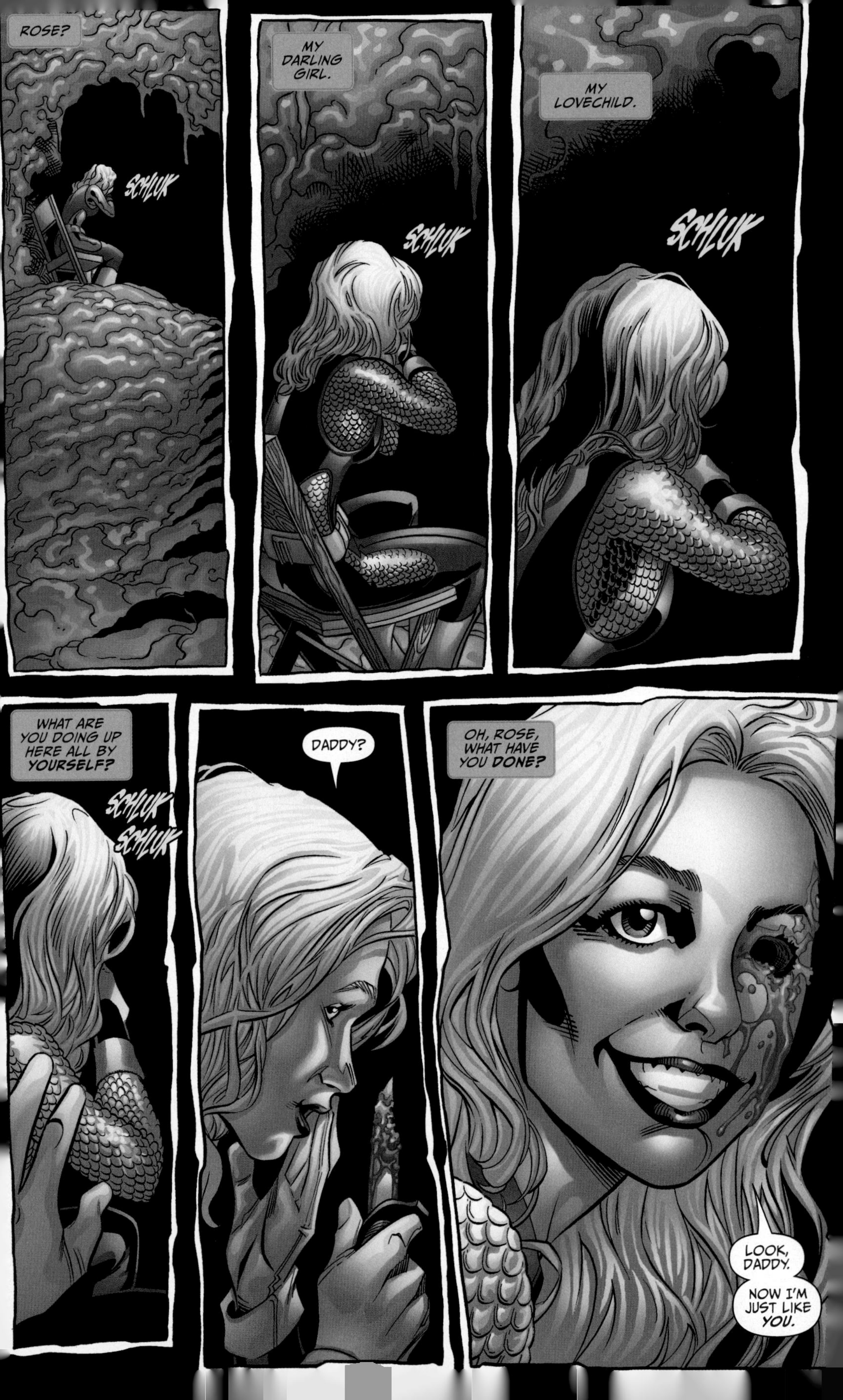
ROSE?
SCHLUK
MY DARLING GIRL.
SCHLUK
MY LOVECHILD.
SCHLUK
WHAT ARE YOU DOING UP HERE ALL BY YOURSELF?
SCHLUK
SCHLUK
DADDY?
OH, ROSE, WHAT HAVE YOU DONE?
LOOK, DADDY.
NOW I'M JUST LIKE YOU.

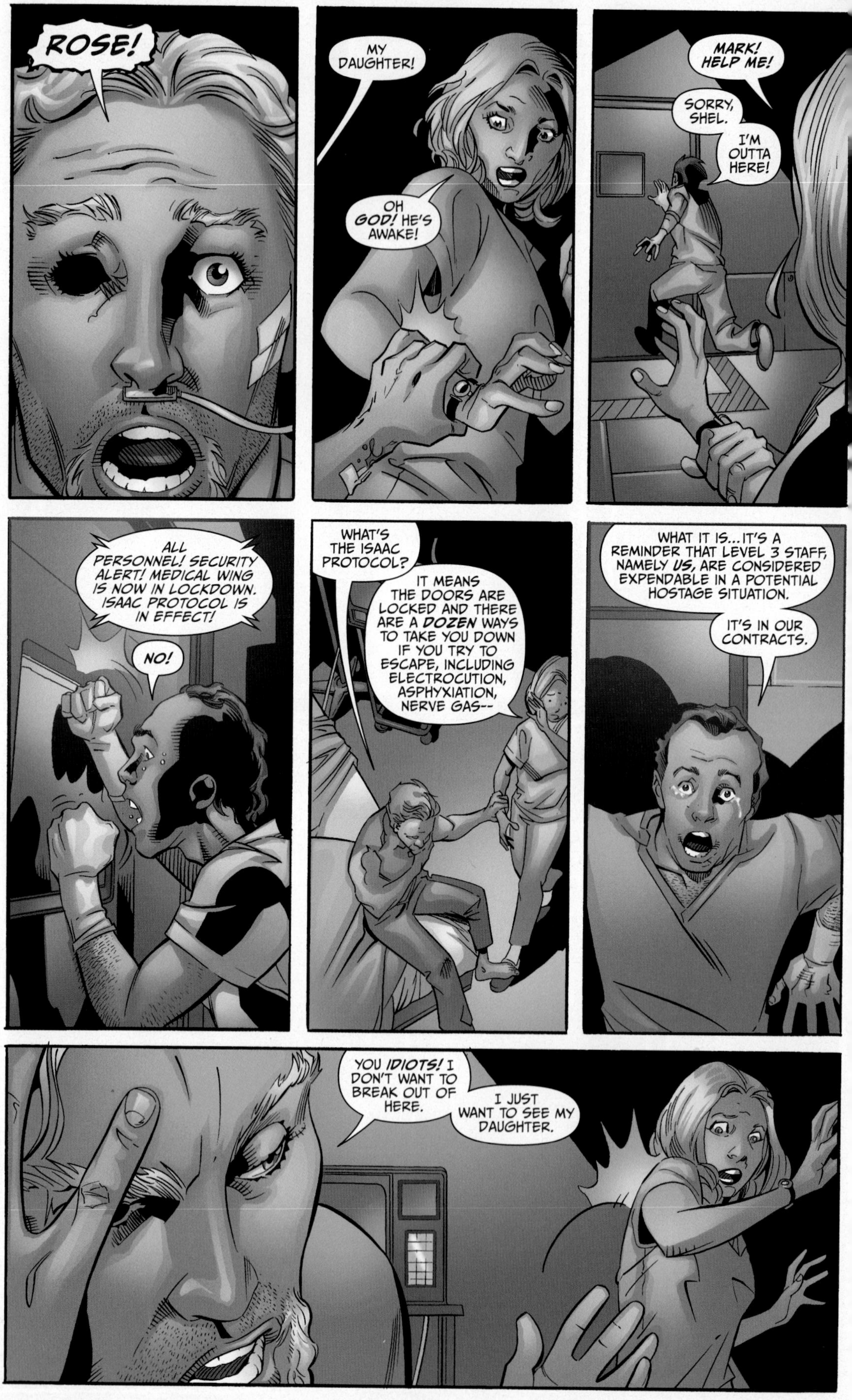
ROSE!
MY DAUGHTER!
OH GOD! HE'S AWAKE!
MARK! HELP ME!
SORRY, SHEL.
I'M OUTTA HERE!
ALL PERSONNEL! SECURITY ALERT! MEDICAL WING IS NOW IN LOCKDOWN. ISAAC PROTOCOL IS IN EFFECT!
NO!
WHAT'S THE ISAAC PROTOCOL?
IT MEANS THE DOORS ARE LOCKED AND THERE ARE A DOZEN WAYS TO TAKE YOU DOWN IF YOU TRY TO ESCAPE, INCLUDING ELECTROCUTION, ASPHYXIATION, NERVE GAS--
WHAT IT IS...IT'S A REMINDER THAT LEVEL 3 STAFF, NAMELY US, ARE CONSIDERED EXPENDABLE IN A POTENTIAL HOSTAGE SITUATION.
IT'S IN OUR CONTRACTS.
YOU IDIOTS! I DON'T WANT TO BREAK OUT OF HERE.
I JUST WANT TO SEE MY DAUGHTER.

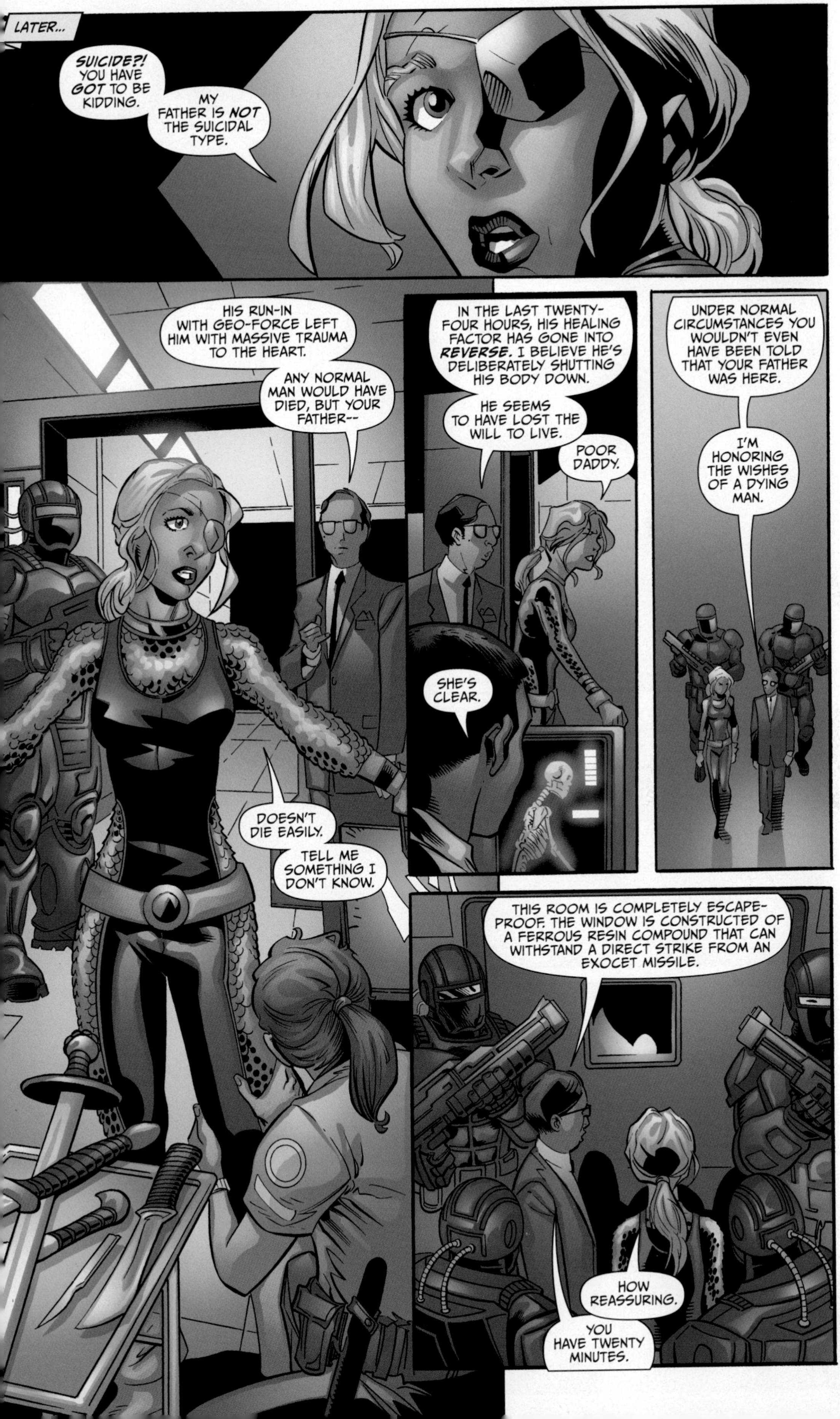
LATER...
SUICIDE?! YOU HAVE GOT TO BE KIDDING.
MY FATHER IS NOT THE SUICIDAL TYPE.
HIS RUN-IN WITH GEO-FORCE LEFT HIM WITH MASSIVE TRAUMA TO THE HEART.
ANY NORMAL MAN WOULD HAVE DIED, BUT YOUR FATHER--
DOESN'T DIE EASILY.
TELL ME SOMETHING I DON'T KNOW.
IN THE LAST TWENTY-FOUR HOURS, HIS HEALING FACTOR HAS GONE INTO REVERSE. I BELIEVE HE'S DELIBERATELY SHUTTING HIS BODY DOWN.
HE SEEMS TO HAVE LOST THE WILL TO LIVE.
POOR DADDY.
SHE'S CLEAR.
UNDER NORMAL CIRCUMSTANCES YOU WOULDN'T EVEN HAVE BEEN TOLD THAT YOUR FATHER WAS HERE.
I'M HONORING THE WISHES OF A DYING MAN.
THIS ROOM IS COMPLETELY ESCAPE-PROOF. THE WINDOW IS CONSTRUCTED OF A FERROUS RESIN COMPOUND THAT CAN WITHSTAND A DIRECT STRIKE FROM AN EXOCET MISSILE.
HOW REASSURING.
YOU HAVE TWENTY MINUTES.

HELLO, ROSE.

THEY LET YOU WEAR YOUR COSTUME.

LAST REQUEST--

OF A DYING MAN.

SO IT'S *TRUE?* YOU'RE REALLY TRYING TO *KILL YOURSELF?*

I'M *SICK* OF IT, ROSE. I'M SO TIRED OF THE CIRCLE OF VIOLENCE I'M TRAPPED IN.

THEY TOOK OUT MY ARTIFICIAL EYE AND...I DON'T KNOW...IT SEEMED TO *TRIGGER* SOMETHING. I'M SEEING THINGS WITH A CLARITY--

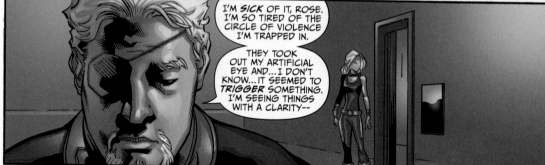

WHAP!

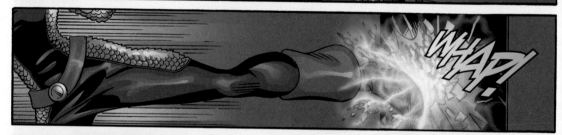

WHAT ARE YOU DOING?

MAKING SURE WE'RE NOT DISTURBED.

BZZAK!

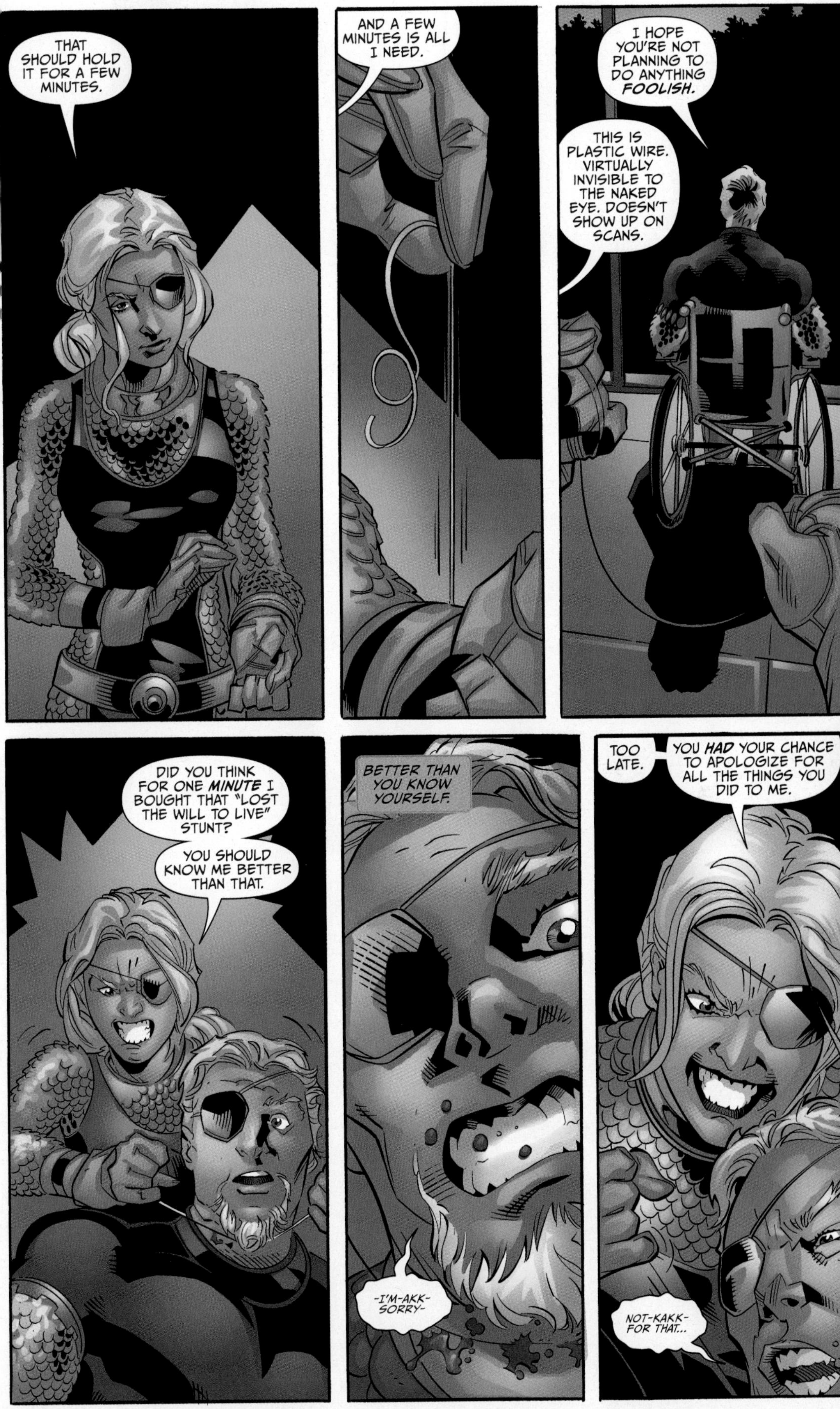
THAT SHOULD HOLD IT FOR A FEW MINUTES.
AND A FEW MINUTES IS ALL I NEED.
I HOPE YOU'RE NOT PLANNING TO DO ANYTHING FOOLISH.
THIS IS PLASTIC WIRE. VIRTUALLY INVISIBLE TO THE NAKED EYE. DOESN'T SHOW UP ON SCANS.
DID YOU THINK FOR ONE MINUTE I BOUGHT THAT "LOST THE WILL TO LIVE" STUNT?
YOU SHOULD KNOW ME BETTER THAN THAT.
BETTER THAN YOU KNOW YOURSELF.
-I'M-AKK-SORRY-
TOO LATE.
YOU HAD YOUR CHANCE TO APOLOGIZE FOR ALL THE THINGS YOU DID TO ME.
NOT-KAKK-FOR THAT...

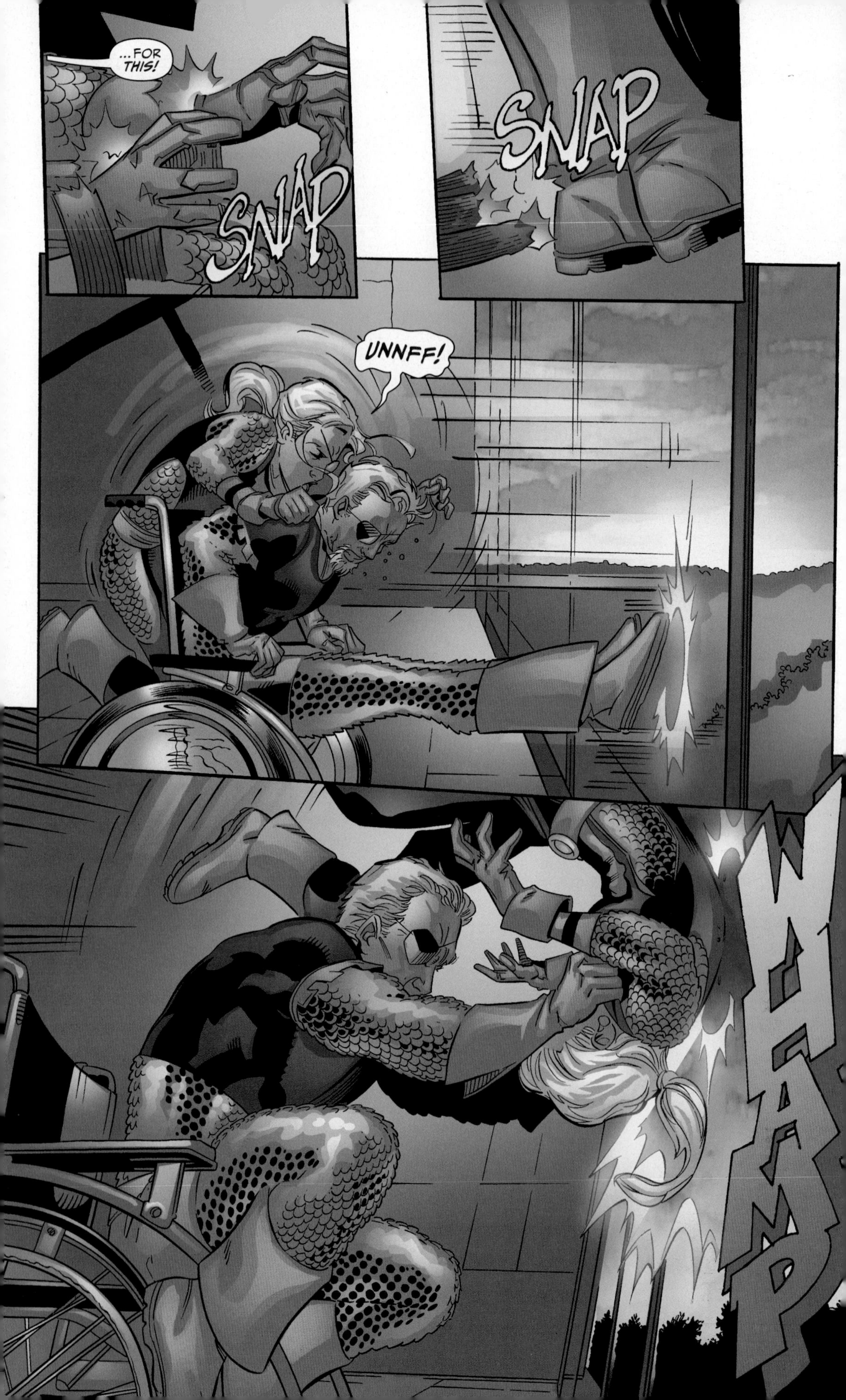
...FOR THIS!
SNAP
SNAP
UNNFF!
WHAMP

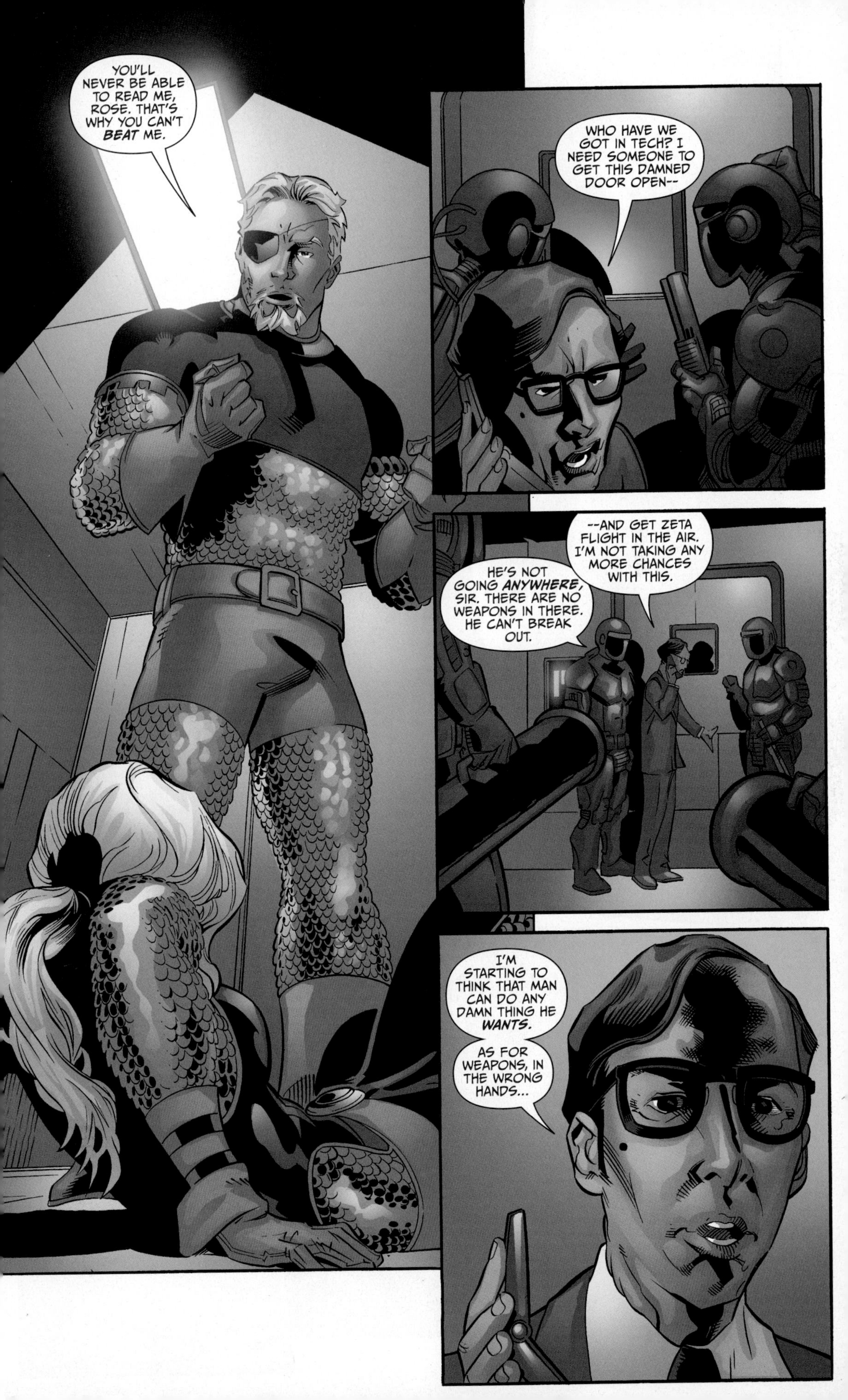
YOU'LL NEVER BE ABLE TO READ ME, ROSE. THAT'S WHY YOU CAN'T *BEAT* ME.
WHO HAVE WE GOT IN TECH? I NEED SOMEONE TO GET THIS DAMNED DOOR OPEN--
--AND GET ZETA FLIGHT IN THE AIR. I'M NOT TAKING ANY MORE CHANCES WITH THIS.
HE'S NOT GOING *ANYWHERE,* SIR. THERE ARE NO WEAPONS IN THERE. HE CAN'T BREAK OUT.
I'M STARTING TO THINK THAT MAN CAN DO ANY DAMN THING HE *WANTS.*
AS FOR WEAPONS, IN THE WRONG HANDS...

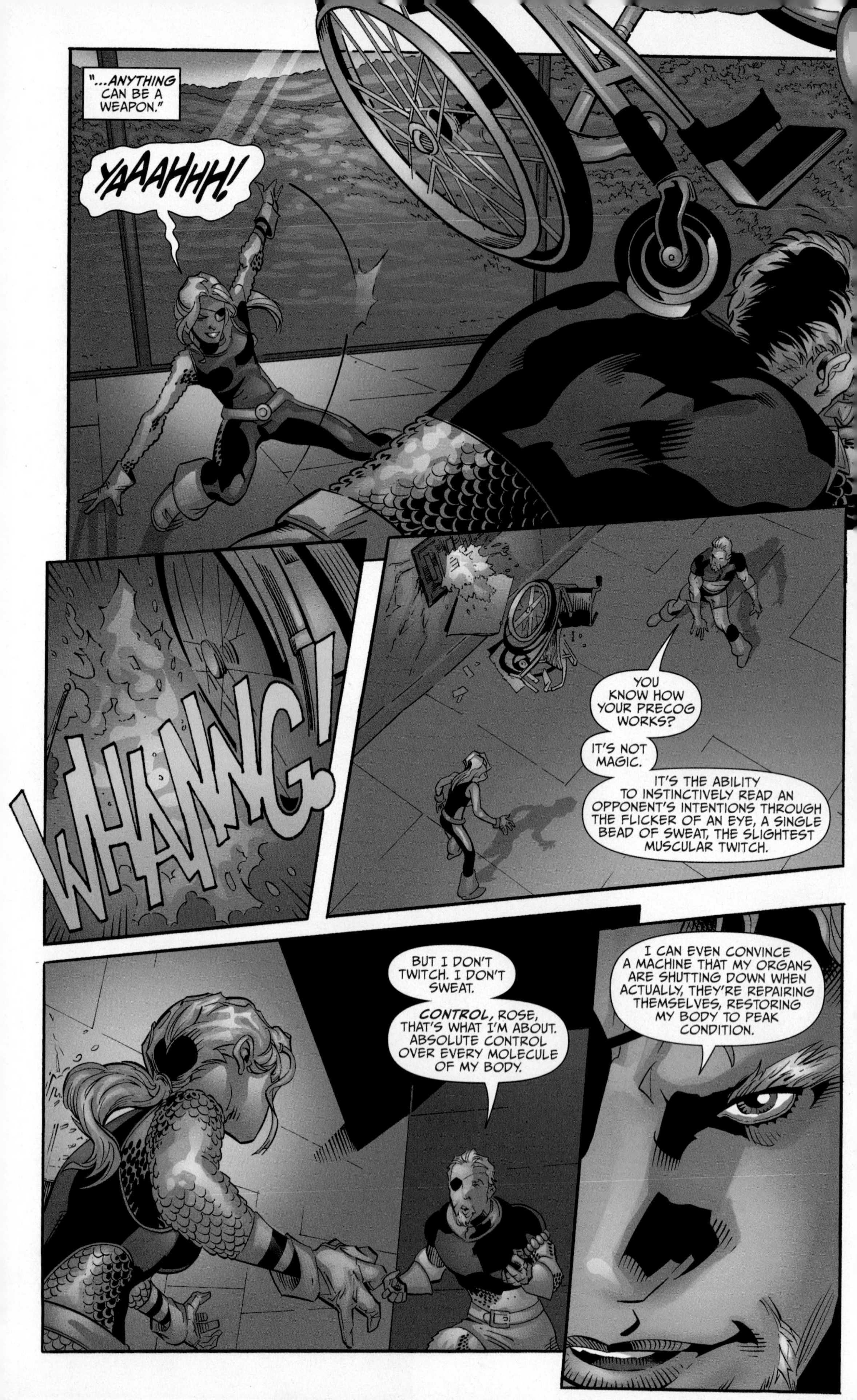
"...ANYTHING CAN BE A WEAPON."
YAAAHHH!
WHANNG!
YOU KNOW HOW YOUR PRECOG WORKS?
IT'S NOT MAGIC.
IT'S THE ABILITY TO INSTINCTIVELY READ AN OPPONENT'S INTENTIONS THROUGH THE FLICKER OF AN EYE, A SINGLE BEAD OF SWEAT, THE SLIGHTEST MUSCULAR TWITCH.
BUT I DON'T TWITCH. I DON'T SWEAT.
CONTROL, ROSE, THAT'S WHAT I'M ABOUT. ABSOLUTE CONTROL OVER EVERY MOLECULE OF MY BODY.
I CAN EVEN CONVINCE A MACHINE THAT MY ORGANS ARE SHUTTING DOWN WHEN ACTUALLY, THEY'RE REPAIRING THEMSELVES, RESTORING MY BODY TO PEAK CONDITION.

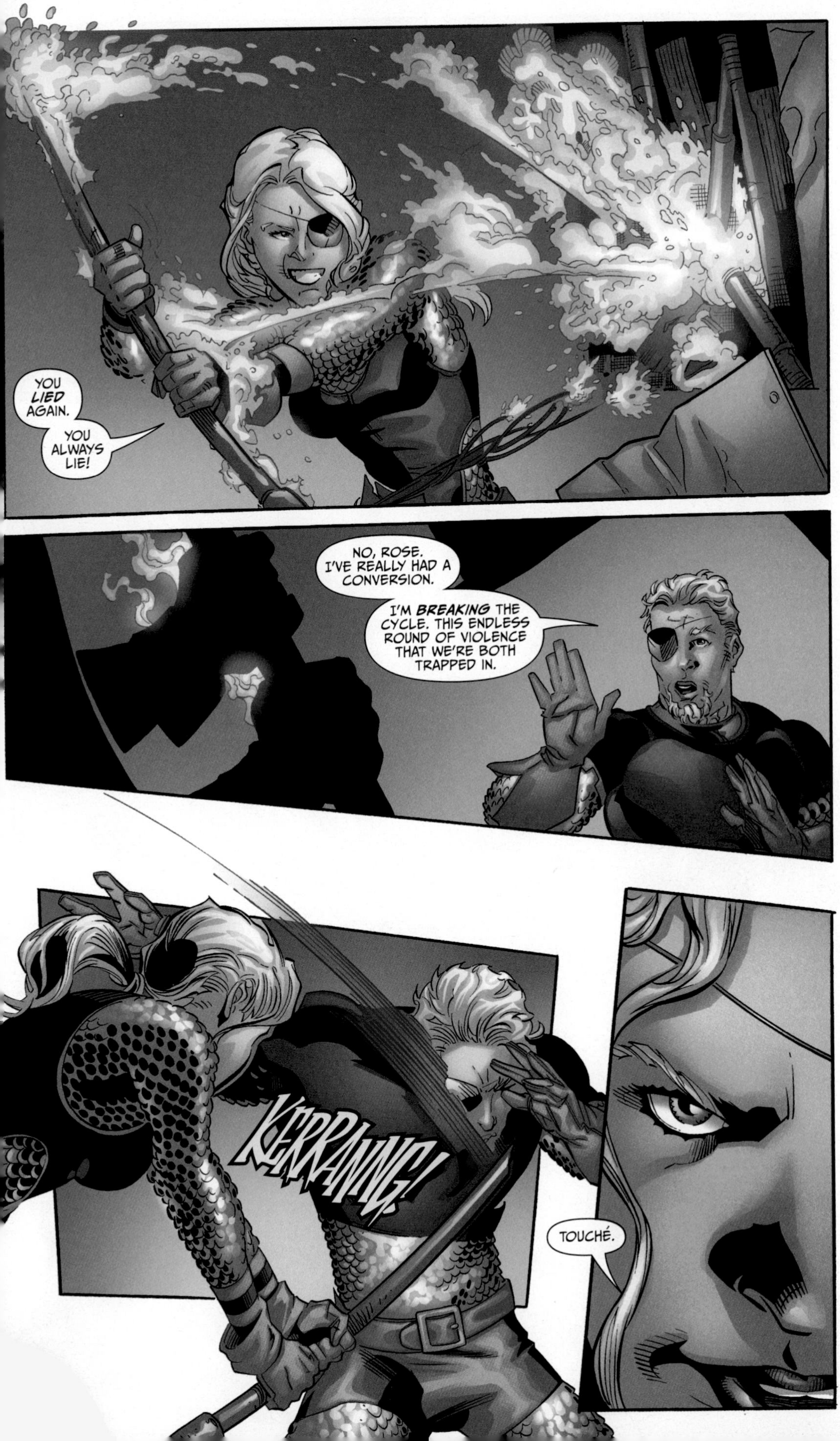

YOU LIED AGAIN.
YOU ALWAYS LIE!
NO, ROSE. I'VE REALLY HAD A CONVERSION.
I'M BREAKING THE CYCLE. THIS ENDLESS ROUND OF VIOLENCE THAT WE'RE BOTH TRAPPED IN.
KERRANG!
TOUCHÉ.

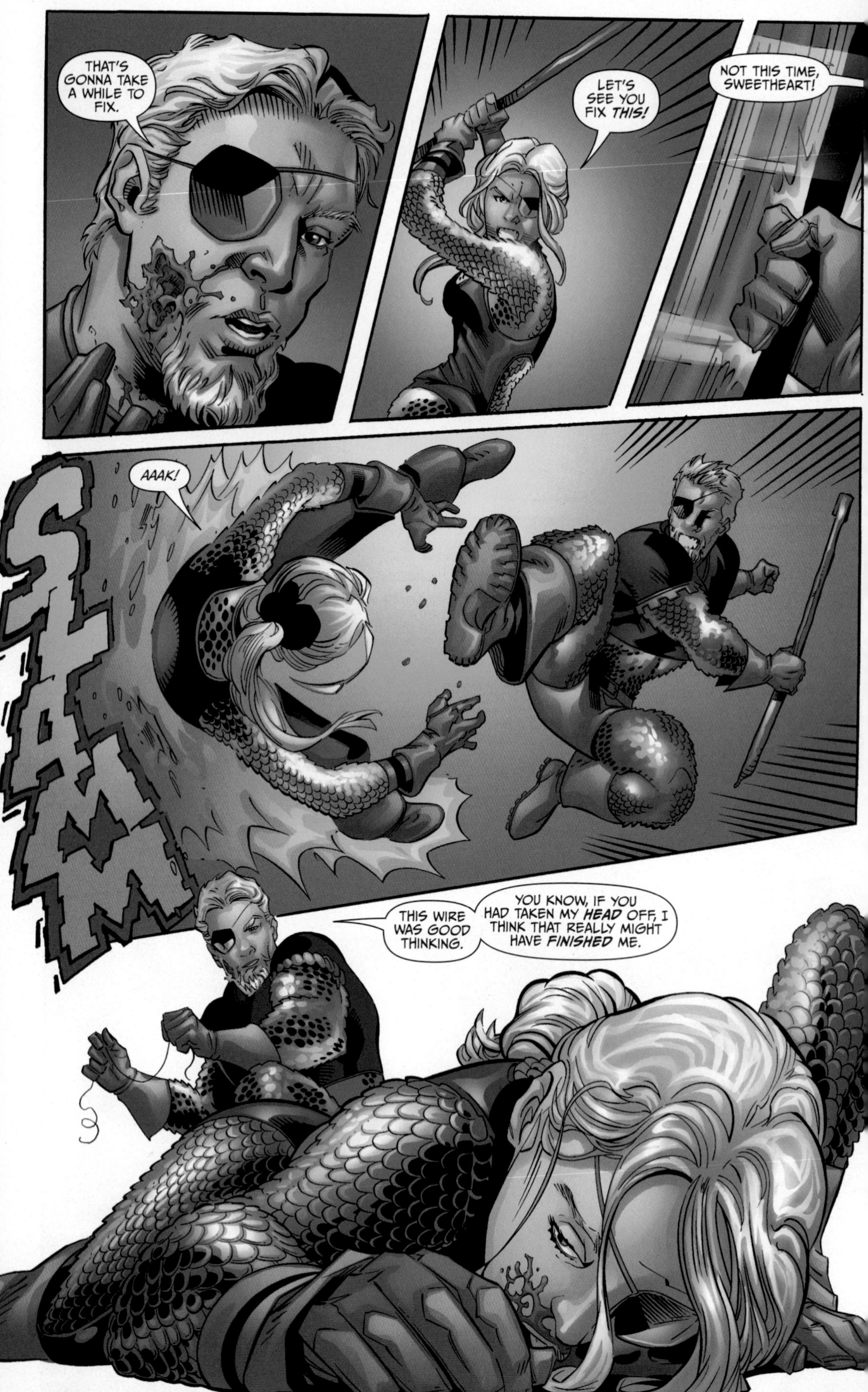
THAT'S GONNA TAKE A WHILE TO FIX.
LET'S SEE YOU FIX *THIS!*
NOT THIS TIME, SWEETHEART!
AAAK!
SLAM
THIS WIRE WAS GOOD THINKING.
YOU KNOW, IF YOU HAD TAKEN MY *HEAD* OFF, I THINK THAT REALLY MIGHT HAVE *FINISHED* ME.

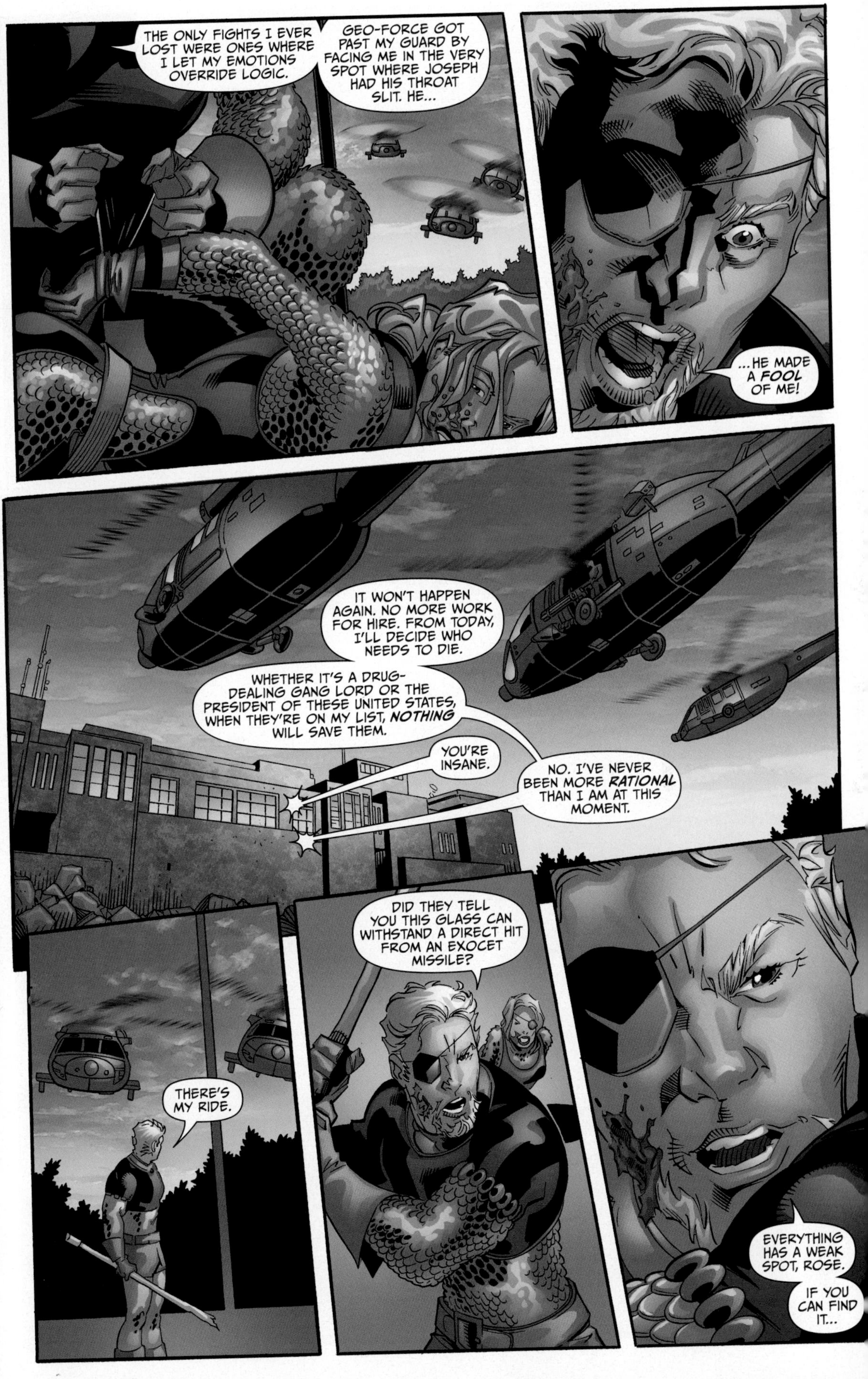
THE ONLY FIGHTS I EVER LOST WERE ONES WHERE I LET MY EMOTIONS OVERRIDE LOGIC.
GEO-FORCE GOT PAST MY GUARD BY FACING ME IN THE VERY SPOT WHERE JOSEPH HAD HIS THROAT SLIT. HE...
...HE MADE A FOOL OF ME!
IT WON'T HAPPEN AGAIN. NO MORE WORK FOR HIRE. FROM TODAY, I'LL DECIDE WHO NEEDS TO DIE.
WHETHER IT'S A DRUG-DEALING GANG LORD OR THE PRESIDENT OF THESE UNITED STATES, WHEN THEY'RE ON MY LIST, NOTHING WILL SAVE THEM.
YOU'RE INSANE.
NO. I'VE NEVER BEEN MORE RATIONAL THAN I AM AT THIS MOMENT.
THERE'S MY RIDE.
DID THEY TELL YOU THIS GLASS CAN WITHSTAND A DIRECT HIT FROM AN EXOCET MISSILE?
EVERYTHING HAS A WEAK SPOT, ROSE.
IF YOU CAN FIND IT...

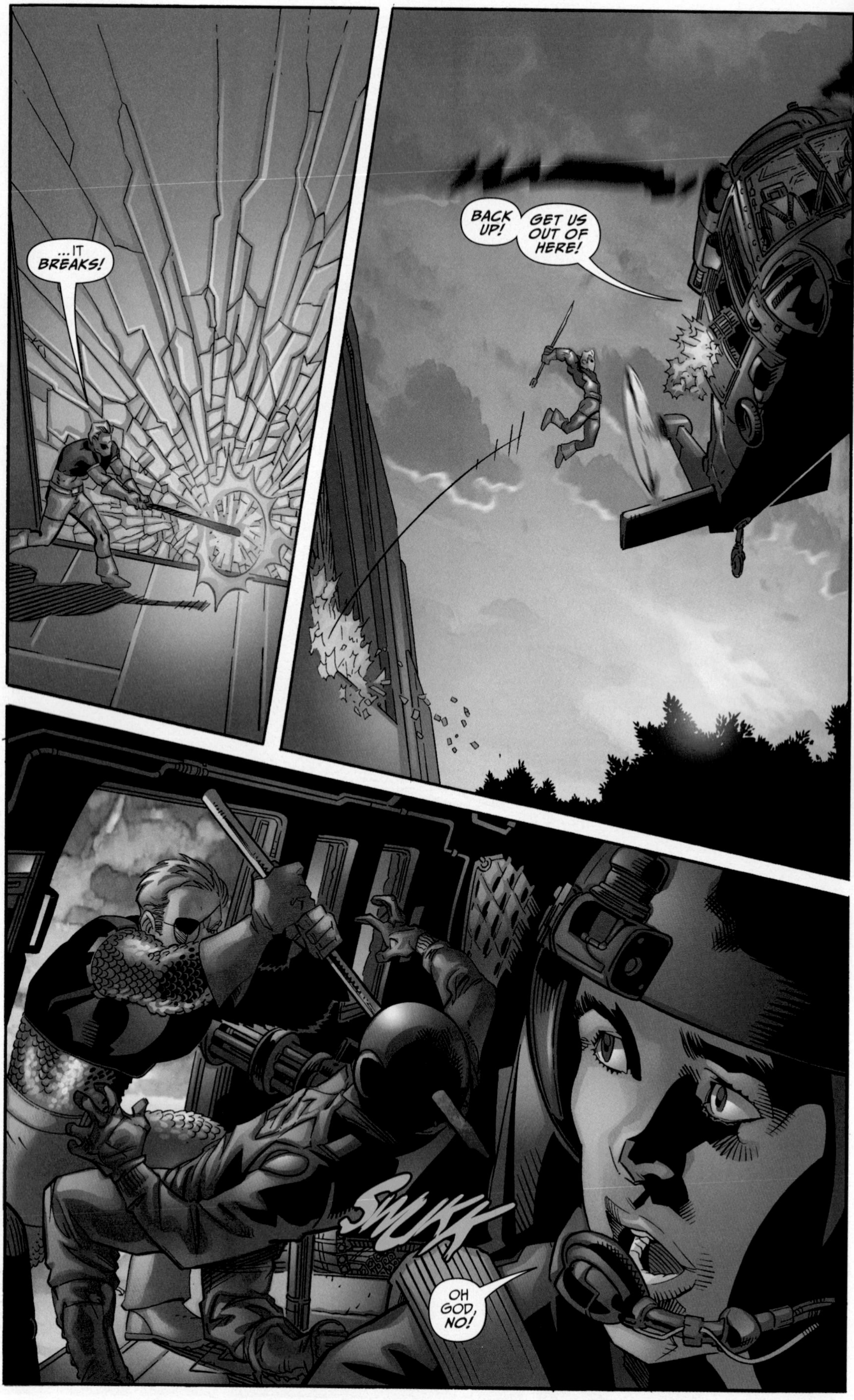
...IT BREAKS!
BACK UP!
GET US OUT OF HERE!
SNIKK
OH GOD, NO!

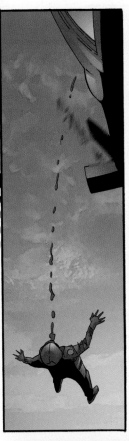

JUMP.

NO. PUH-*PLEASE.* I C-CAN'T. IT'S T-TOO HIGH!

YOUR CHOICE.

NICE-LOOKING HARDWARE.

LET'S SEE HOW IT HANDLES.

SWEET.

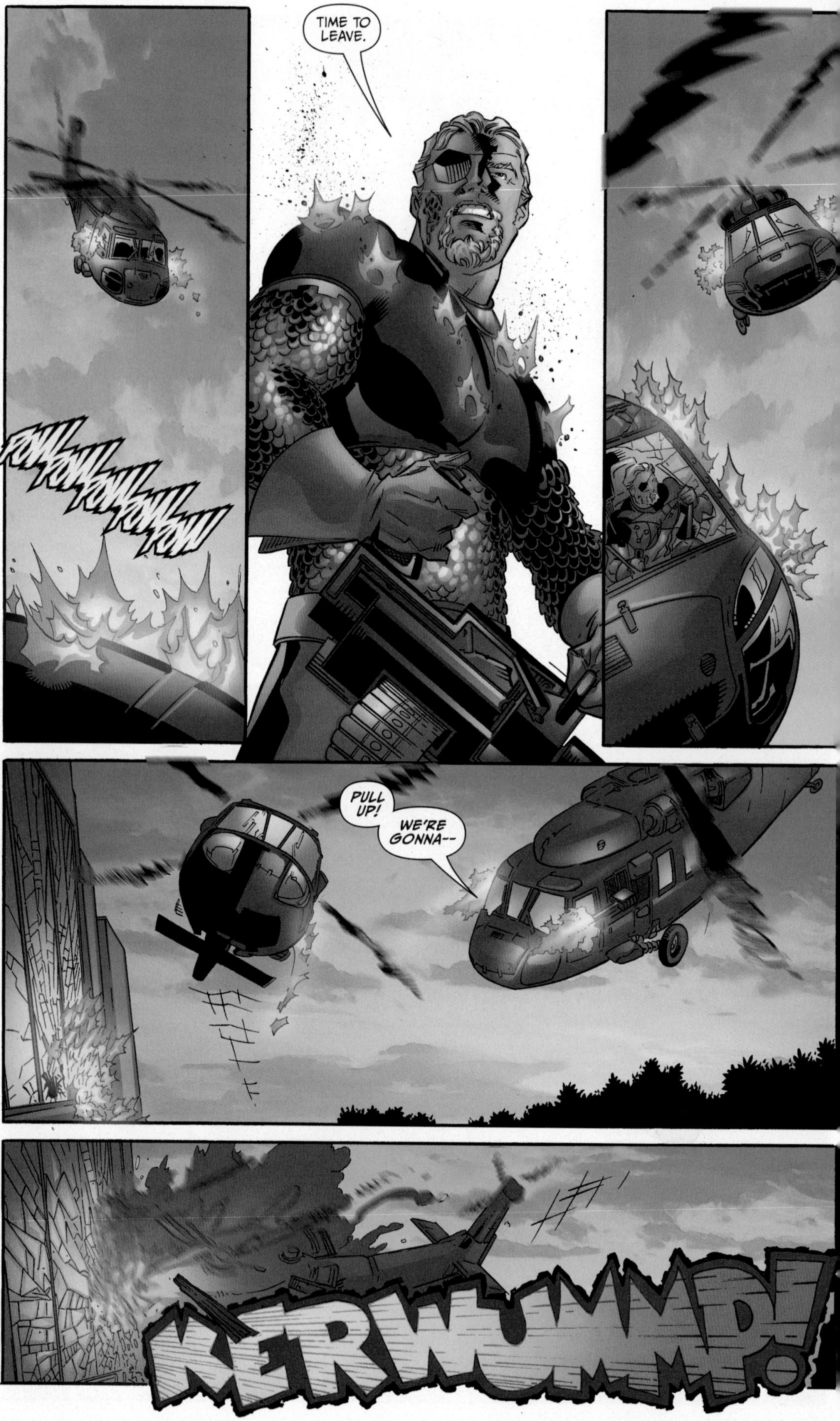

TIME TO LEAVE.
POW POW POW POW POW POW POW
PULL UP!
WE'RE GONNA--
KERWUMMP!

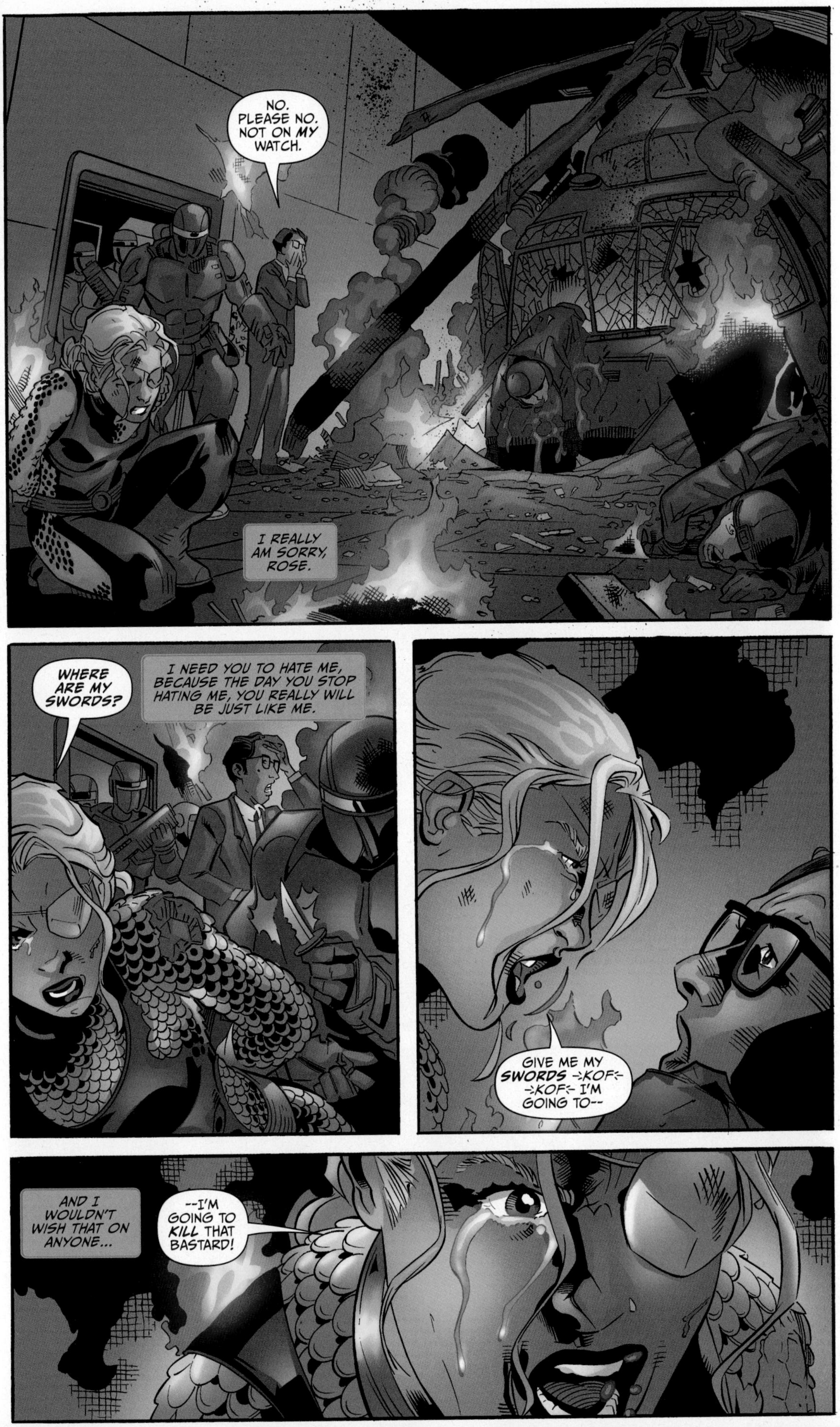
NO. PLEASE NO. NOT ON MY WATCH.
I REALLY AM SORRY, ROSE.
WHERE ARE MY SWORDS?
I NEED YOU TO HATE ME, BECAUSE THE DAY YOU STOP HATING ME, YOU REALLY WILL BE JUST LIKE ME.
GIVE ME MY SWORDS -KOF- -KOF- I'M GOING TO--
AND I WOULDN'T WISH THAT ON ANYONE...
--I'M GOING TO KILL THAT BASTARD!

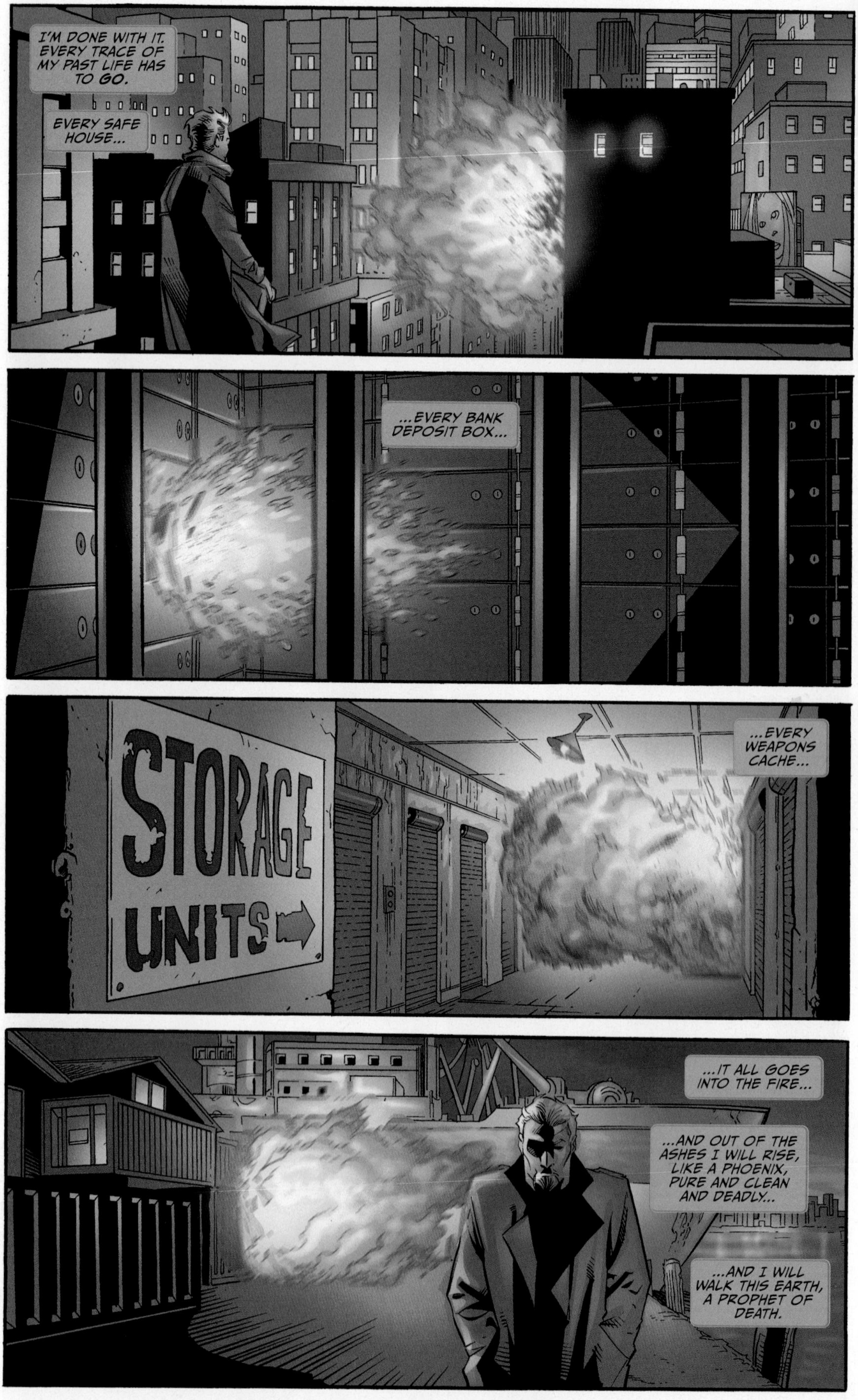

I'M DONE WITH IT. EVERY TRACE OF MY PAST LIFE HAS TO GO.
EVERY SAFE HOUSE...
...EVERY BANK DEPOSIT BOX...
STORAGE UNITS
...EVERY WEAPONS CACHE...
...IT ALL GOES INTO THE FIRE...
...AND OUT OF THE ASHES I WILL RISE, LIKE A PHOENIX, PURE AND CLEAN AND DEADLY...
...AND I WILL WALK THIS EARTH, A PROPHET OF DEATH.

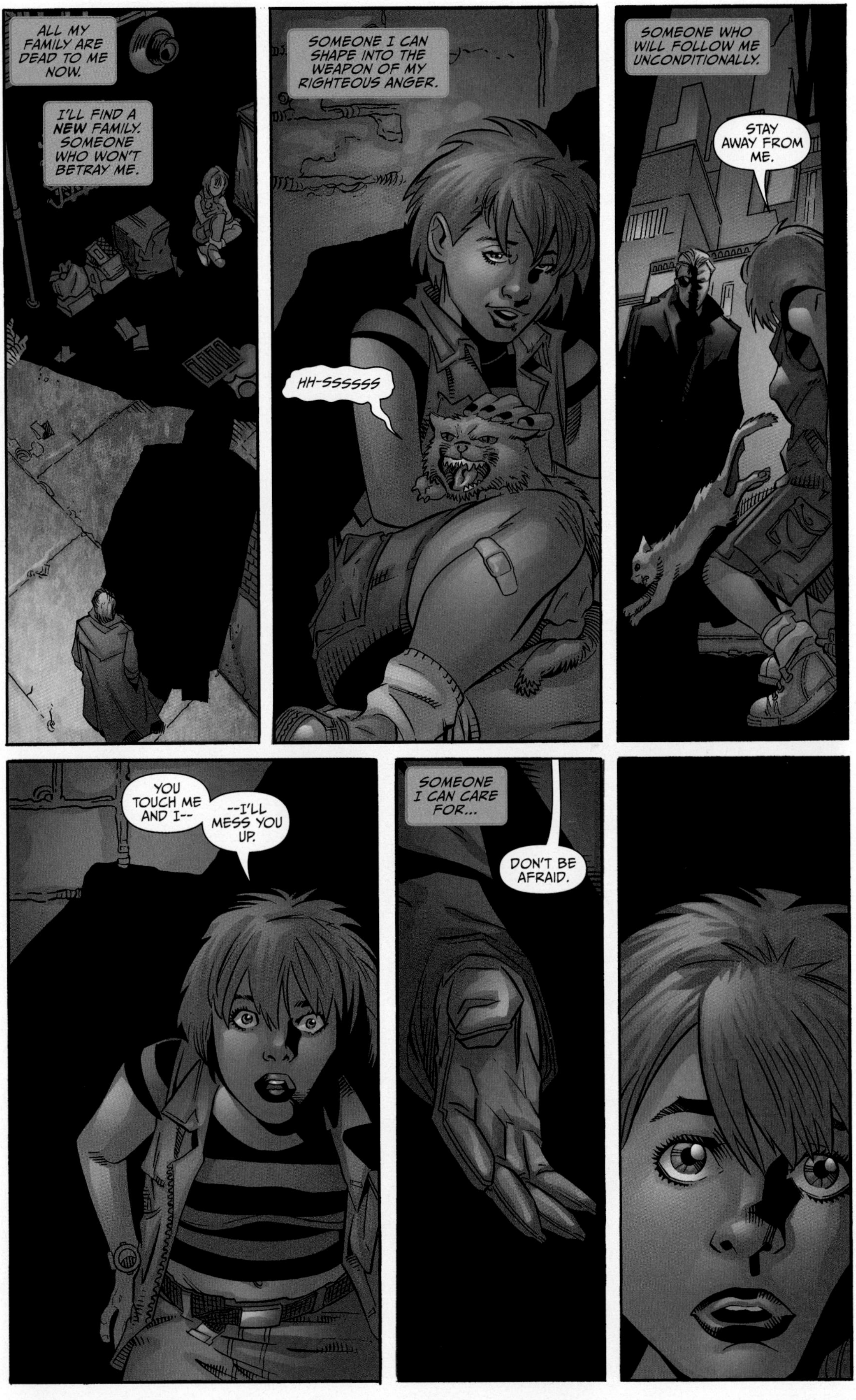

ALL MY FAMILY ARE DEAD TO ME NOW.
I'LL FIND A NEW FAMILY. SOMEONE WHO WON'T BETRAY ME.
SOMEONE I CAN SHAPE INTO THE WEAPON OF MY RIGHTEOUS ANGER.
HH-SSSSSS
SOMEONE WHO WILL FOLLOW ME UNCONDITIONALLY.
STAY AWAY FROM ME.
YOU TOUCH ME AND I--
--I'LL MESS YOU UP.
SOMEONE I CAN CARE FOR...
DON'T BE AFRAID.

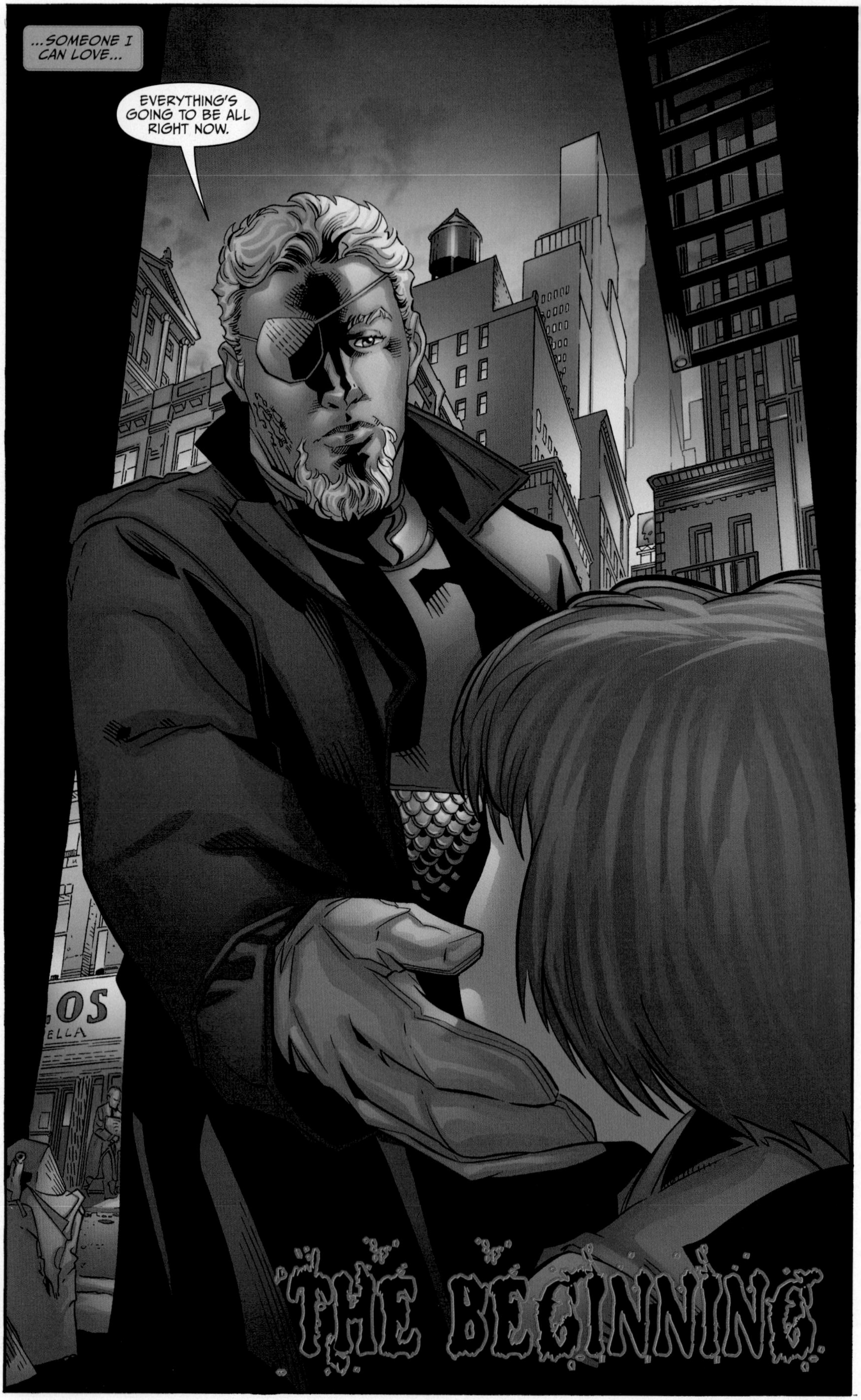
...SOMEONE I CAN LOVE...
EVERYTHING'S GOING TO BE ALL RIGHT NOW.
THE BEGINNING

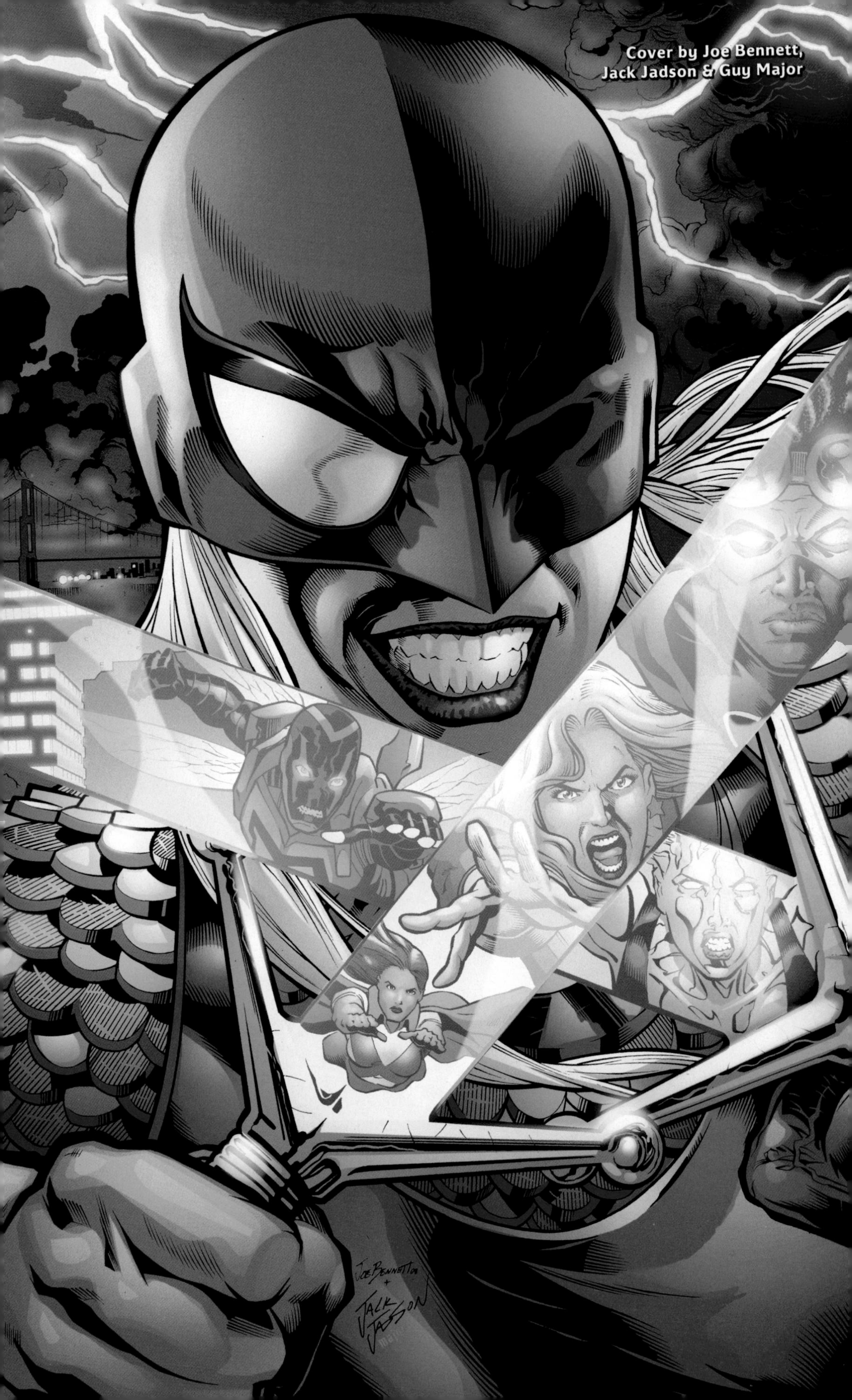

Cover by Joe Bennett, Jack Jadson & Guy Major

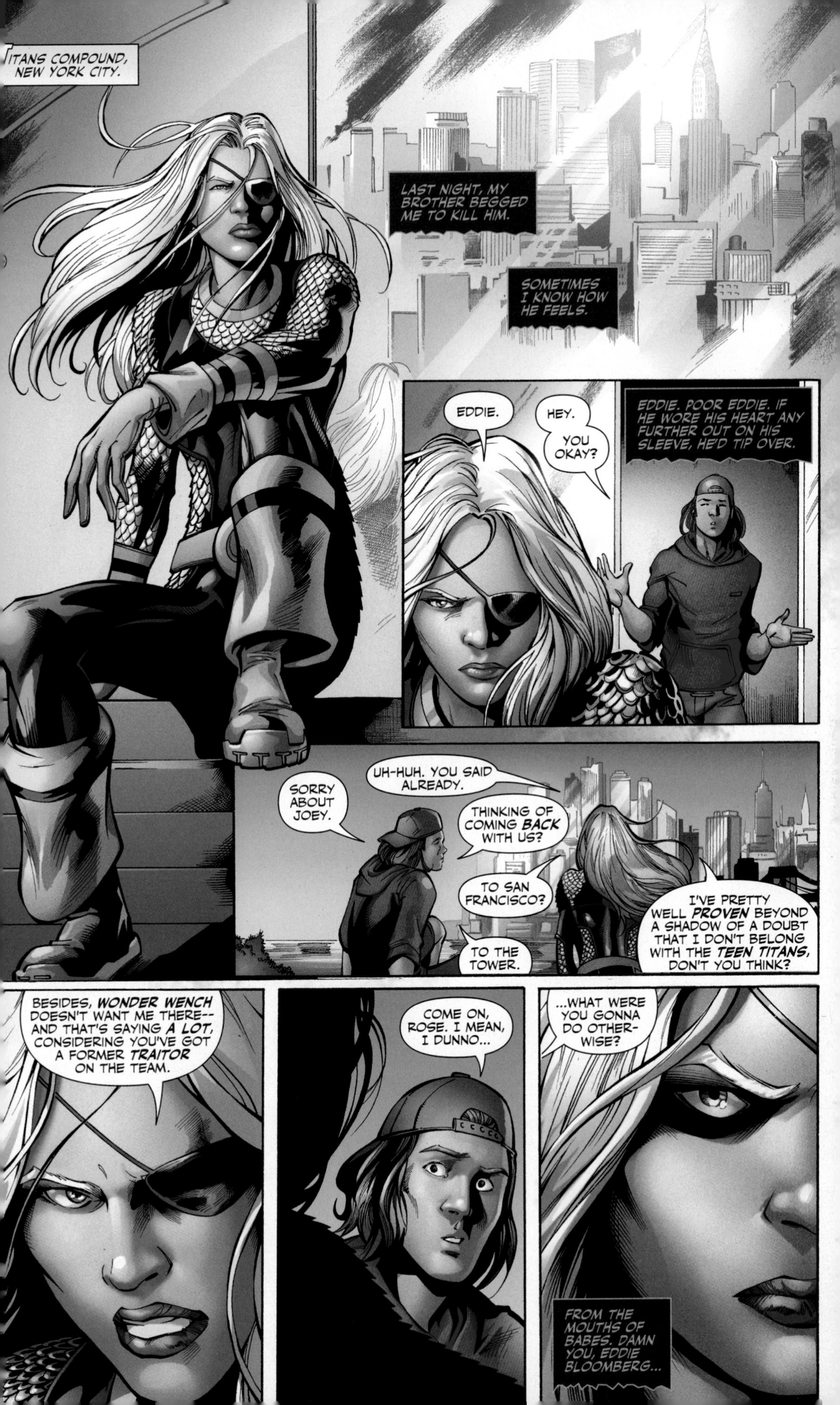

ITANS COMPOUND, NEW YORK CITY.
LAST NIGHT, MY BROTHER BEGGED ME TO KILL HIM.
SOMETIMES I KNOW HOW HE FEELS.
EDDIE.
HEY.
YOU OKAY?
EDDIE. POOR EDDIE. IF HE WORE HIS HEART ANY FURTHER OUT ON HIS SLEEVE, HE'D TIP OVER.
SORRY ABOUT JOEY.
UH-HUH. YOU SAID ALREADY.
THINKING OF COMING BACK WITH US?
TO SAN FRANCISCO?
TO THE TOWER.
I'VE PRETTY WELL PROVEN BEYOND A SHADOW OF A DOUBT THAT I DON'T BELONG WITH THE TEEN TITANS, DON'T YOU THINK?
BESIDES, WONDER WENCH DOESN'T WANT ME THERE-- AND THAT'S SAYING A LOT, CONSIDERING YOU'VE GOT A FORMER TRAITOR ON THE TEAM.
COME ON, ROSE. I MEAN, I DUNNO...
...WHAT WERE YOU GONNA DO OTHER-WISE?
FROM THE MOUTHS OF BABES. DAMN YOU, EDDIE BLOOMBERG...

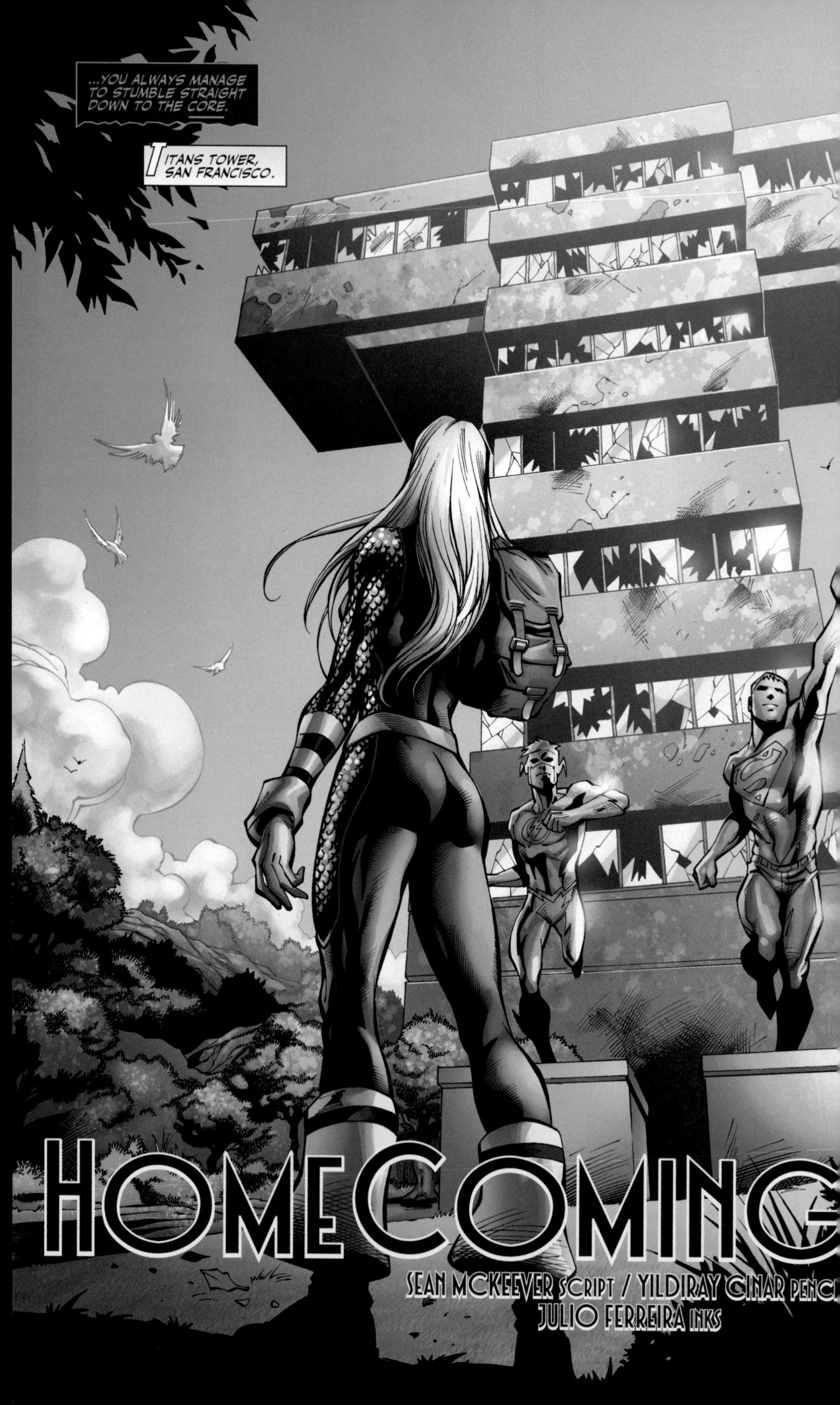
...YOU ALWAYS MANAGE TO STUMBLE STRAIGHT DOWN TO THE CORE.
TITANS TOWER, SAN FRANCISCO.
HOMECOMING
SEAN MCKEEVER SCRIPT / YILDIRAY CINAR PENCI
JULIO FERREIRA INKS

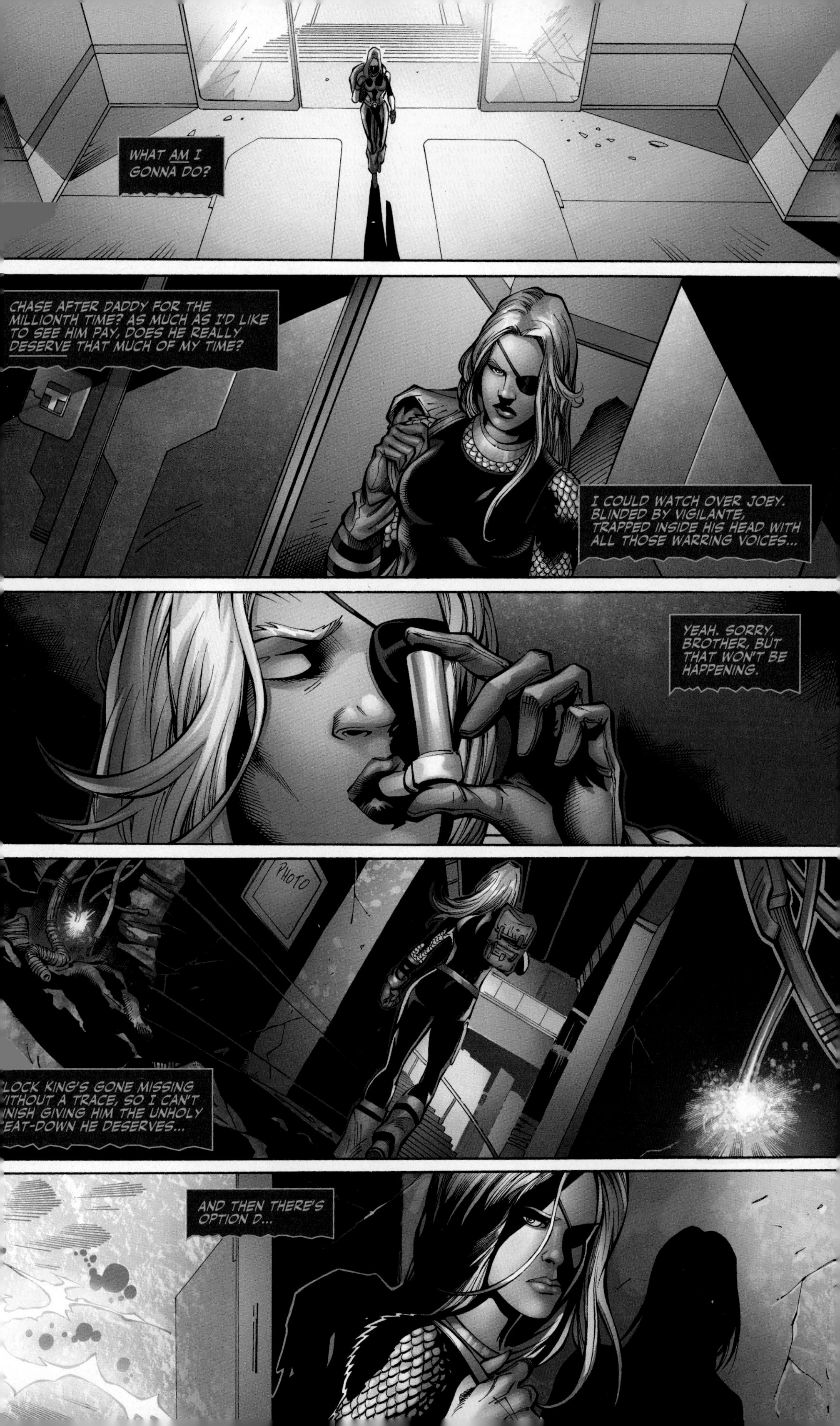

WHAT AM I GONNA DO?
CHASE AFTER DADDY FOR THE MILLIONTH TIME? AS MUCH AS I'D LIKE TO SEE HIM PAY, DOES HE REALLY DESERVE THAT MUCH OF MY TIME?
I COULD WATCH OVER JOEY. BLINDED BY VIGILANTE, TRAPPED INSIDE HIS HEAD WITH ALL THOSE WARRING VOICES...
YEAH. SORRY, BROTHER, BUT THAT WON'T BE HAPPENING.
PHOTO
LOCK KING'S GONE MISSING WITHOUT A TRACE, SO I CAN'T FINISH GIVING HIM THE UNHOLY BEAT-DOWN HE DESERVES...
AND THEN THERE'S OPTION D...

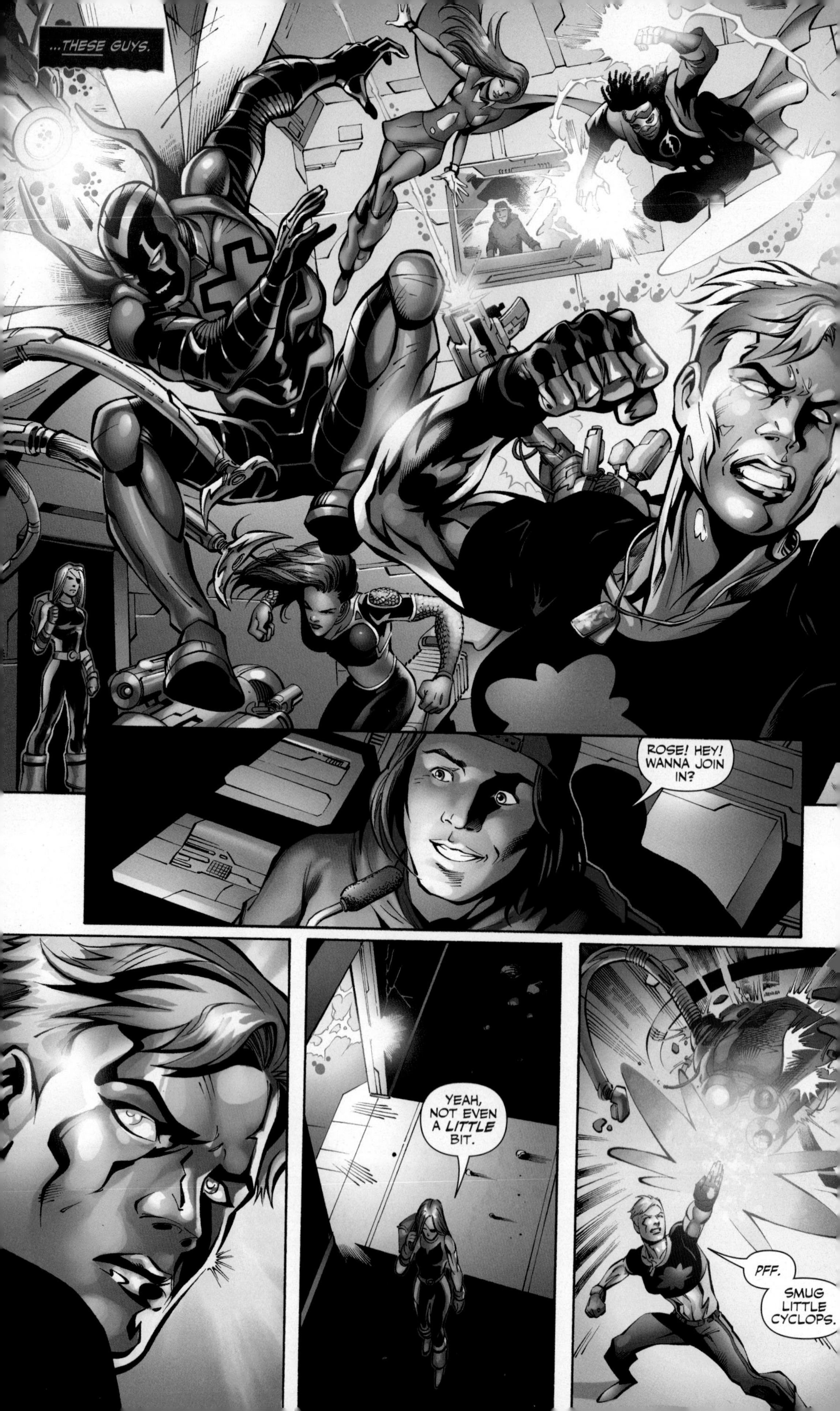
...THESE GUYS.
ROSE! HEY! WANNA JOIN IN?
YEAH, NOT EVEN A LITTLE BIT.
PFF.
SMUG LITTLE CYCLOPS.

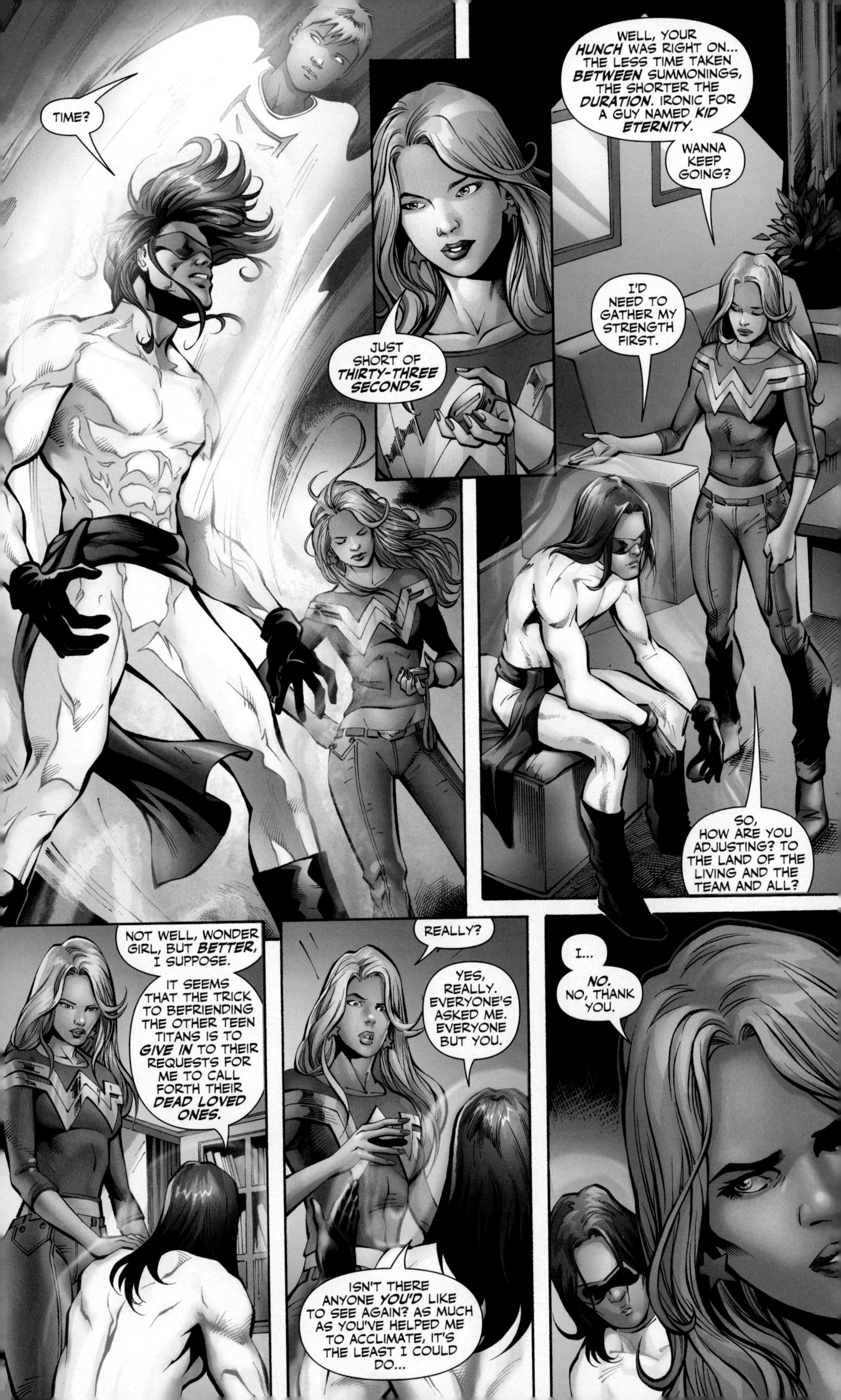
TIME?
JUST SHORT OF THIRTY-THREE SECONDS.
WELL, YOUR HUNCH WAS RIGHT ON... THE LESS TIME TAKEN BETWEEN SUMMONINGS, THE SHORTER THE DURATION. IRONIC FOR A GUY NAMED KID ETERNITY.
WANNA KEEP GOING?
I'D NEED TO GATHER MY STRENGTH FIRST.
SO, HOW ARE YOU ADJUSTING? TO THE LAND OF THE LIVING AND THE TEAM AND ALL?
NOT WELL, WONDER GIRL, BUT BETTER, I SUPPOSE.
IT SEEMS THAT THE TRICK TO BEFRIENDING THE OTHER TEEN TITANS IS TO GIVE IN TO THEIR REQUESTS FOR ME TO CALL FORTH THEIR DEAD LOVED ONES.
REALLY?
YES, REALLY. EVERYONE'S ASKED ME. EVERYONE BUT YOU.
ISN'T THERE ANYONE YOU'D LIKE TO SEE AGAIN? AS MUCH AS YOU'VE HELPED ME TO ACCLIMATE, IT'S THE LEAST I COULD DO...
I...
NO. NO, THANK YOU.

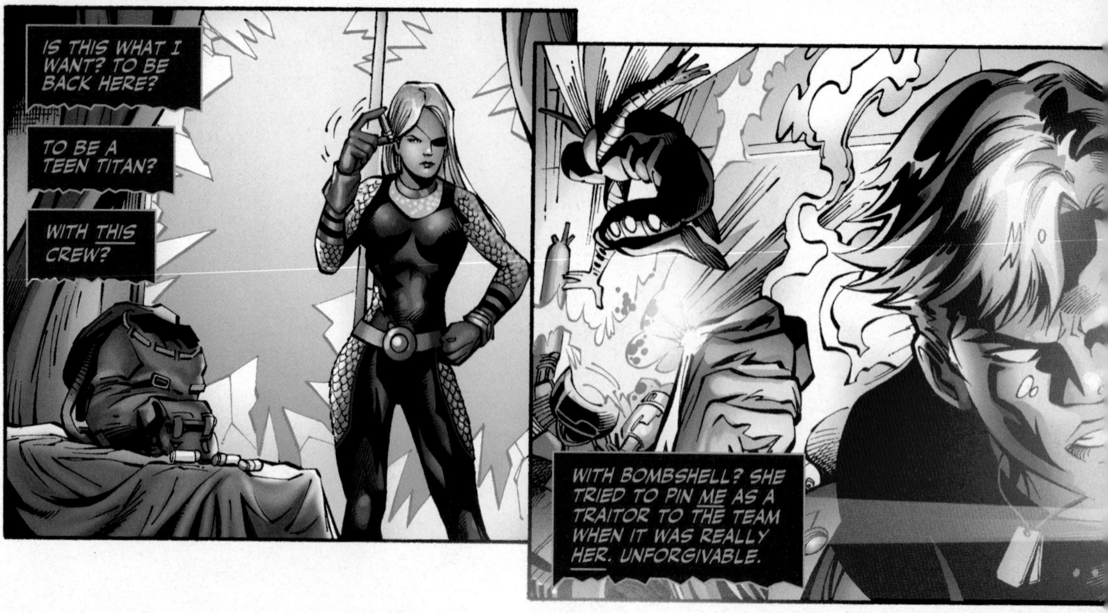
IS THIS WHAT I WANT? TO BE BACK HERE?
TO BE A TEEN TITAN?
WITH THIS CREW?
WITH BOMBSHELL? SHE TRIED TO PIN ME AS A TRAITOR TO THE TEAM WHEN IT WAS REALLY HER. UNFORGIVABLE.

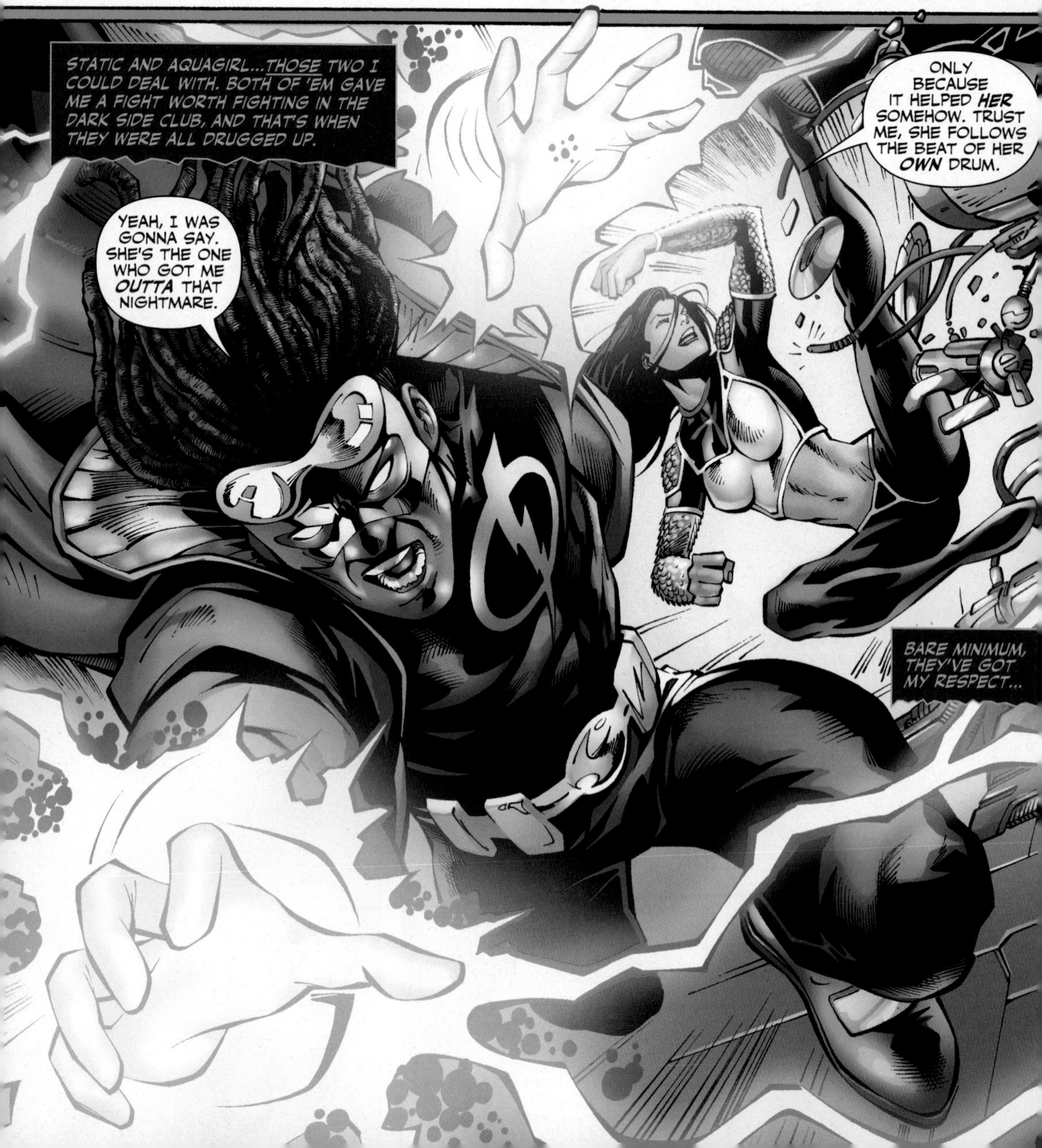
STATIC AND AQUAGIRL...THOSE TWO I COULD DEAL WITH. BOTH OF 'EM GAVE ME A FIGHT WORTH FIGHTING IN THE DARK SIDE CLUB, AND THAT'S WHEN THEY WERE ALL DRUGGED UP.
YEAH, I WAS GONNA SAY. SHE'S THE ONE WHO GOT ME OUTTA THAT NIGHTMARE.
ONLY BECAUSE IT HELPED HER SOMEHOW. TRUST ME, SHE FOLLOWS THE BEAT OF HER OWN DRUM.
BARE MINIMUM, THEY'VE GOT MY RESPECT...

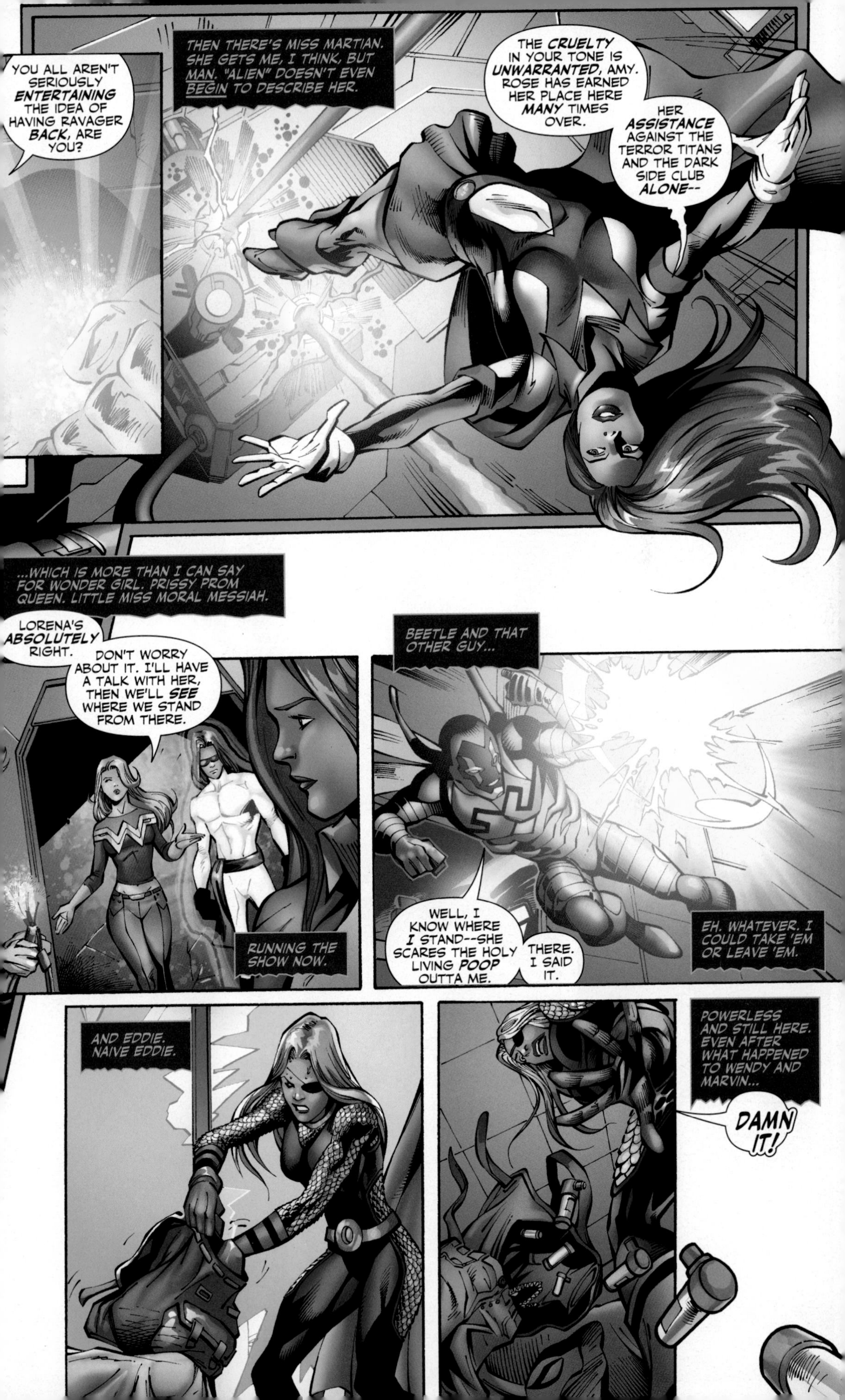

YOU ALL AREN'T SERIOUSLY ENTERTAINING THE IDEA OF HAVING RAVAGER BACK, ARE YOU?
THEN THERE'S MISS MARTIAN. SHE GETS ME, I THINK, BUT MAN. "ALIEN" DOESN'T EVEN BEGIN TO DESCRIBE HER.
THE CRUELTY IN YOUR TONE IS UNWARRANTED, AMY. ROSE HAS EARNED HER PLACE HERE MANY TIMES OVER.
HER ASSISTANCE AGAINST THE TERROR TITANS AND THE DARK SIDE CLUB ALONE--
...WHICH IS MORE THAN I CAN SAY FOR WONDER GIRL. PRISSY PROM QUEEN. LITTLE MISS MORAL MESSIAH.
LORENA'S ABSOLUTELY RIGHT.
DON'T WORRY ABOUT IT. I'LL HAVE A TALK WITH HER, THEN WE'LL SEE WHERE WE STAND FROM THERE.
RUNNING THE SHOW NOW.
BEETLE AND THAT OTHER GUY...
WELL, I KNOW WHERE I STAND--SHE SCARES THE HOLY LIVING POOP OUTTA ME.
THERE. I SAID IT.
EH. WHATEVER. I COULD TAKE 'EM OR LEAVE 'EM.
AND EDDIE. NAIVE EDDIE.
POWERLESS AND STILL HERE. EVEN AFTER WHAT HAPPENED TO WENDY AND MARVIN...
DAMN IT!

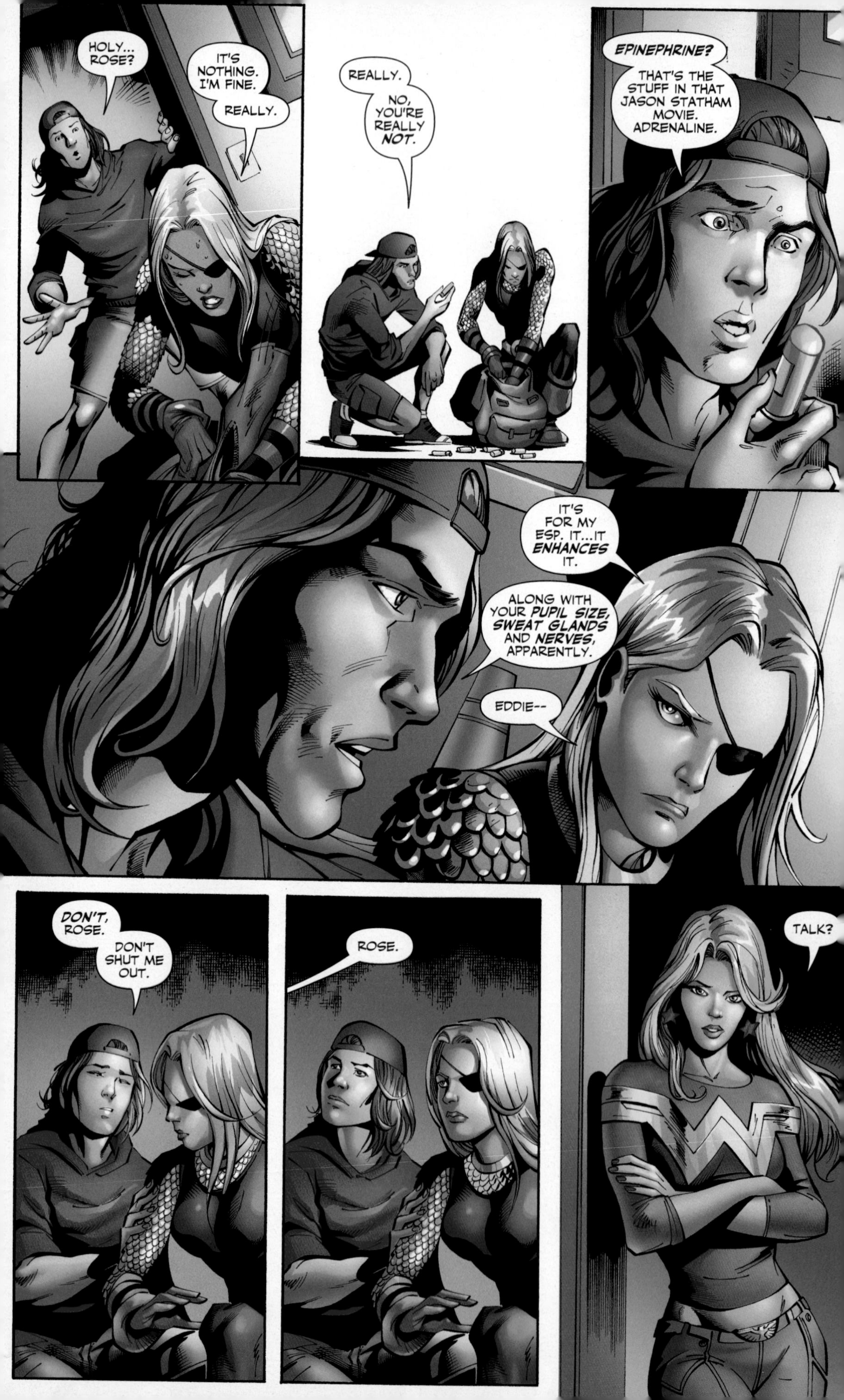
HOLY... ROSE?
IT'S NOTHING. I'M FINE.
REALLY.
REALLY.
NO, YOU'RE REALLY NOT.
EPINEPHRINE?
THAT'S THE STUFF IN THAT JASON STATHAM MOVIE. ADRENALINE.
IT'S FOR MY ESP. IT...IT ENHANCES IT.
ALONG WITH YOUR PUPIL SIZE, SWEAT GLANDS AND NERVES, APPARENTLY.
EDDIE--
DON'T, ROSE.
DON'T SHUT ME OUT.
ROSE.
TALK?

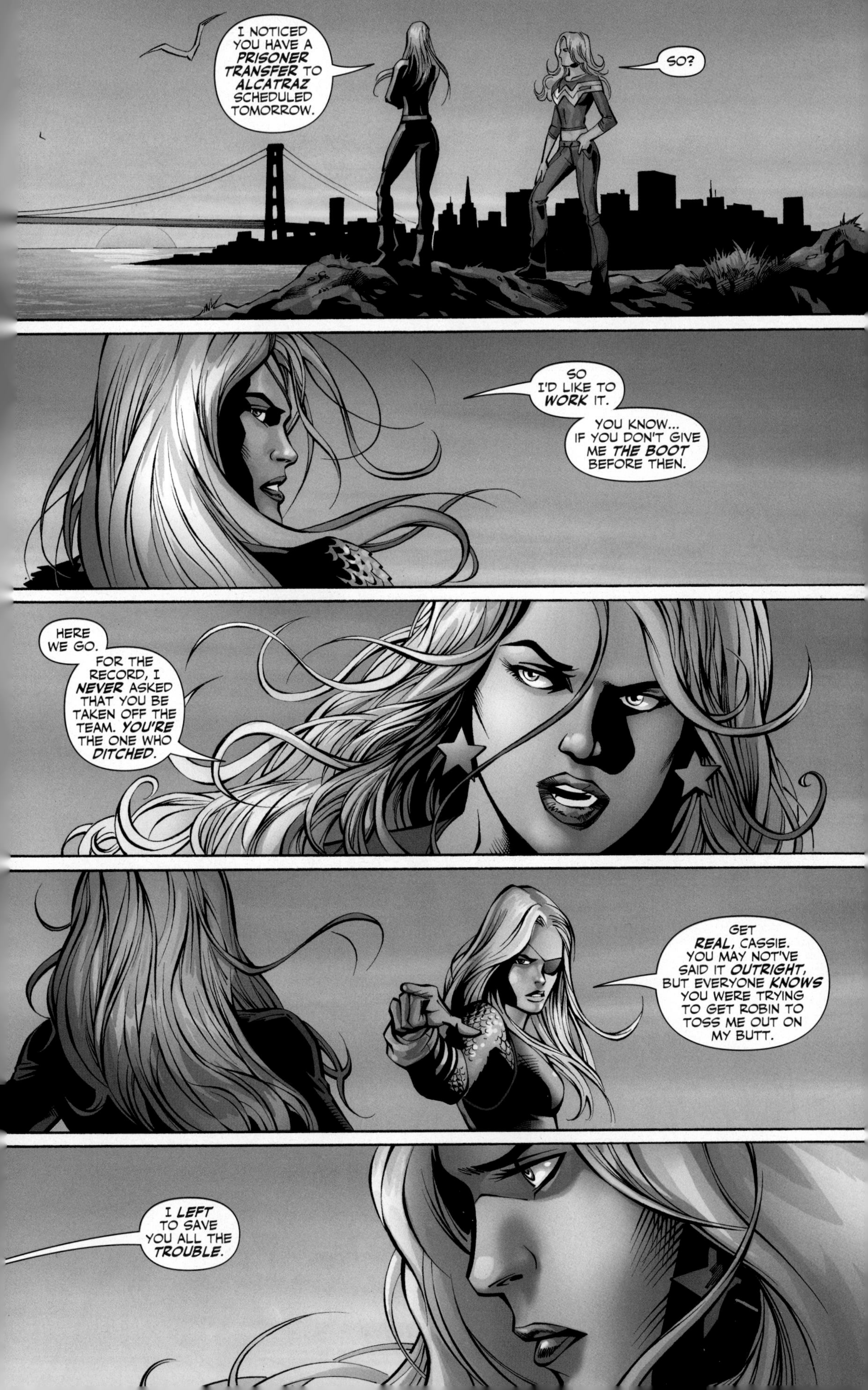
I NOTICED YOU HAVE A PRISONER TRANSFER TO ALCATRAZ SCHEDULED TOMORROW.
SO?
SO I'D LIKE TO WORK IT.
YOU KNOW... IF YOU DON'T GIVE ME THE BOOT BEFORE THEN.
HERE WE GO.
FOR THE RECORD, I NEVER ASKED THAT YOU BE TAKEN OFF THE TEAM. YOU'RE THE ONE WHO DITCHED.
GET REAL, CASSIE. YOU MAY NOT'VE SAID IT OUTRIGHT, BUT EVERYONE KNOWS YOU WERE TRYING TO GET ROBIN TO TOSS ME OUT ON MY BUTT.
I LEFT TO SAVE YOU ALL THE TROUBLE.

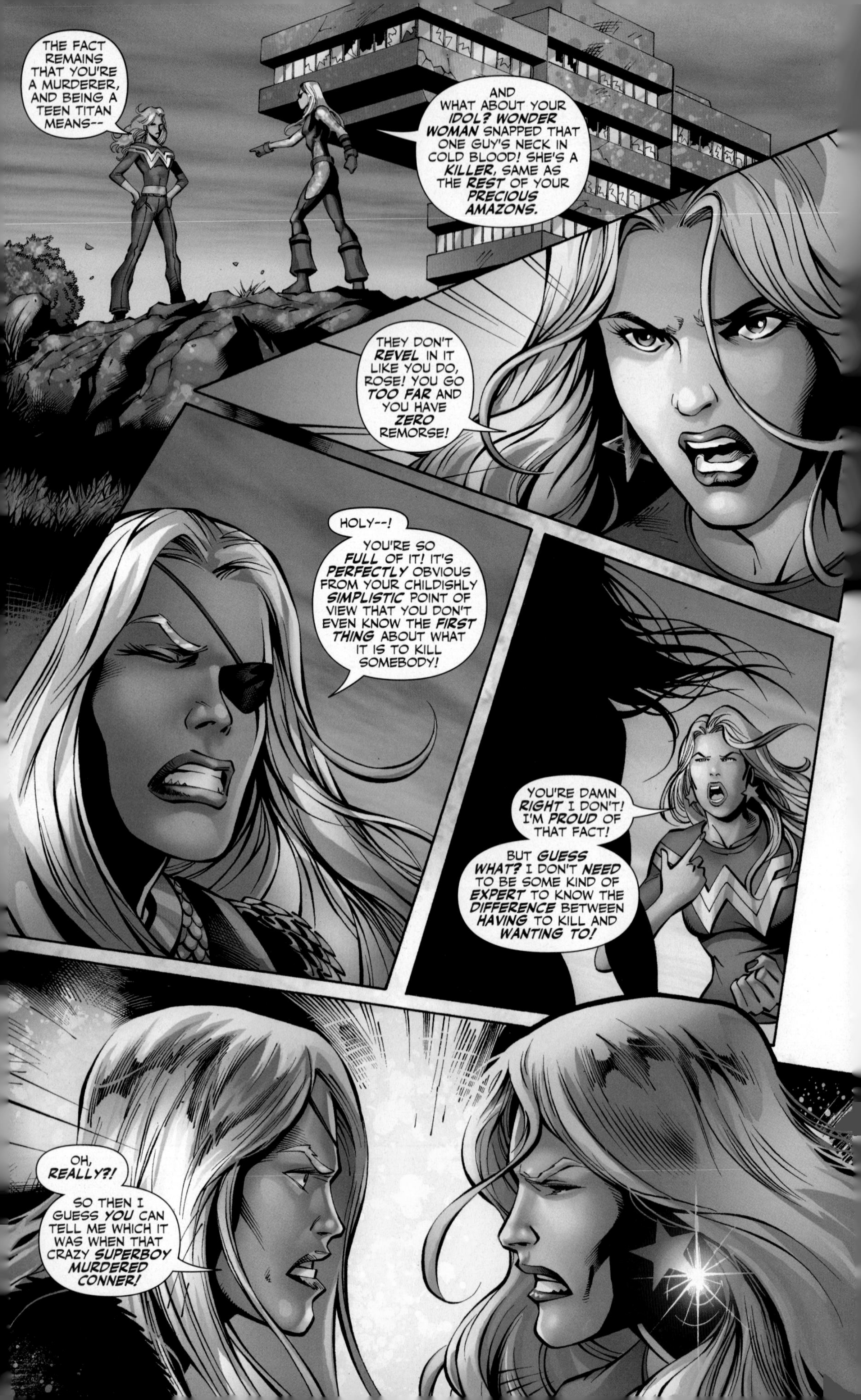
THE FACT REMAINS THAT YOU'RE A MURDERER, AND BEING A TEEN TITAN MEANS--
AND WHAT ABOUT YOUR IDOL? WONDER WOMAN SNAPPED THAT ONE GUY'S NECK IN COLD BLOOD! SHE'S A KILLER, SAME AS THE REST OF YOUR PRECIOUS AMAZONS.
THEY DON'T REVEL IN IT LIKE YOU DO, ROSE! YOU GO TOO FAR AND YOU HAVE ZERO REMORSE!
HOLY--!
YOU'RE SO FULL OF IT! IT'S PERFECTLY OBVIOUS FROM YOUR CHILDISHLY SIMPLISTIC POINT OF VIEW THAT YOU DON'T EVEN KNOW THE FIRST THING ABOUT WHAT IT IS TO KILL SOMEBODY!
YOU'RE DAMN RIGHT I DON'T! I'M PROUD OF THAT FACT!
BUT GUESS WHAT? I DON'T NEED TO BE SOME KIND OF EXPERT TO KNOW THE DIFFERENCE BETWEEN HAVING TO KILL AND WANTING TO!
OH, REALLY?!
SO THEN I GUESS YOU CAN TELL ME WHICH IT WAS WHEN THAT CRAZY SUPERBOY MURDERED CONNER!

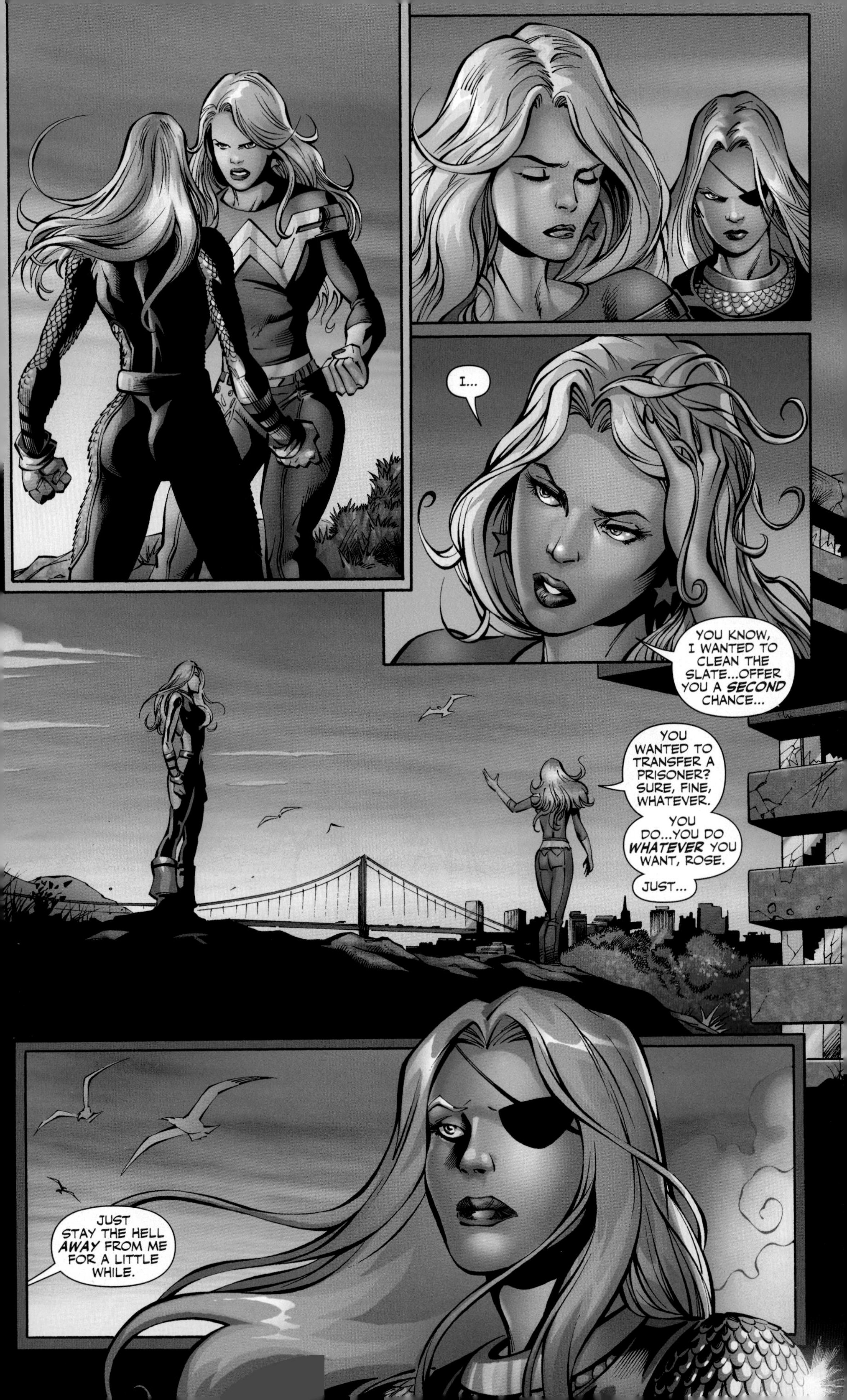
I...
YOU KNOW, I WANTED TO CLEAN THE SLATE...OFFER YOU A SECOND CHANCE...
YOU WANTED TO TRANSFER A PRISONER? SURE, FINE, WHATEVER.
YOU DO...YOU DO WHATEVER YOU WANT, ROSE.
JUST...
JUST STAY THE HELL AWAY FROM ME FOR A LITTLE WHILE.

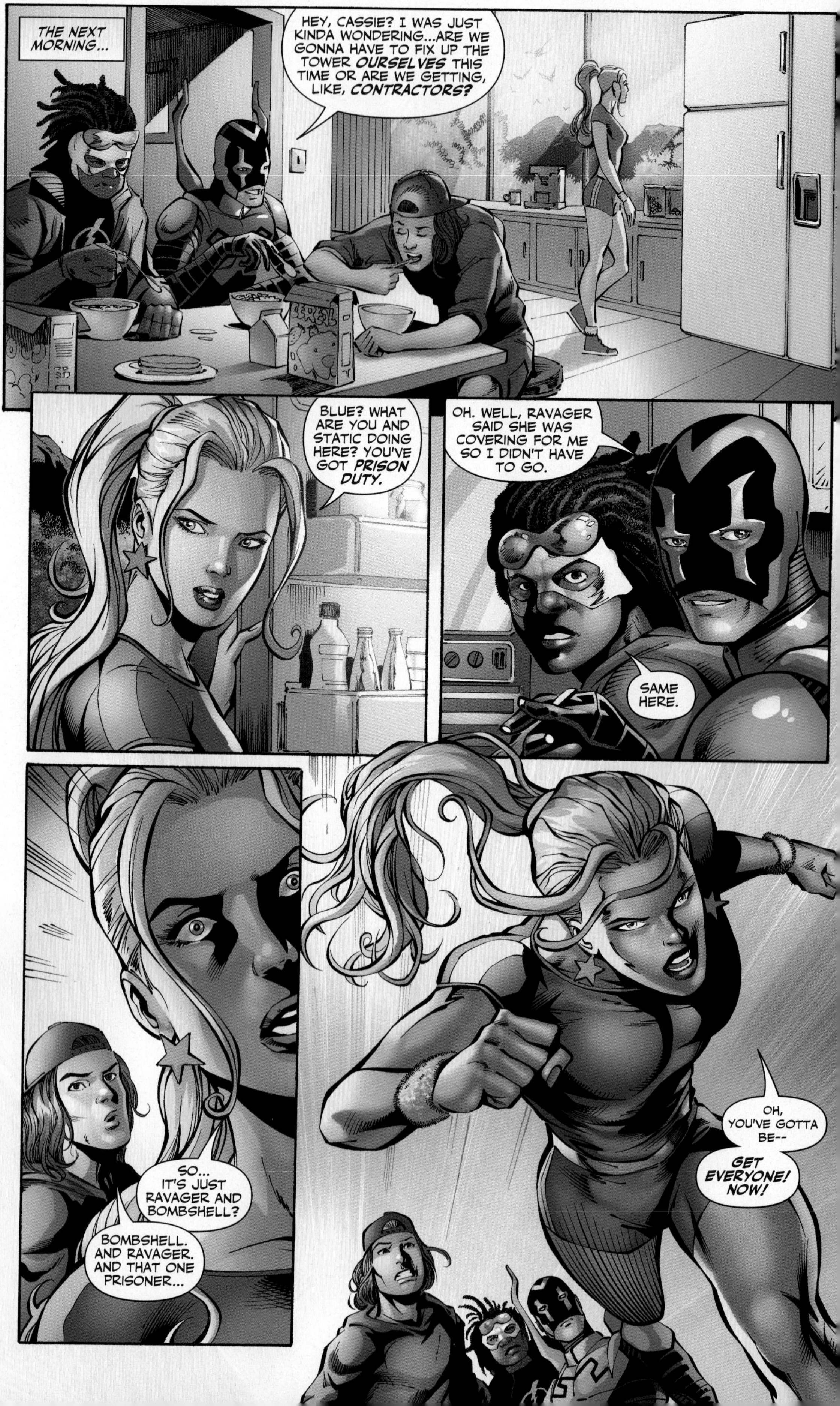
THE NEXT MORNING...
HEY, CASSIE? I WAS JUST KINDA WONDERING...ARE WE GONNA HAVE TO FIX UP THE TOWER OURSELVES THIS TIME OR ARE WE GETTING, LIKE, CONTRACTORS?
BLUE? WHAT ARE YOU AND STATIC DOING HERE? YOU'VE GOT PRISON DUTY.
OH. WELL, RAVAGER SAID SHE WAS COVERING FOR ME SO I DIDN'T HAVE TO GO.
SAME HERE.
SO... IT'S JUST RAVAGER AND BOMBSHELL?
BOMBSHELL. AND RAVAGER. AND THAT ONE PRISONER...
OH, YOU'VE GOTTA BE--
GET EVERYONE! NOW!

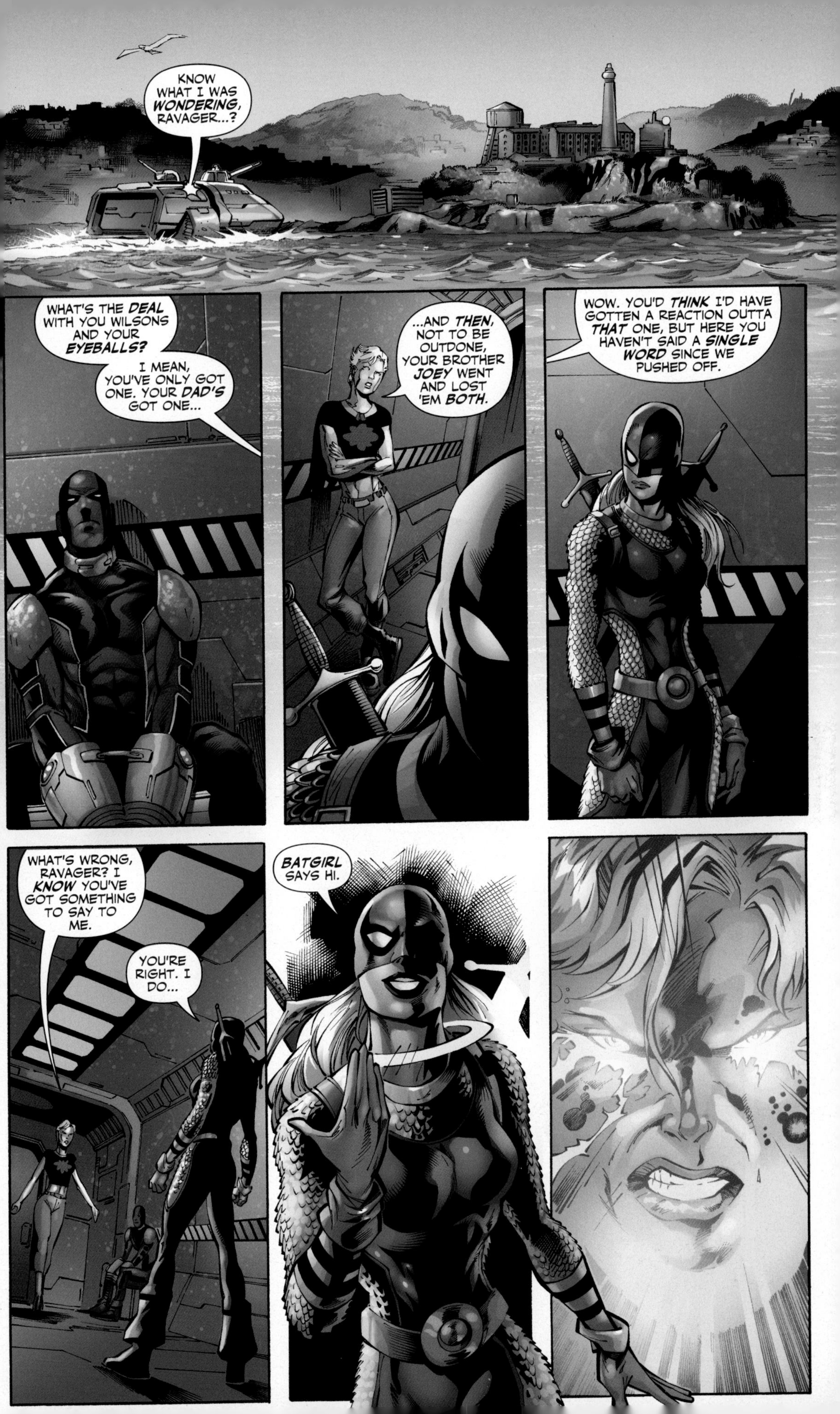
KNOW WHAT I WAS WONDERING, RAVAGER...?
WHAT'S THE DEAL WITH YOU WILSONS AND YOUR EYEBALLS?
I MEAN, YOU'VE ONLY GOT ONE. YOUR DAD'S GOT ONE...
...AND THEN, NOT TO BE OUTDONE, YOUR BROTHER JOEY WENT AND LOST 'EM BOTH.
WOW. YOU'D THINK I'D HAVE GOTTEN A REACTION OUTTA THAT ONE, BUT HERE YOU HAVEN'T SAID A SINGLE WORD SINCE WE PUSHED OFF.
WHAT'S WRONG, RAVAGER? I KNOW YOU'VE GOT SOMETHING TO SAY TO ME.
YOU'RE RIGHT. I DO...
BATGIRL SAYS HI.

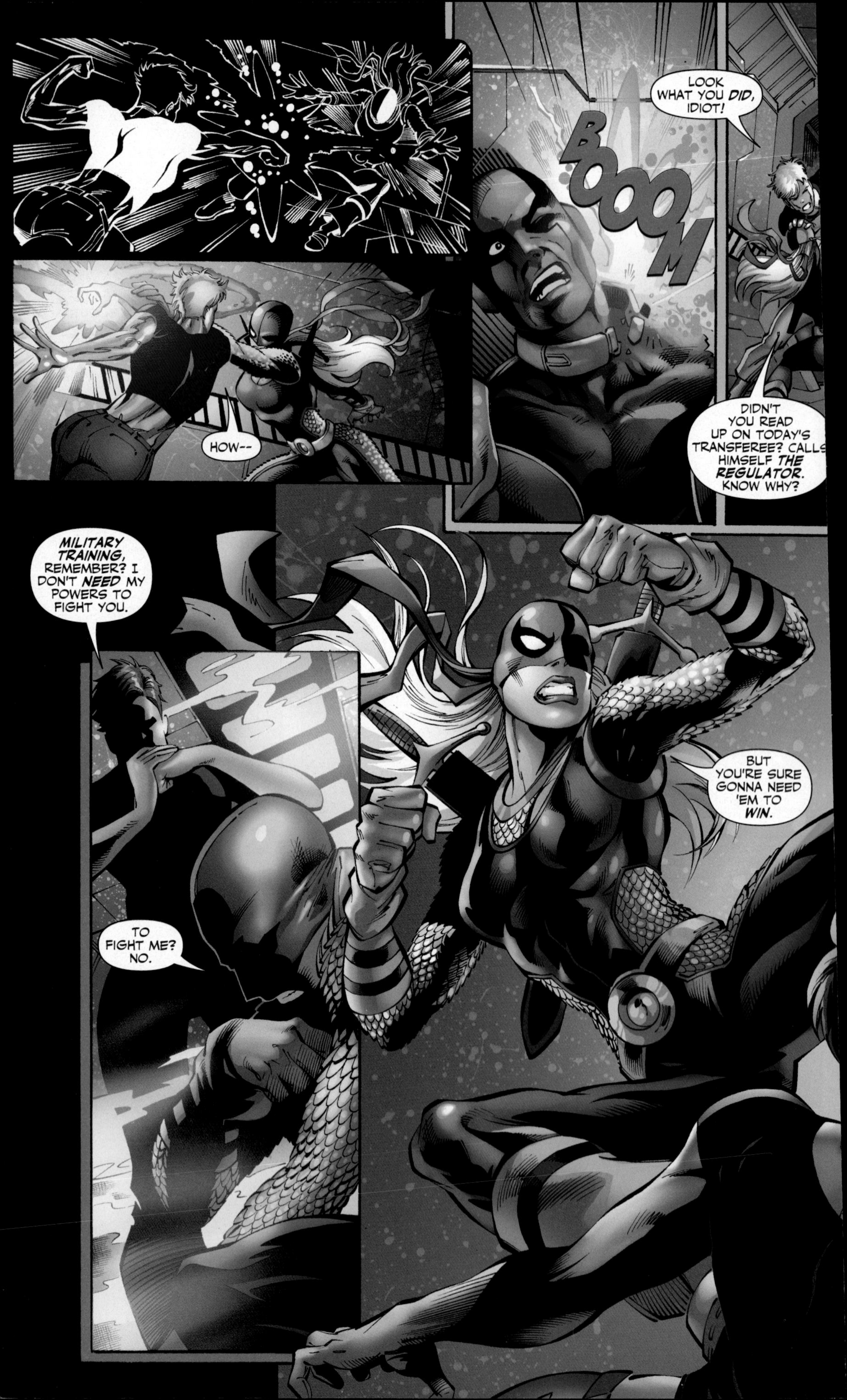
HOW--
LOOK WHAT YOU *DID*, IDIOT!
BOOOOM
DIDN'T YOU READ UP ON TODAY'S TRANSFEREE? CALLS HIMSELF ***THE REGULATOR***. KNOW WHY?
MILITARY TRAINING, REMEMBER? I DON'T ***NEED*** MY POWERS TO FIGHT YOU.
BUT YOU'RE SURE GONNA NEED 'EM TO ***WIN***.
TO FIGHT ME? NO.

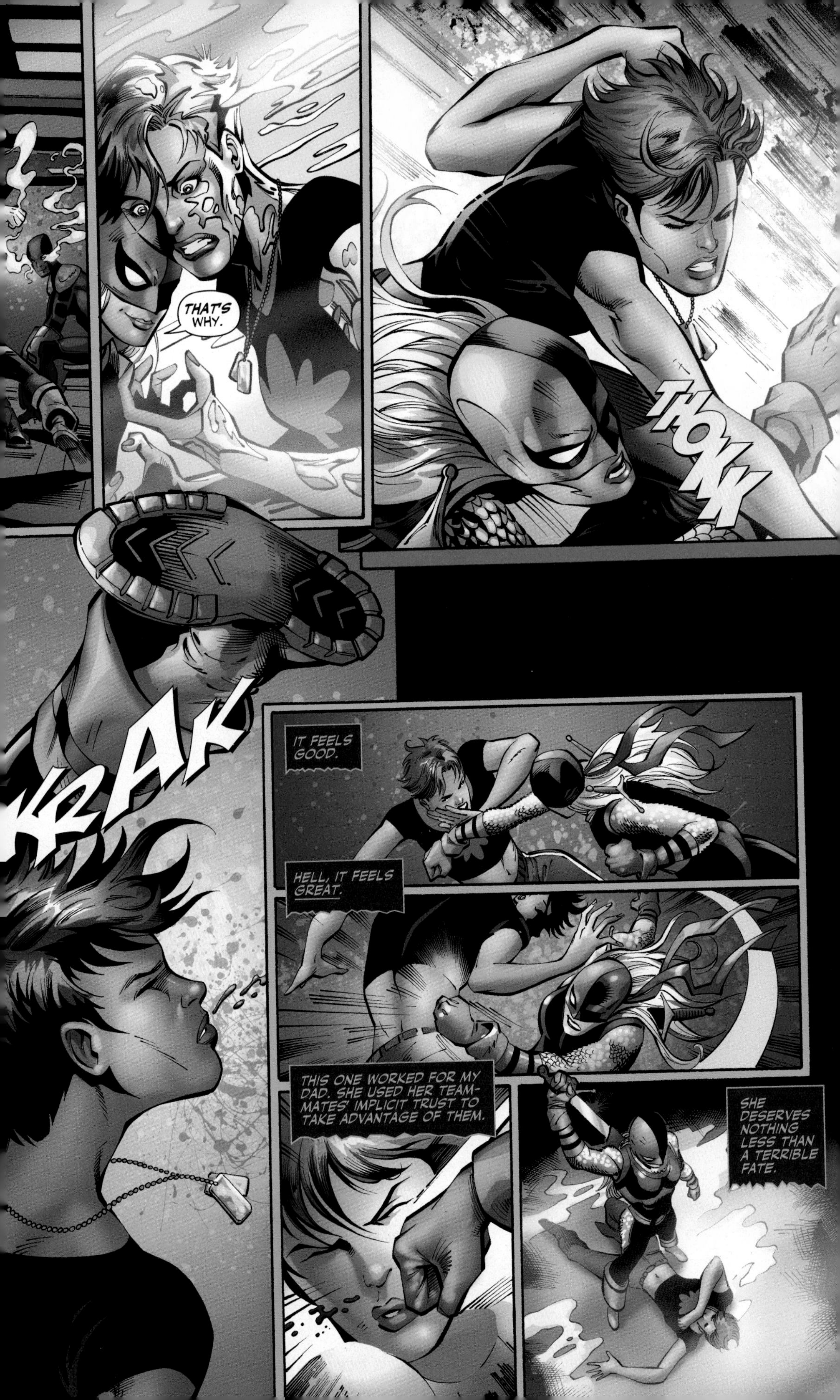
THAT'S WHY.
THONK
KRAK
IT FEELS GOOD.
HELL, IT FEELS GREAT.
THIS ONE WORKED FOR MY DAD. SHE USED HER TEAM-MATES' IMPLICIT TRUST TO TAKE ADVANTAGE OF THEM.
SHE DESERVES NOTHING LESS THAN A TERRIBLE FATE.

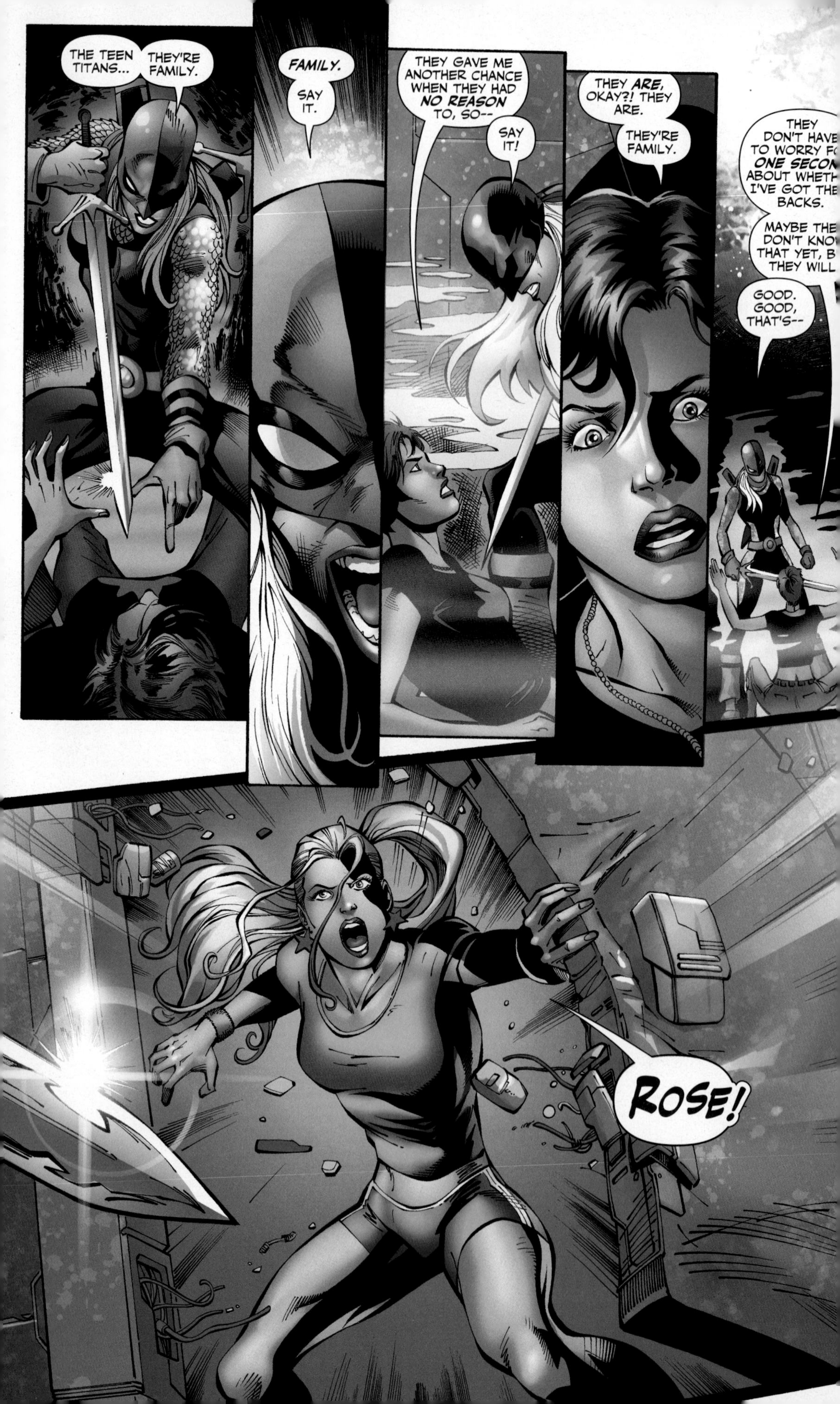
THE TEEN TITANS...
THEY'RE FAMILY.
FAMILY.
SAY IT.
THEY GAVE ME ANOTHER CHANCE WHEN THEY HAD NO REASON TO, SO--
SAY IT!
THEY ARE, OKAY?! THEY ARE.
THEY'RE FAMILY.
GOOD. GOOD, THAT'S--
ROSE!

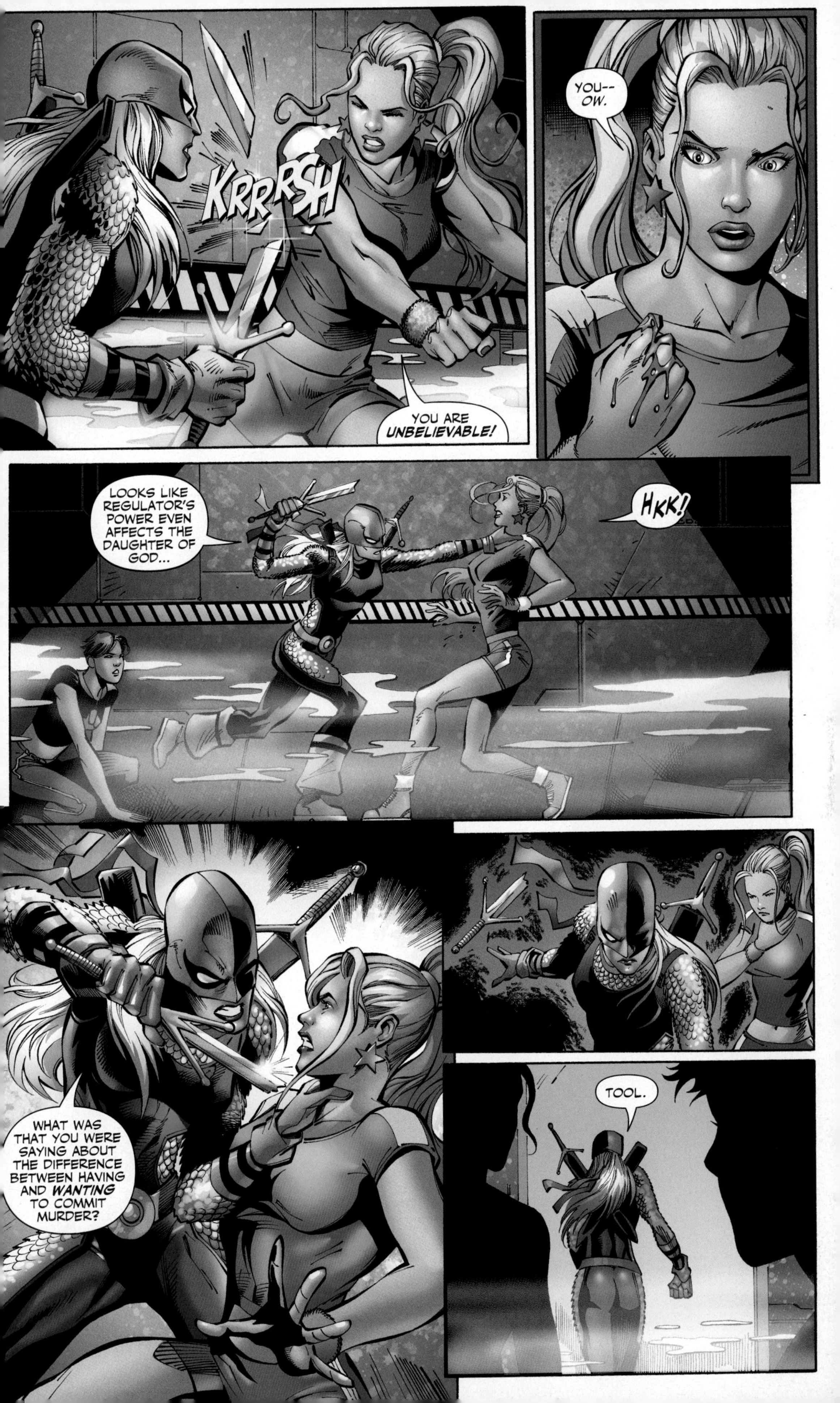
KRRRSH
YOU ARE UNBELIEVABLE!
YOU-- OW.
LOOKS LIKE REGULATOR'S POWER EVEN AFFECTS THE DAUGHTER OF GOD...
HKK!
WHAT WAS THAT YOU WERE SAYING ABOUT THE DIFFERENCE BETWEEN HAVING AND WANTING TO COMMIT MURDER?
TOOL.

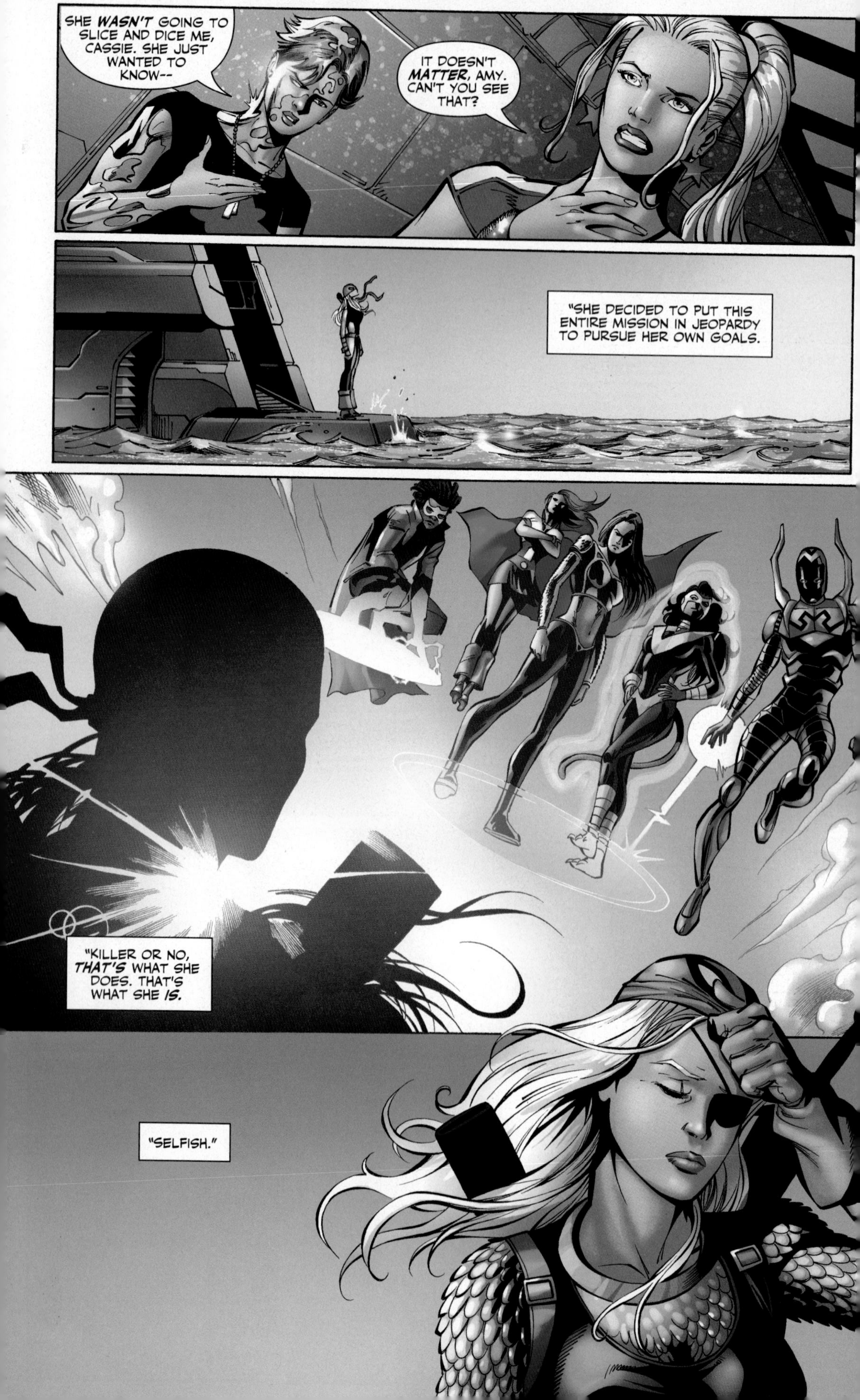
SHE WASN'T GOING TO SLICE AND DICE ME, CASSIE. SHE JUST WANTED TO KNOW--
IT DOESN'T MATTER, AMY. CAN'T YOU SEE THAT?
"SHE DECIDED TO PUT THIS ENTIRE MISSION IN JEOPARDY TO PURSUE HER OWN GOALS.
"KILLER OR NO, THAT'S WHAT SHE DOES. THAT'S WHAT SHE IS.
"SELFISH."

FOUND ME.

FIGURED YOU MIGHT BE UP HERE.

YOU ALWAYS LIKED THIS SPOT, DIDN'T YOU? THE VIEW. THE PRIVACY.

WHAT ABOUT YOU? STILL COME UP HERE TO THINK?

NOT REALLY. NOT ANYMORE.

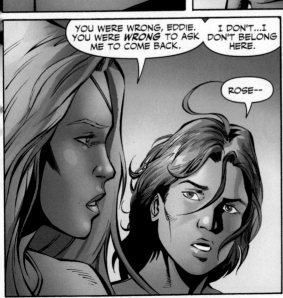

YOU WERE WRONG, EDDIE. YOU WERE WRONG TO ASK ME TO COME BACK.

I DON'T...I DON'T BELONG HERE.

ROSE--

AND NEITHER DO YOU.

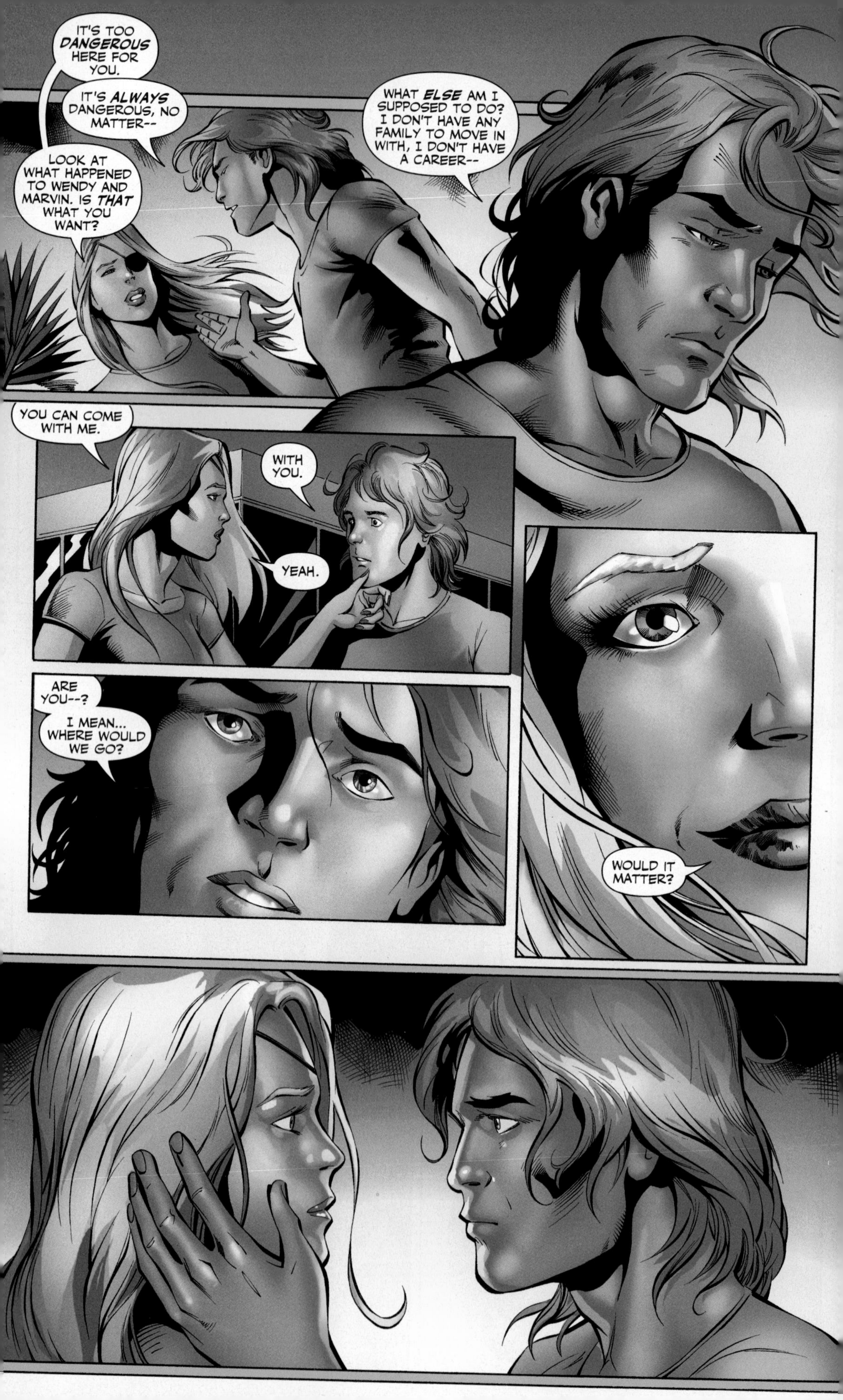
IT'S TOO DANGEROUS HERE FOR YOU.
IT'S ALWAYS DANGEROUS, NO MATTER--
LOOK AT WHAT HAPPENED TO WENDY AND MARVIN. IS THAT WHAT YOU WANT?
WHAT ELSE AM I SUPPOSED TO DO? I DON'T HAVE ANY FAMILY TO MOVE IN WITH, I DON'T HAVE A CAREER--
YOU CAN COME WITH ME.
WITH YOU.
YEAH.
ARE YOU--?
I MEAN... WHERE WOULD WE GO?
WOULD IT MATTER?

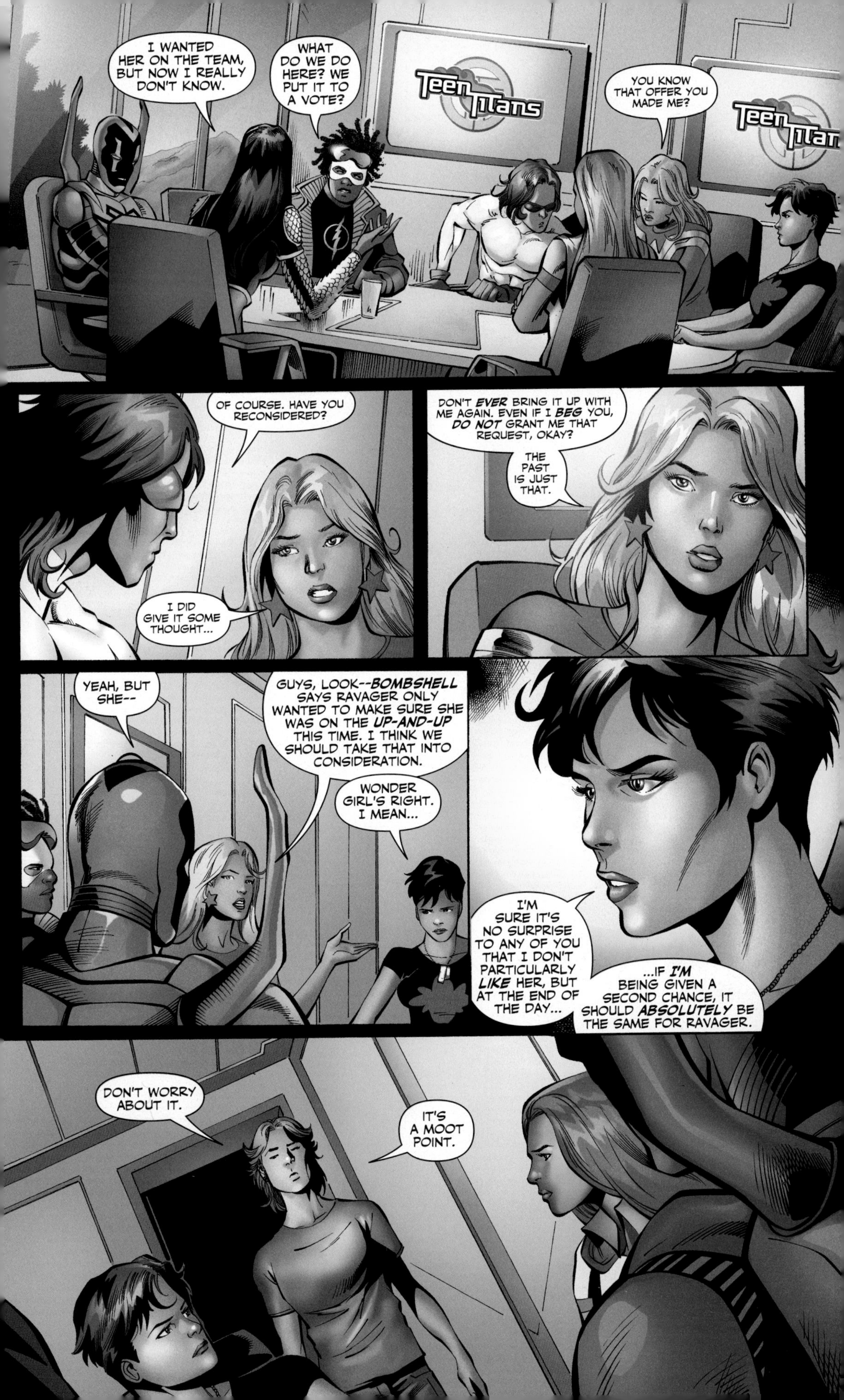
I WANTED HER ON THE TEAM, BUT NOW I REALLY DON'T KNOW.
WHAT DO WE DO HERE? WE PUT IT TO A VOTE?
TEEN TITANS
YOU KNOW THAT OFFER YOU MADE ME?
TEEN TITANS
OF COURSE. HAVE YOU RECONSIDERED?
I DID GIVE IT SOME THOUGHT...
DON'T *EVER* BRING IT UP WITH ME AGAIN. EVEN IF I *BEG* YOU, *DO NOT* GRANT ME THAT REQUEST, OKAY?
THE PAST IS JUST THAT.
YEAH, BUT SHE--
GUYS, LOOK--*BOMBSHELL* SAYS RAVAGER ONLY WANTED TO MAKE SURE SHE WAS ON THE *UP-AND-UP* THIS TIME. I THINK WE SHOULD TAKE THAT INTO CONSIDERATION.
WONDER GIRL'S RIGHT. I MEAN...
I'M SURE IT'S NO SURPRISE TO ANY OF YOU THAT I DON'T PARTICULARLY *LIKE* HER, BUT AT THE END OF THE DAY...
...IF *I'M* BEING GIVEN A SECOND CHANCE, IT SHOULD *ABSOLUTELY* BE THE SAME FOR RAVAGER.
DON'T WORRY ABOUT IT.
IT'S A MOOT POINT.

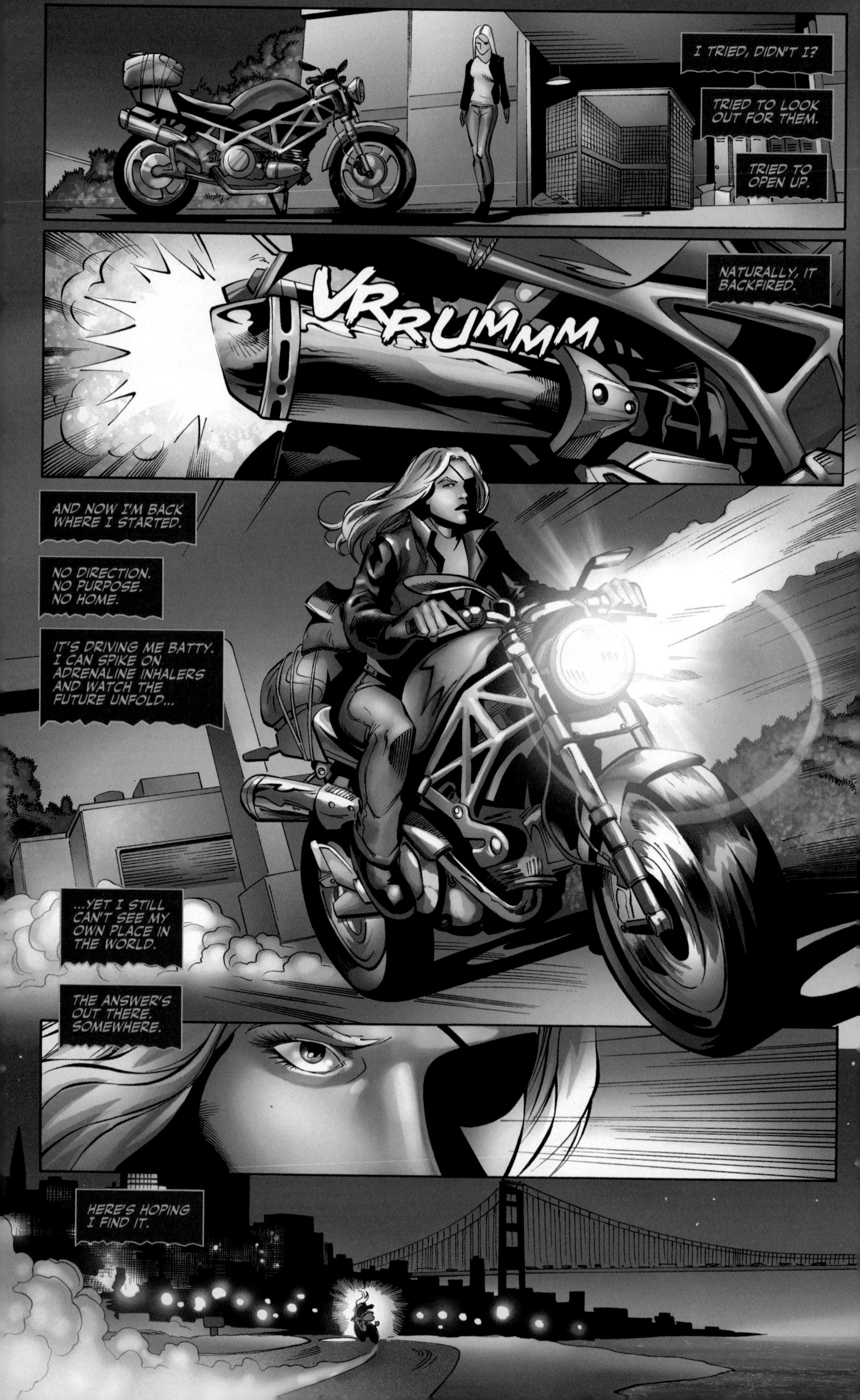

I TRIED, DIDN'T I?
TRIED TO LOOK OUT FOR THEM.
TRIED TO OPEN UP.
VRRUMMM
NATURALLY, IT BACKFIRED.
AND NOW I'M BACK WHERE I STARTED.
NO DIRECTION. NO PURPOSE. NO HOME.
IT'S DRIVING ME BATTY. I CAN SPIKE ON ADRENALINE INHALERS AND WATCH THE FUTURE UNFOLD...
...YET I STILL CAN'T SEE MY OWN PLACE IN THE WORLD.
THE ANSWER'S OUT THERE. SOMEWHERE.
HERE'S HOPING I FIND IT.

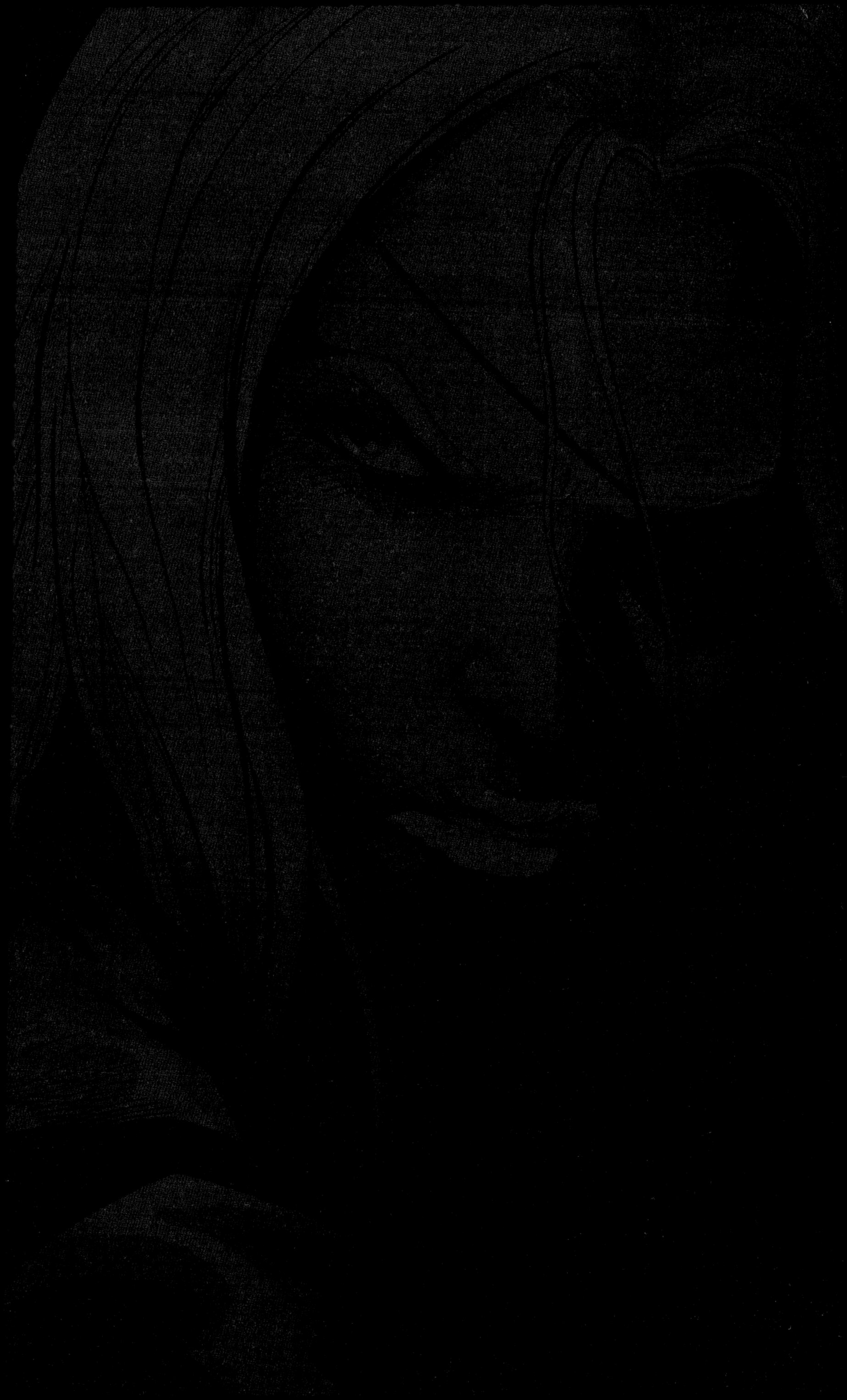

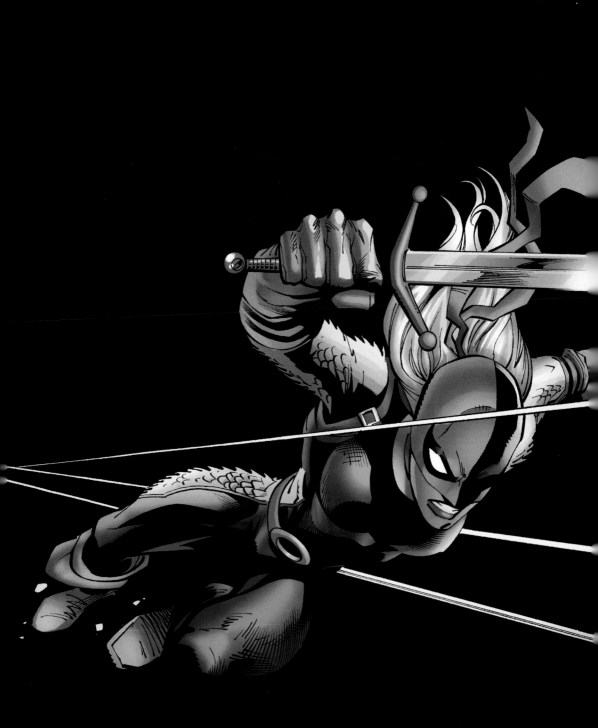

RAVAGER IN FRESH HELL

YILDIRAY CINAR draws
SEAN McKEEVER writes
JULIO FERREIRA inks

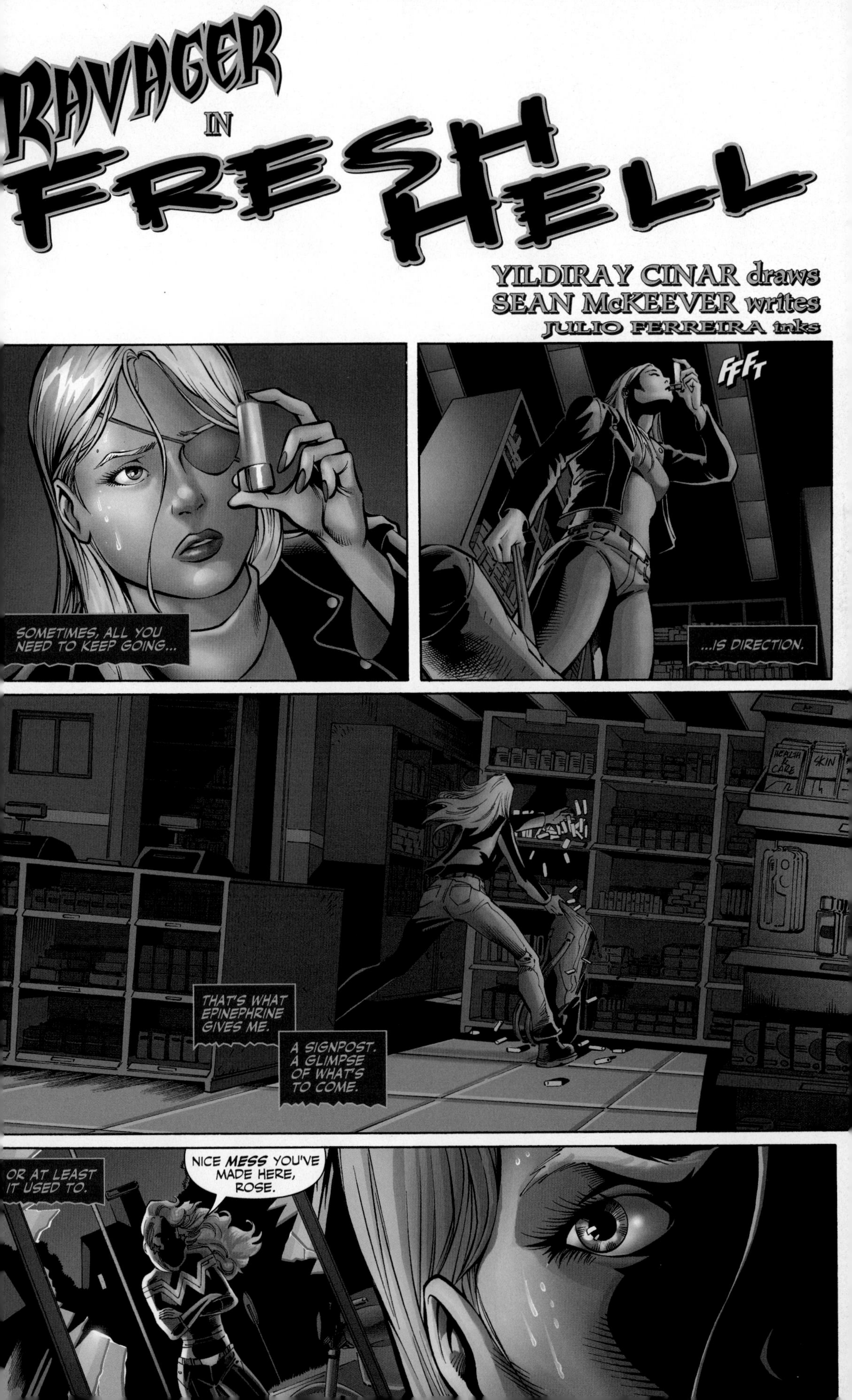

SOMETIMES, ALL YOU NEED TO KEEP GOING...
FFFT
...IS DIRECTION.
THAT'S WHAT EPINEPHRINE GIVES ME.
A SIGNPOST. A GLIMPSE OF WHAT'S TO COME.
OR AT LEAST IT USED TO.
NICE MESS YOU'VE MADE HERE, ROSE.

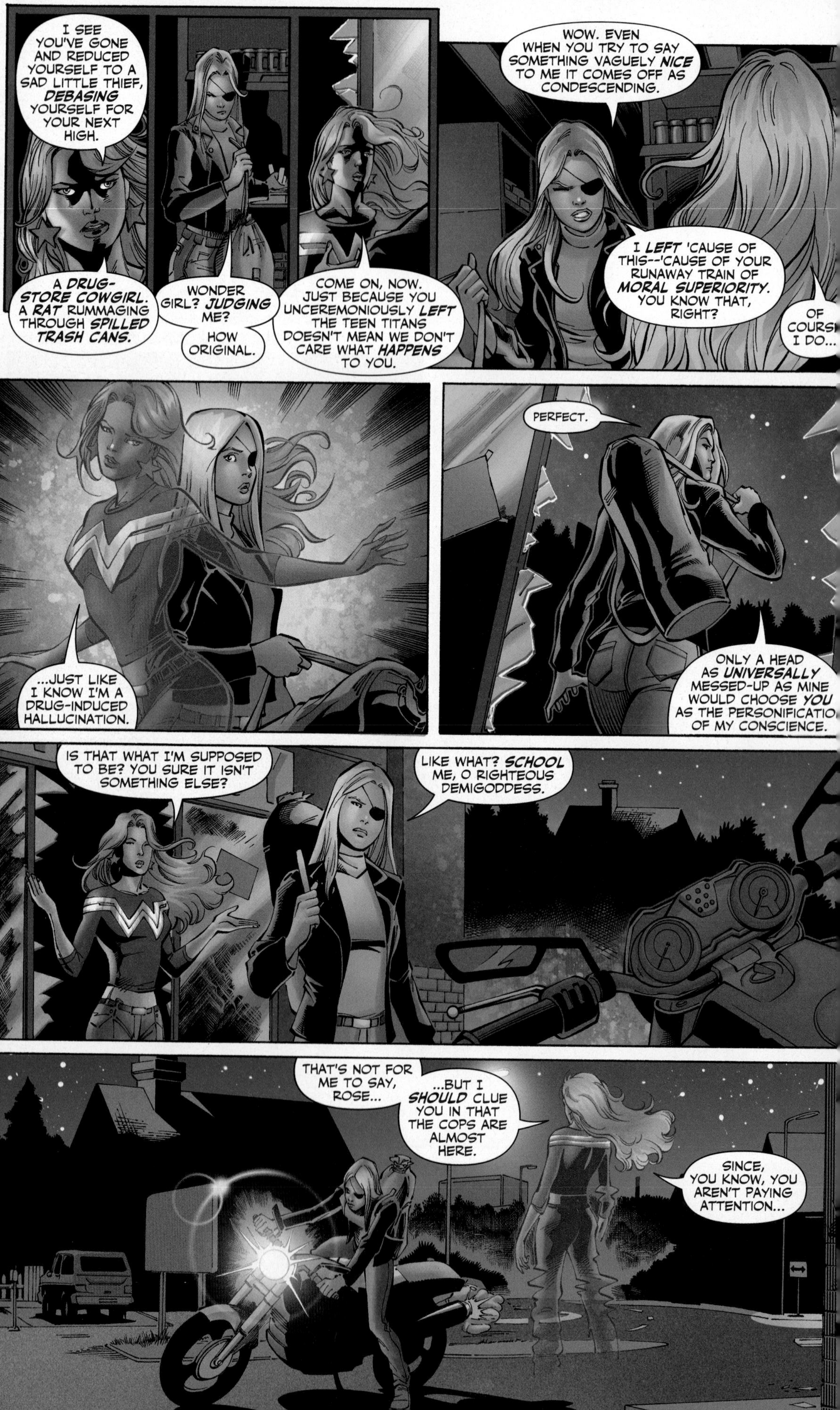
I SEE YOU'VE GONE AND REDUCED YOURSELF TO A SAD LITTLE THIEF, DEBASING YOURSELF FOR YOUR NEXT HIGH.
A DRUG-STORE COWGIRL. A RAT RUMMAGING THROUGH SPILLED TRASH CANS.
WONDER GIRL? JUDGING ME?
HOW ORIGINAL.
COME ON, NOW. JUST BECAUSE YOU UNCEREMONIOUSLY LEFT THE TEEN TITANS DOESN'T MEAN WE DON'T CARE WHAT HAPPENS TO YOU.
WOW. EVEN WHEN YOU TRY TO SAY SOMETHING VAGUELY NICE TO ME IT COMES OFF AS CONDESCENDING.
I LEFT 'CAUSE OF THIS--'CAUSE OF YOUR RUNAWAY TRAIN OF MORAL SUPERIORITY. YOU KNOW THAT, RIGHT?
OF COURS I DO...
...JUST LIKE I KNOW I'M A DRUG-INDUCED HALLUCINATION.
PERFECT.
ONLY A HEAD AS UNIVERSALLY MESSED-UP AS MINE WOULD CHOOSE YOU AS THE PERSONIFICATIO OF MY CONSCIENCE.
IS THAT WHAT I'M SUPPOSED TO BE? YOU SURE IT ISN'T SOMETHING ELSE?
LIKE WHAT? SCHOOL ME, O RIGHTEOUS DEMIGODDESS.
THAT'S NOT FOR ME TO SAY, ROSE...
...BUT I SHOULD CLUE YOU IN THAT THE COPS ARE ALMOST HERE.
SINCE, YOU KNOW, YOU AREN'T PAYING ATTENTION...

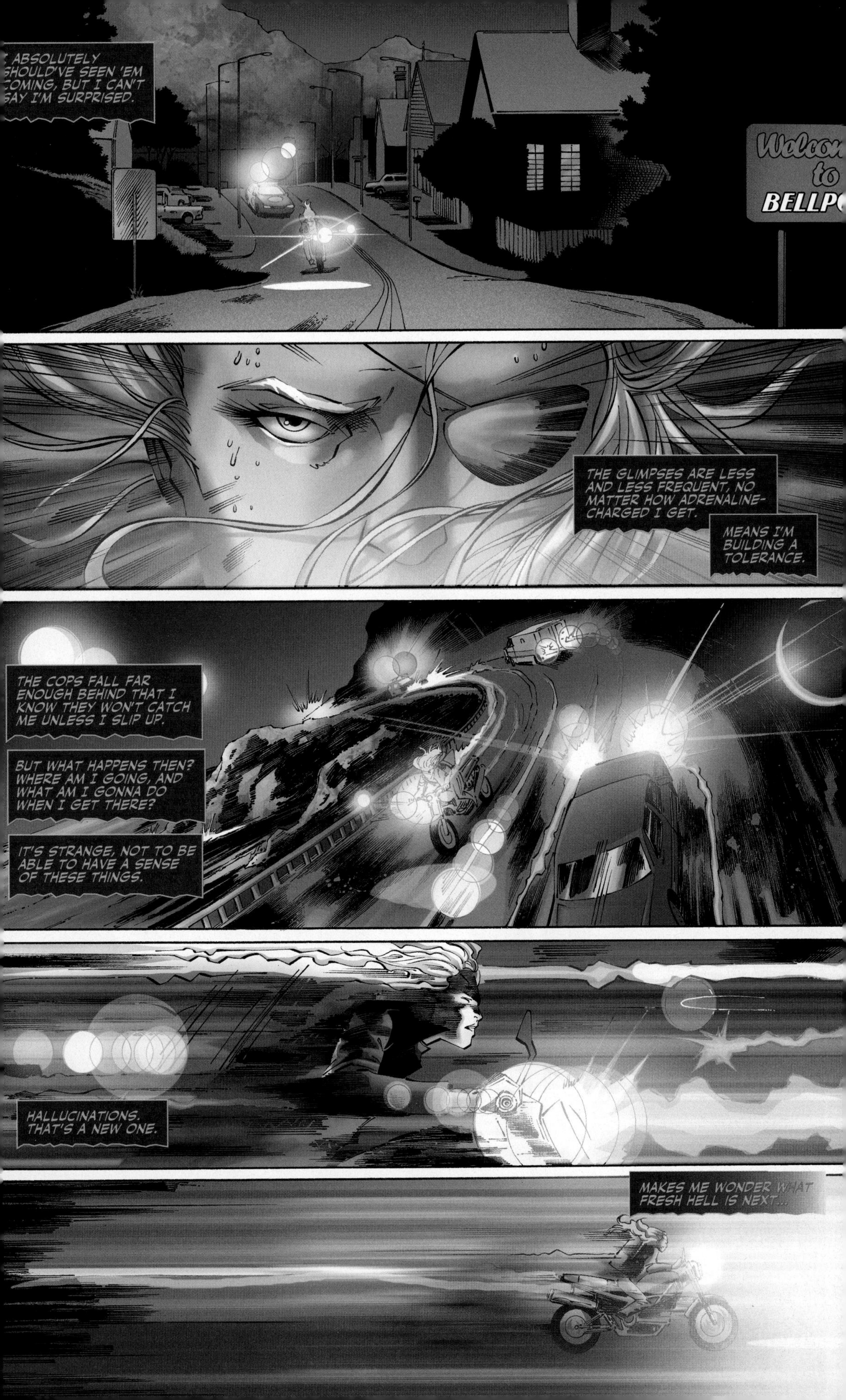
I ABSOLUTELY SHOULD'VE SEEN 'EM COMING, BUT I CAN'T SAY I'M SURPRISED.
Welcome to BELLP
THE GLIMPSES ARE LESS AND LESS FREQUENT, NO MATTER HOW ADRENALINE-CHARGED I GET.
MEANS I'M BUILDING A TOLERANCE.
THE COPS FALL FAR ENOUGH BEHIND THAT I KNOW THEY WON'T CATCH ME UNLESS I SLIP UP.
BUT WHAT HAPPENS THEN? WHERE AM I GOING, AND WHAT AM I GONNA DO WHEN I GET THERE?
IT'S STRANGE, NOT TO BE ABLE TO HAVE A SENSE OF THESE THINGS.
HALLUCINATIONS. THAT'S A NEW ONE.
MAKES ME WONDER WHAT FRESH HELL IS NEXT...

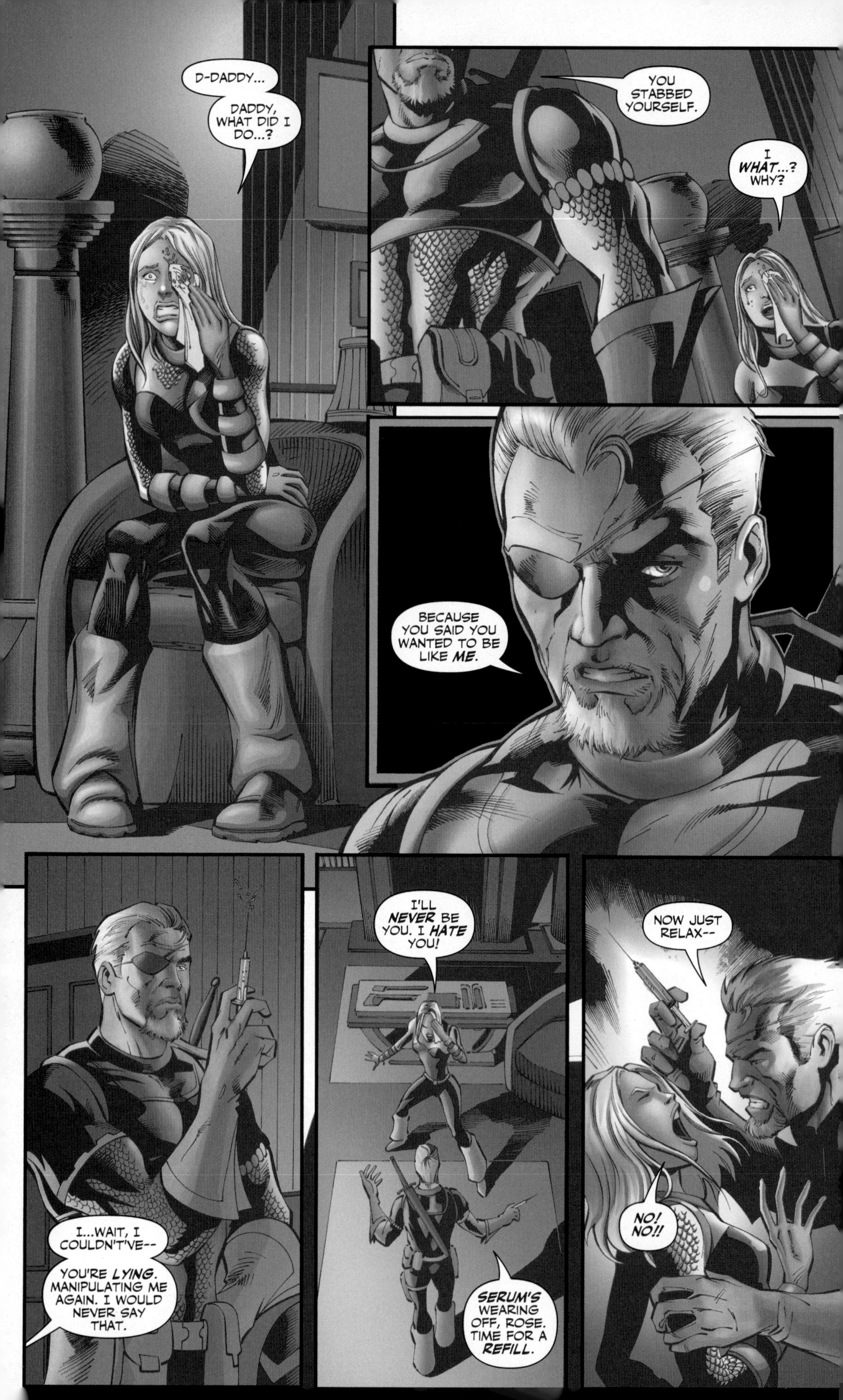
D-DADDY...
DADDY, WHAT DID I DO...?
YOU STABBED YOURSELF.
I *WHAT*...? WHY?
BECAUSE YOU SAID YOU WANTED TO BE LIKE *ME*.
I...WAIT, I COULDN'T'VE--
YOU'RE *LYING*. MANIPULATING ME AGAIN. I WOULD NEVER SAY THAT.
I'LL *NEVER* BE YOU. I *HATE* YOU!
SERUM'S WEARING OFF, ROSE. TIME FOR A *REFILL*.
NOW JUST RELAX--
NO! NO!!

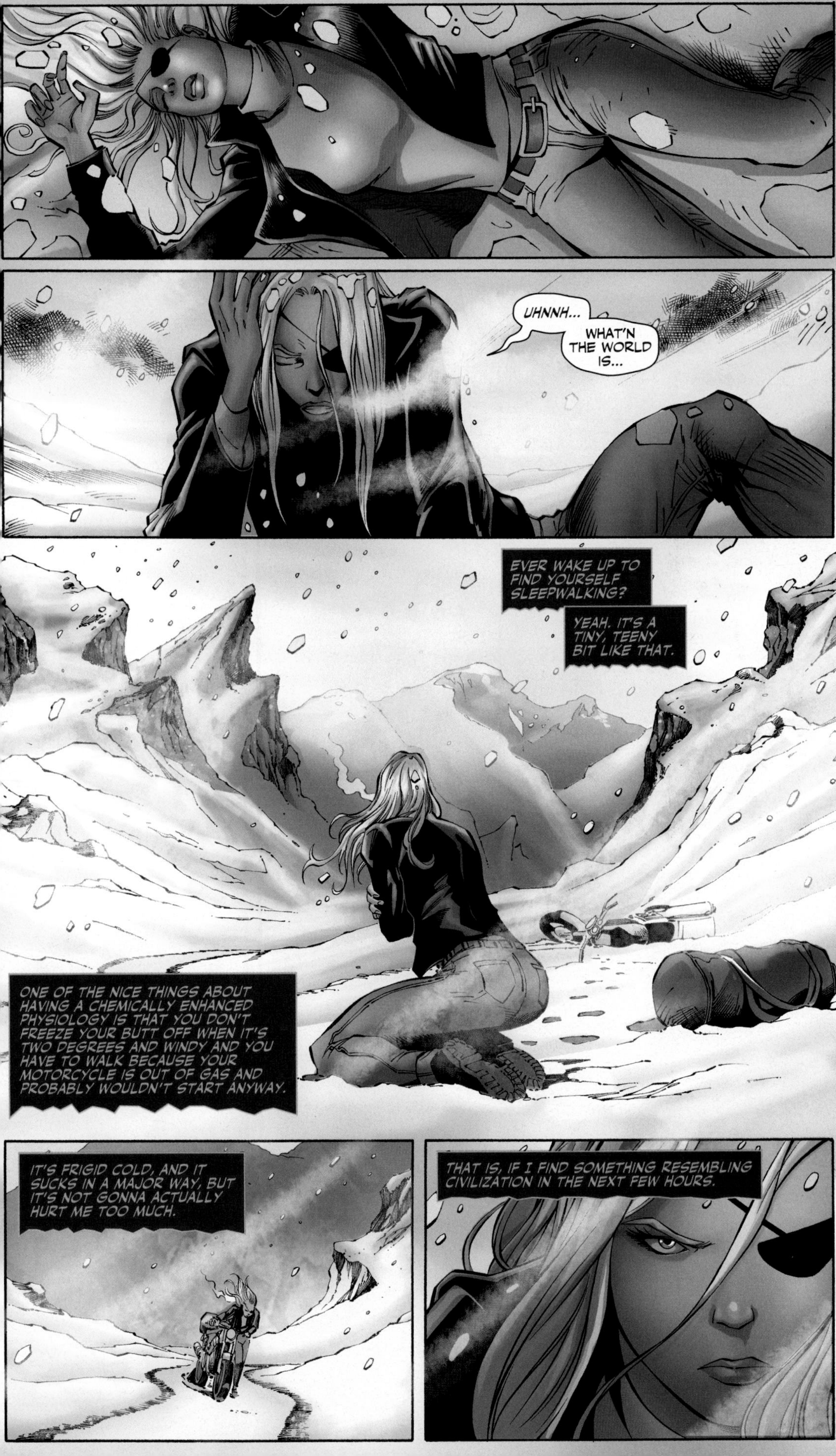

UHNNH... WHAT'N THE WORLD IS...
EVER WAKE UP TO FIND YOURSELF SLEEPWALKING?
YEAH. IT'S A TINY, TEENY BIT LIKE THAT.
ONE OF THE NICE THINGS ABOUT HAVING A CHEMICALLY ENHANCED PHYSIOLOGY IS THAT YOU DON'T FREEZE YOUR BUTT OFF WHEN IT'S TWO DEGREES AND WINDY AND YOU HAVE TO WALK BECAUSE YOUR MOTORCYCLE IS OUT OF GAS AND PROBABLY WOULDN'T START ANYWAY.
IT'S FRIGID COLD, AND IT SUCKS IN A MAJOR WAY, BUT IT'S NOT GONNA ACTUALLY HURT ME TOO MUCH.
THAT IS, IF I FIND SOMETHING RESEMBLING CIVILIZATION IN THE NEXT FEW HOURS.

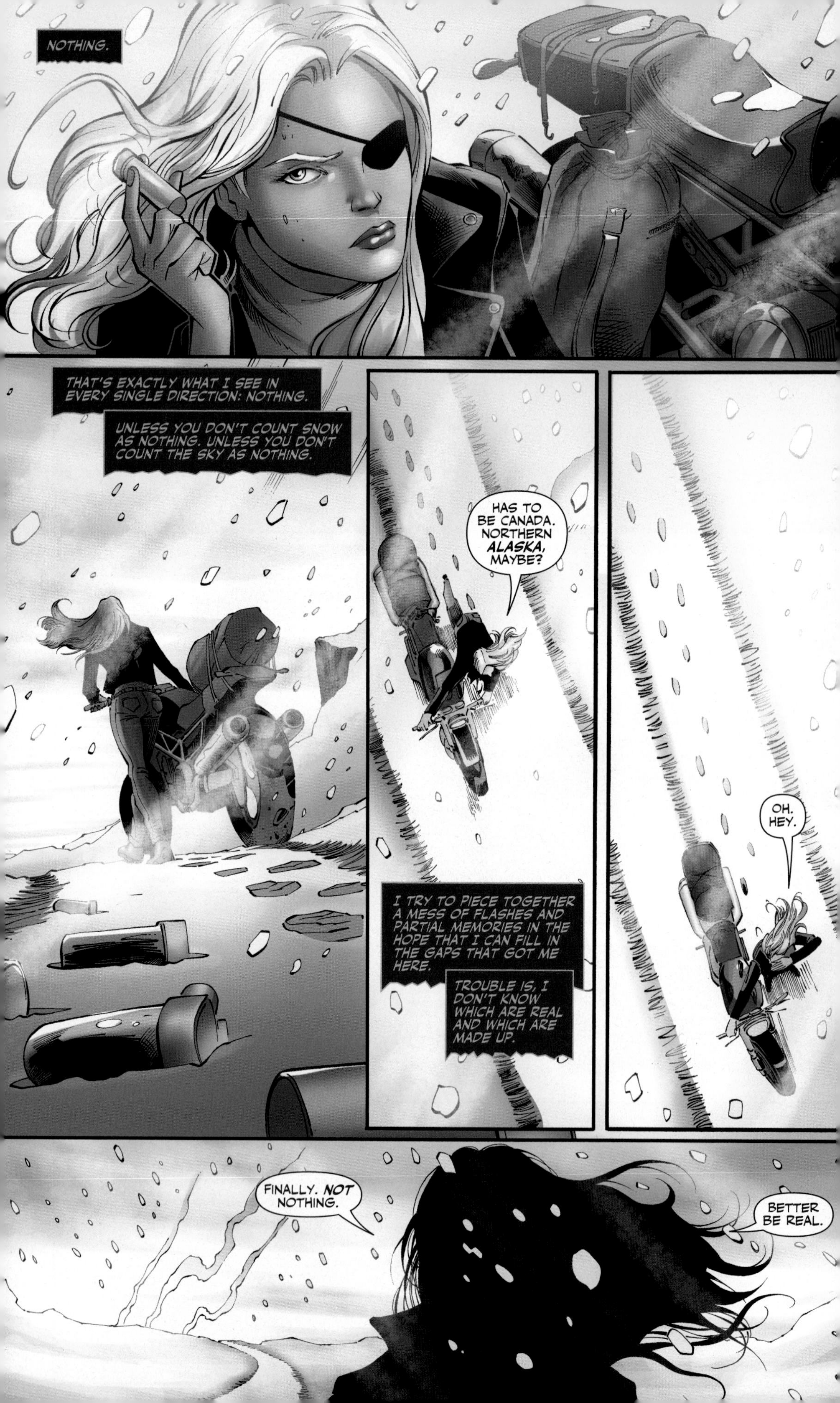
NOTHING.
THAT'S EXACTLY WHAT I SEE IN EVERY SINGLE DIRECTION: NOTHING.
UNLESS YOU DON'T COUNT SNOW AS NOTHING. UNLESS YOU DON'T COUNT THE SKY AS NOTHING.
HAS TO BE CANADA. NORTHERN ALASKA, MAYBE?
I TRY TO PIECE TOGETHER A MESS OF FLASHES AND PARTIAL MEMORIES IN THE HOPE THAT I CAN FILL IN THE GAPS THAT GOT ME HERE.
TROUBLE IS, I DON'T KNOW WHICH ARE REAL AND WHICH ARE MADE UP.
OH. HEY.
FINALLY. NOT NOTHING.
BETTER BE REAL.

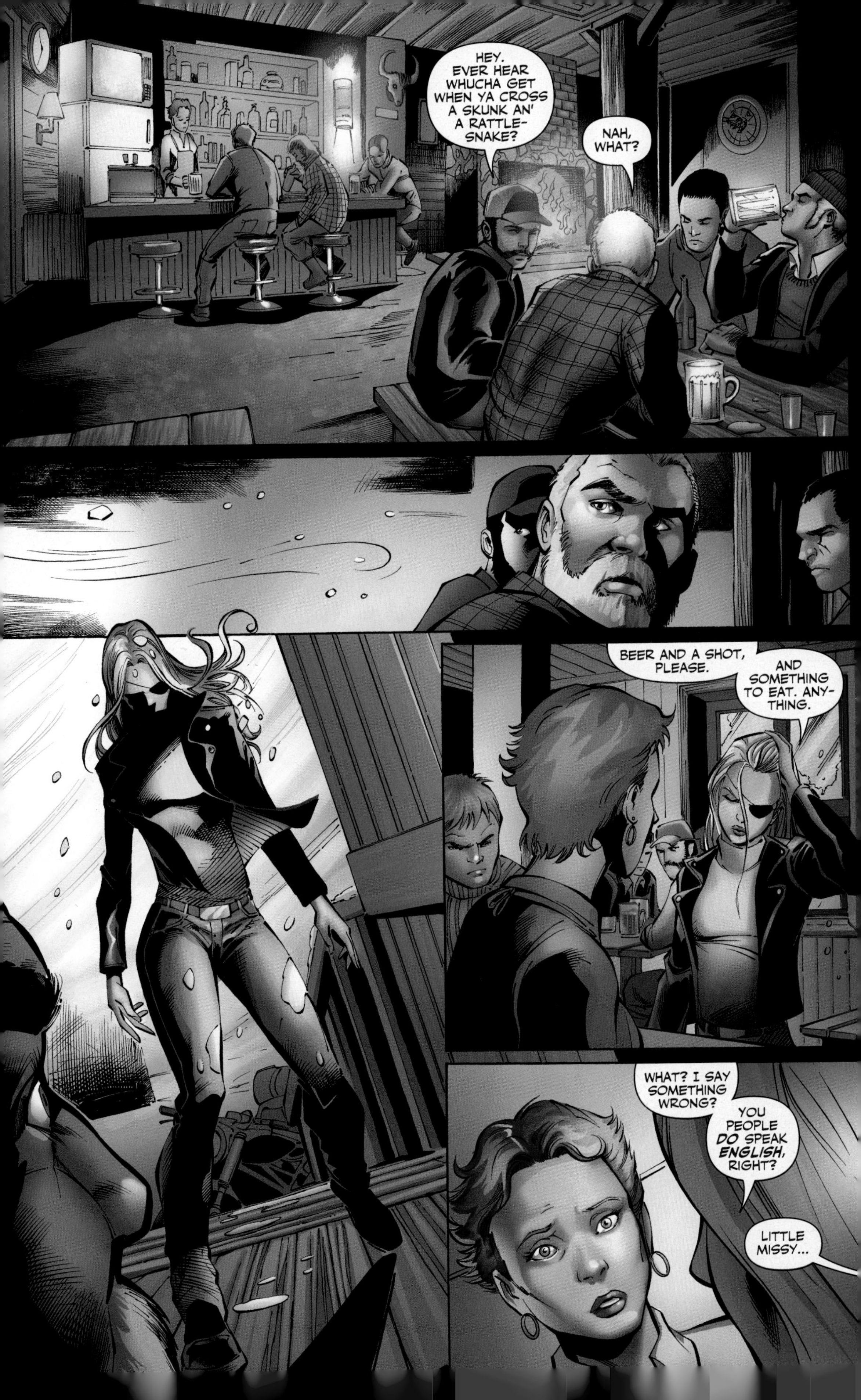
HEY. EVER HEAR WHUCHA GET WHEN YA CROSS A SKUNK AN' A RATTLE-SNAKE?
NAH, WHAT?
BEER AND A SHOT, PLEASE.
AND SOMETHING TO EAT. ANY-THING.
WHAT? I SAY SOMETHING WRONG?
YOU PEOPLE *DO* SPEAK *ENGLISH*, RIGHT?
LITTLE MISSY...

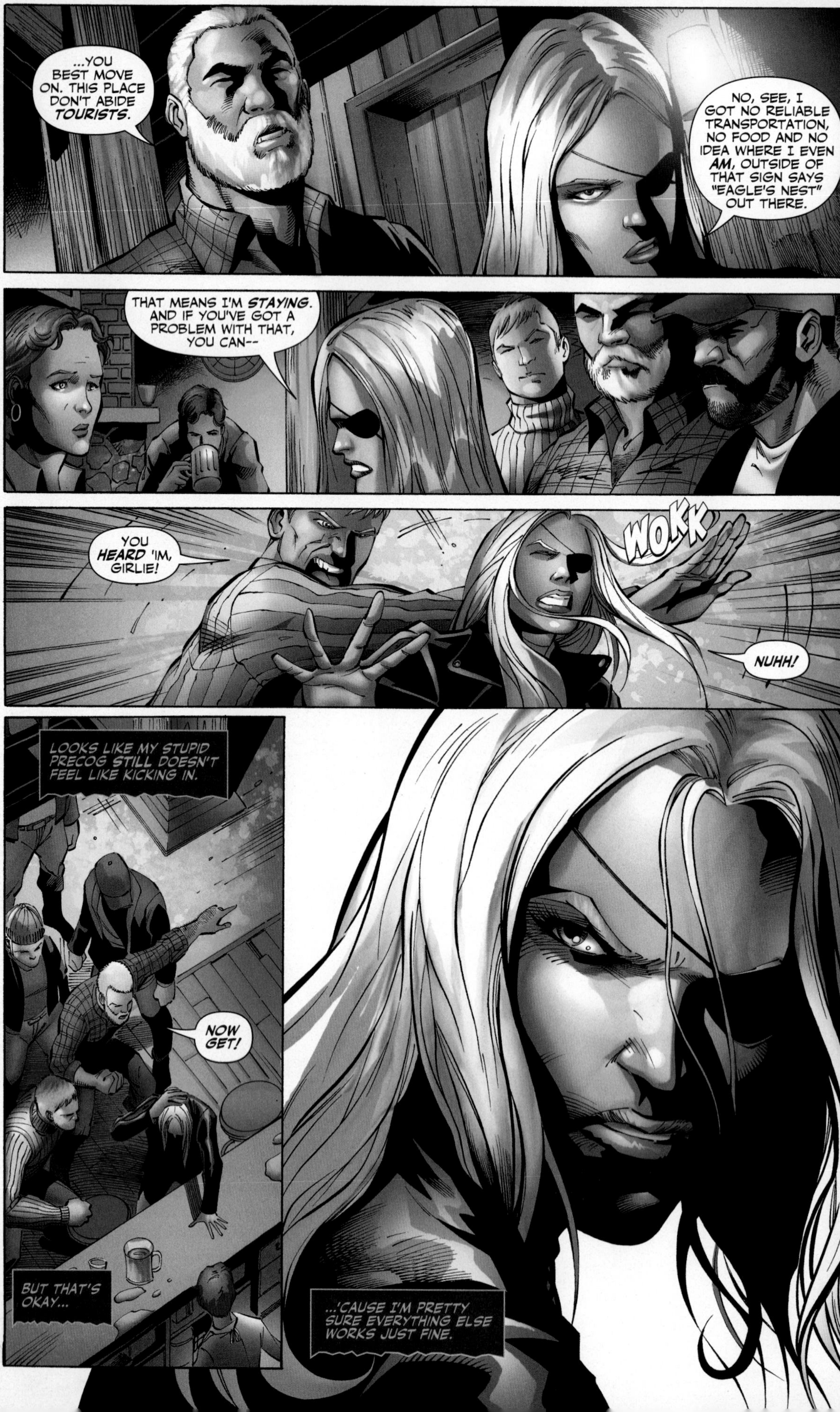
...YOU BEST MOVE ON. THIS PLACE DON'T ABIDE TOURISTS.
NO, SEE, I GOT NO RELIABLE TRANSPORTATION, NO FOOD AND NO IDEA WHERE I EVEN AM, OUTSIDE OF THAT SIGN SAYS "EAGLE'S NEST" OUT THERE.
THAT MEANS I'M STAYING. AND IF YOU'VE GOT A PROBLEM WITH THAT, YOU CAN--
YOU HEARD 'IM, GIRLIE!
WOKK
NUHH!
LOOKS LIKE MY STUPID PRECOG STILL DOESN'T FEEL LIKE KICKING IN.
NOW GET!
BUT THAT'S OKAY...
...'CAUSE I'M PRETTY SURE EVERYTHING ELSE WORKS JUST FINE.

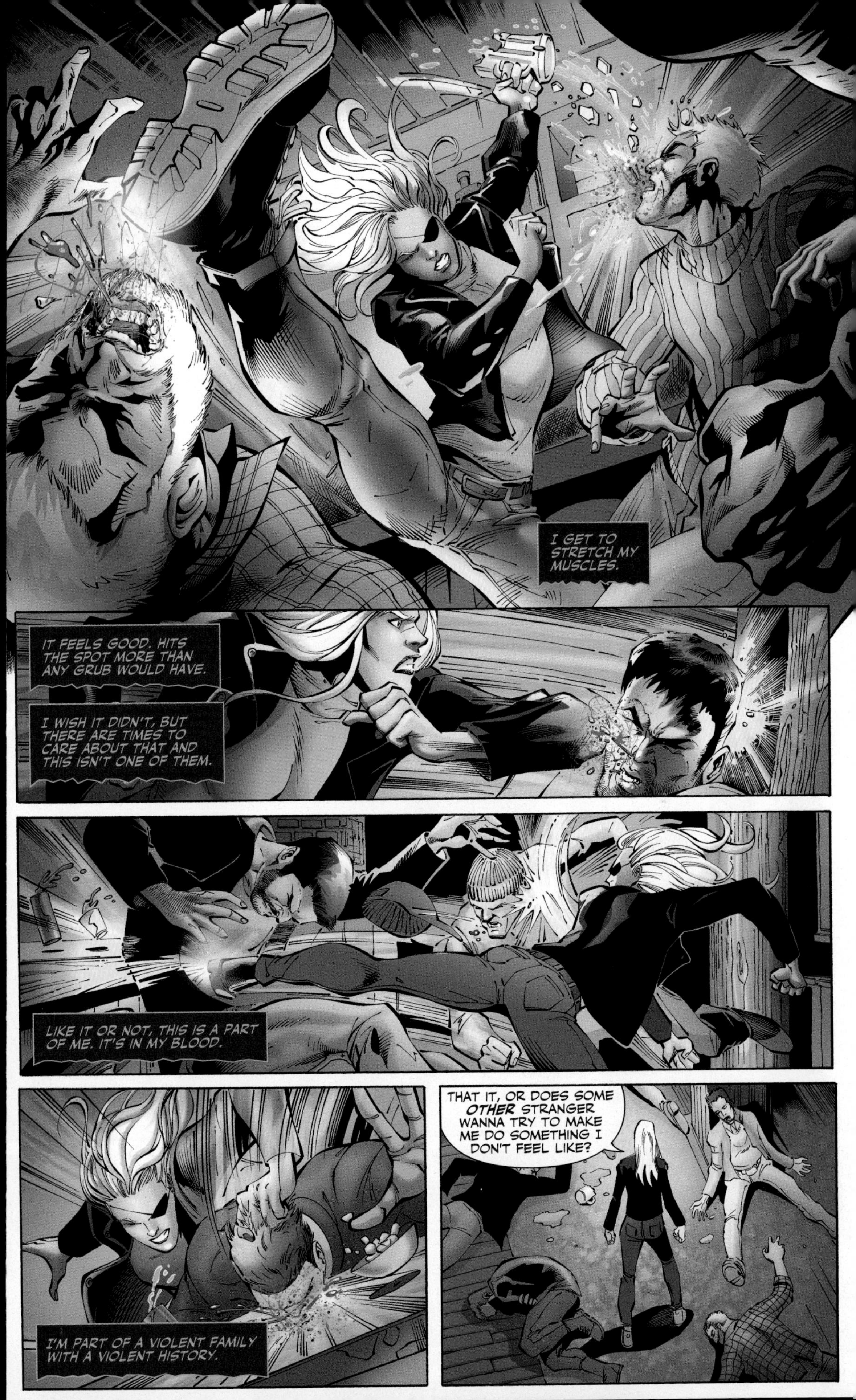
I GET TO STRETCH MY MUSCLES.
IT FEELS GOOD. HITS THE SPOT MORE THAN ANY GRUB WOULD HAVE.
I WISH IT DIDN'T, BUT THERE ARE TIMES TO CARE ABOUT THAT AND THIS ISN'T ONE OF THEM.
LIKE IT OR NOT, THIS IS A PART OF ME. IT'S IN MY BLOOD.
I'M PART OF A VIOLENT FAMILY WITH A VIOLENT HISTORY.
THAT IT, OR DOES SOME OTHER STRANGER WANNA TRY TO MAKE ME DO SOMETHING I DON'T FEEL LIKE?

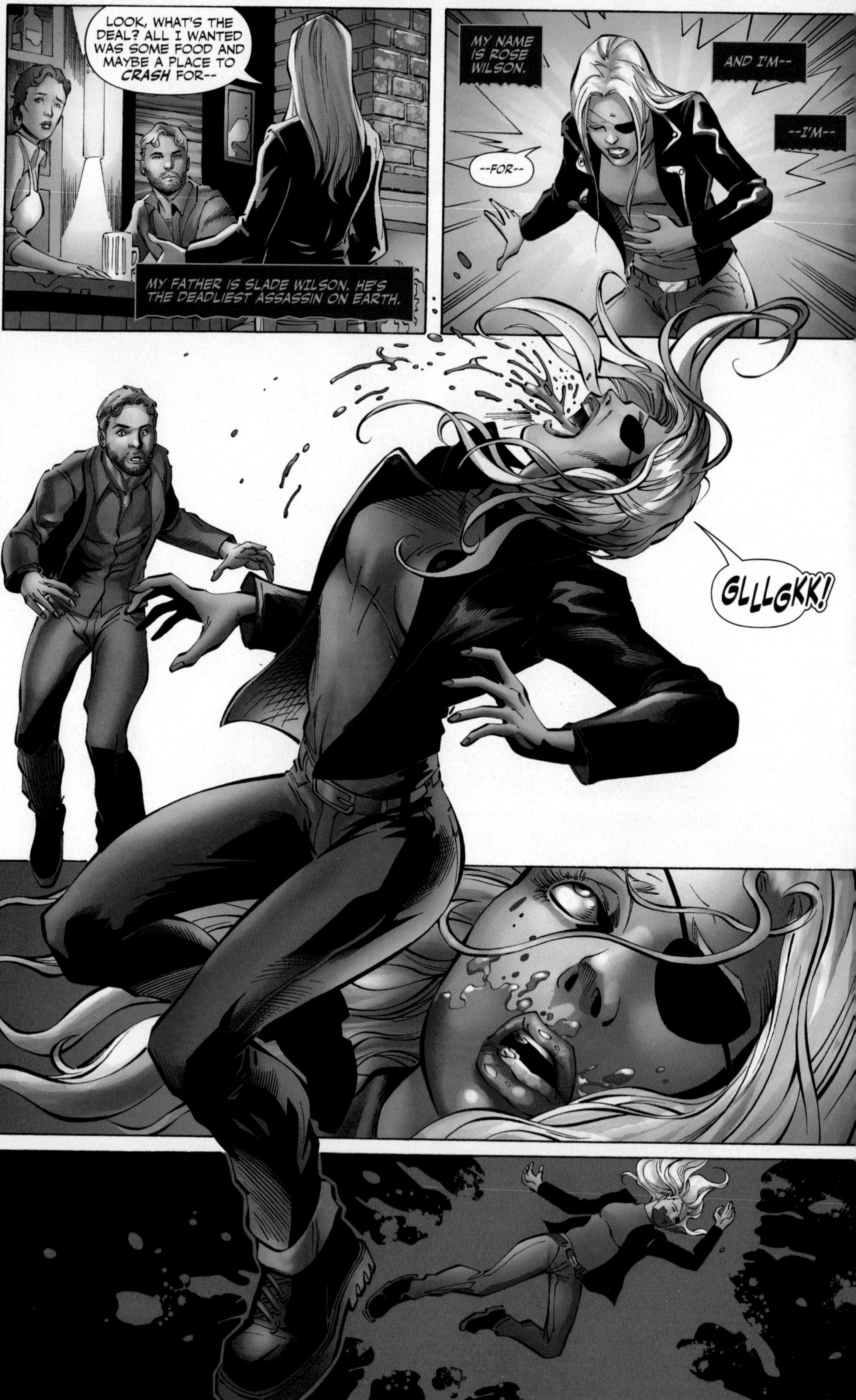
LOOK, WHAT'S THE DEAL? ALL I WANTED WAS SOME FOOD AND MAYBE A PLACE TO *CRASH* FOR--
MY FATHER IS SLADE WILSON. HE'S THE DEADLIEST ASSASSIN ON EARTH.
MY NAME IS ROSE WILSON.
--FOR--
AND I'M--
--I'M--
GLLLGKK!

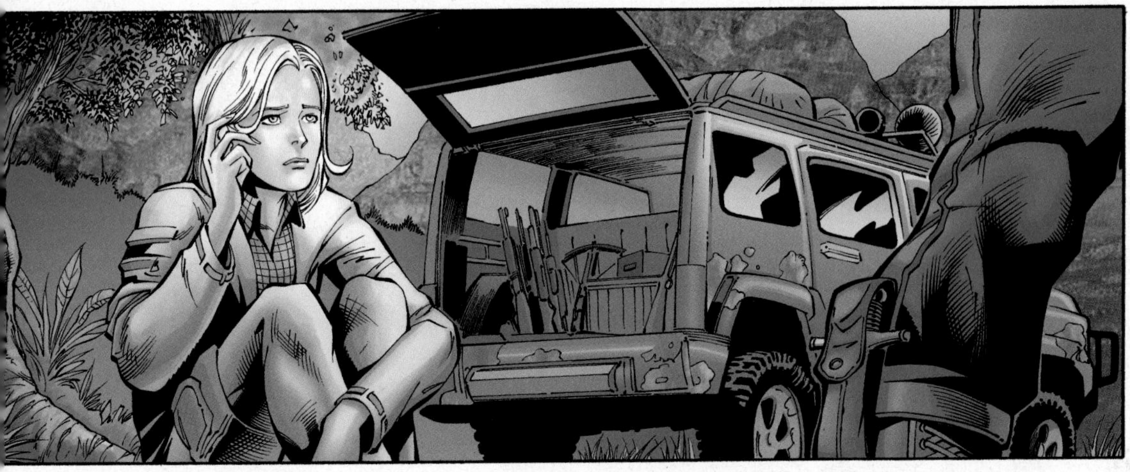

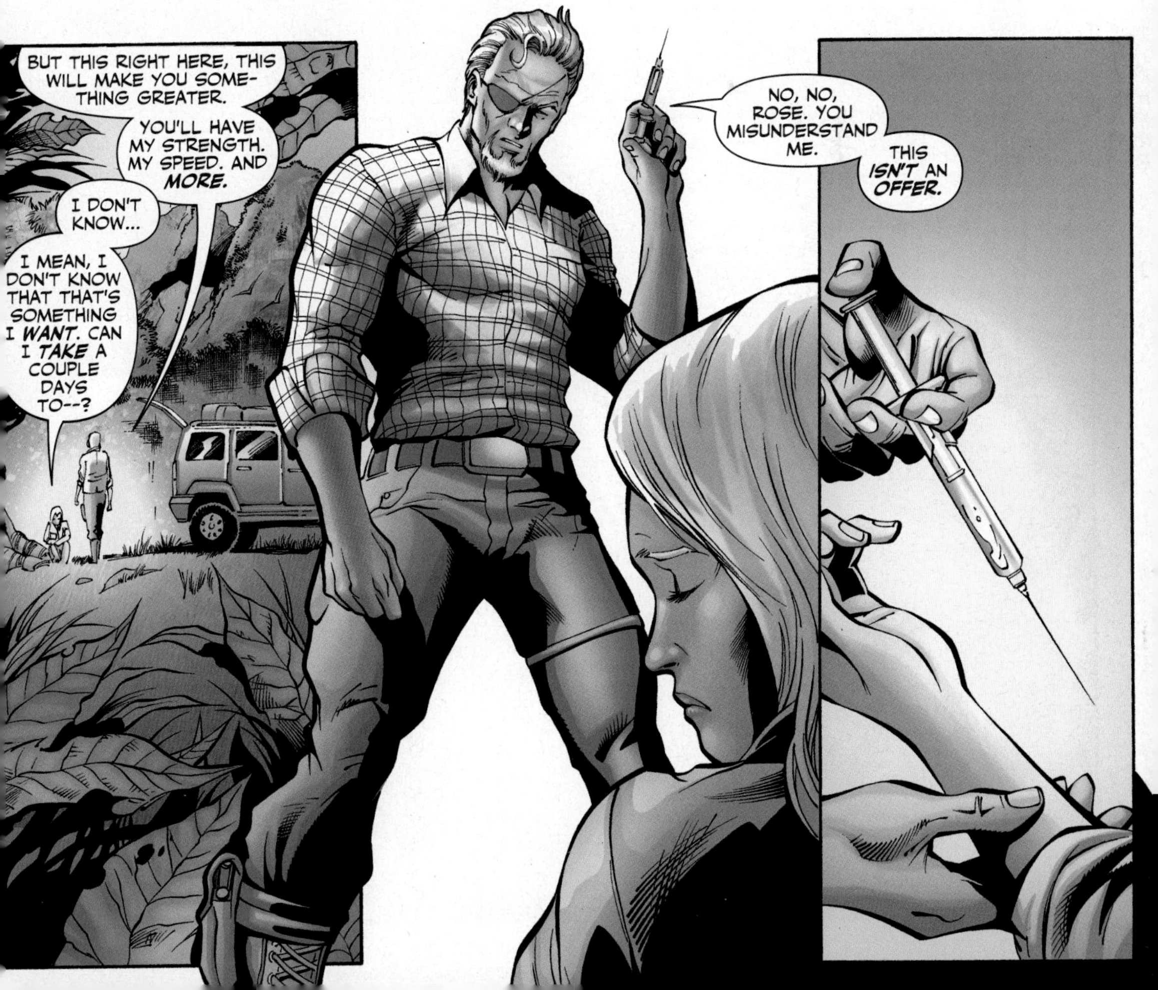

BUT THIS RIGHT HERE, THIS WILL MAKE YOU SOMETHING GREATER.
YOU'LL HAVE MY STRENGTH. MY SPEED. AND MORE.
I DON'T KNOW...
I MEAN, I DON'T KNOW THAT THAT'S SOMETHING I WANT. CAN I TAKE A COUPLE DAYS TO--?
NO, NO, ROSE. YOU MISUNDERSTAND ME.
THIS ISN'T AN OFFER.

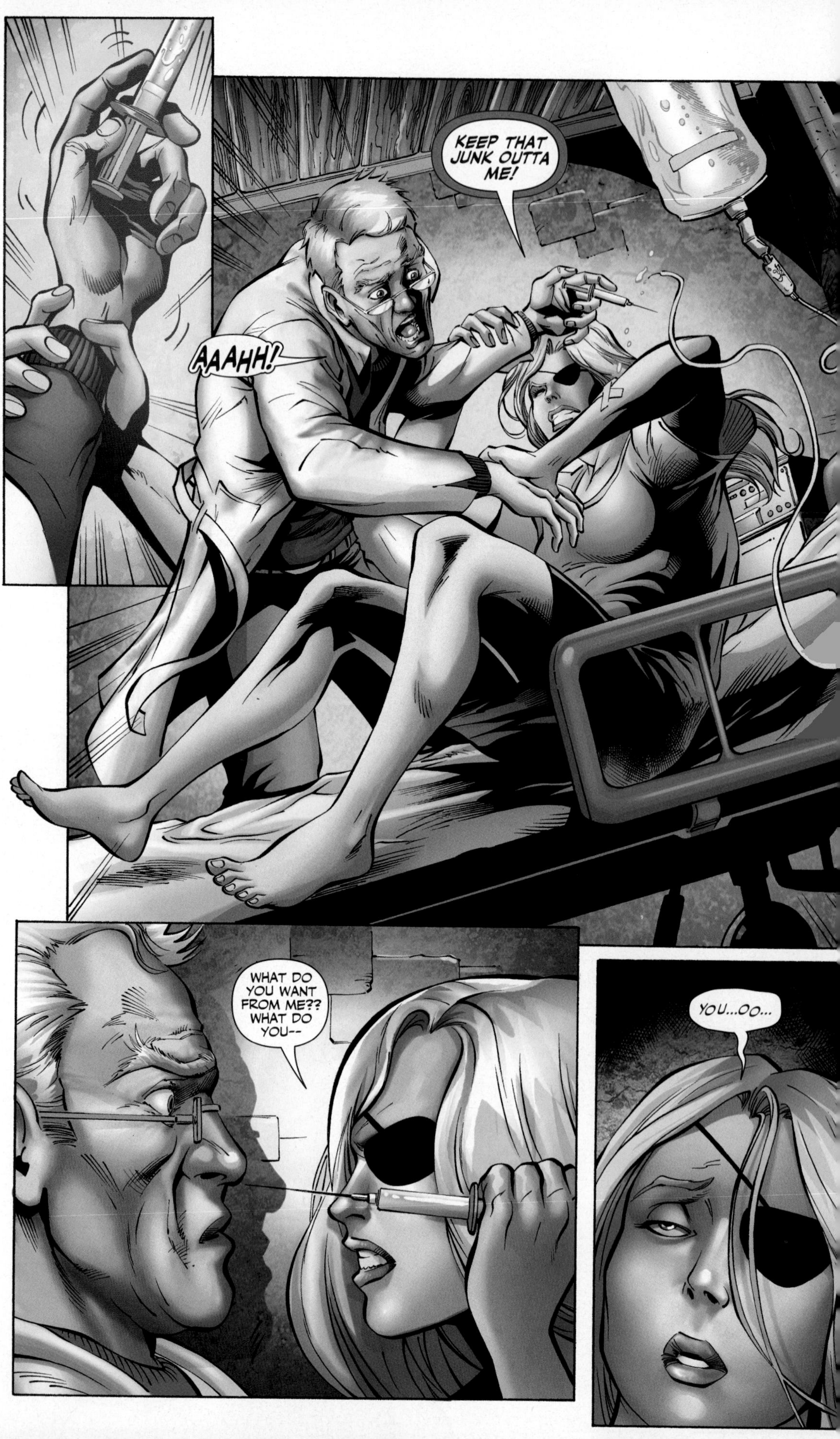
KEEP THAT JUNK OUTTA ME!
AAAHH!
WHAT DO YOU WANT FROM ME?? WHAT DO YOU--
YOU...OO...

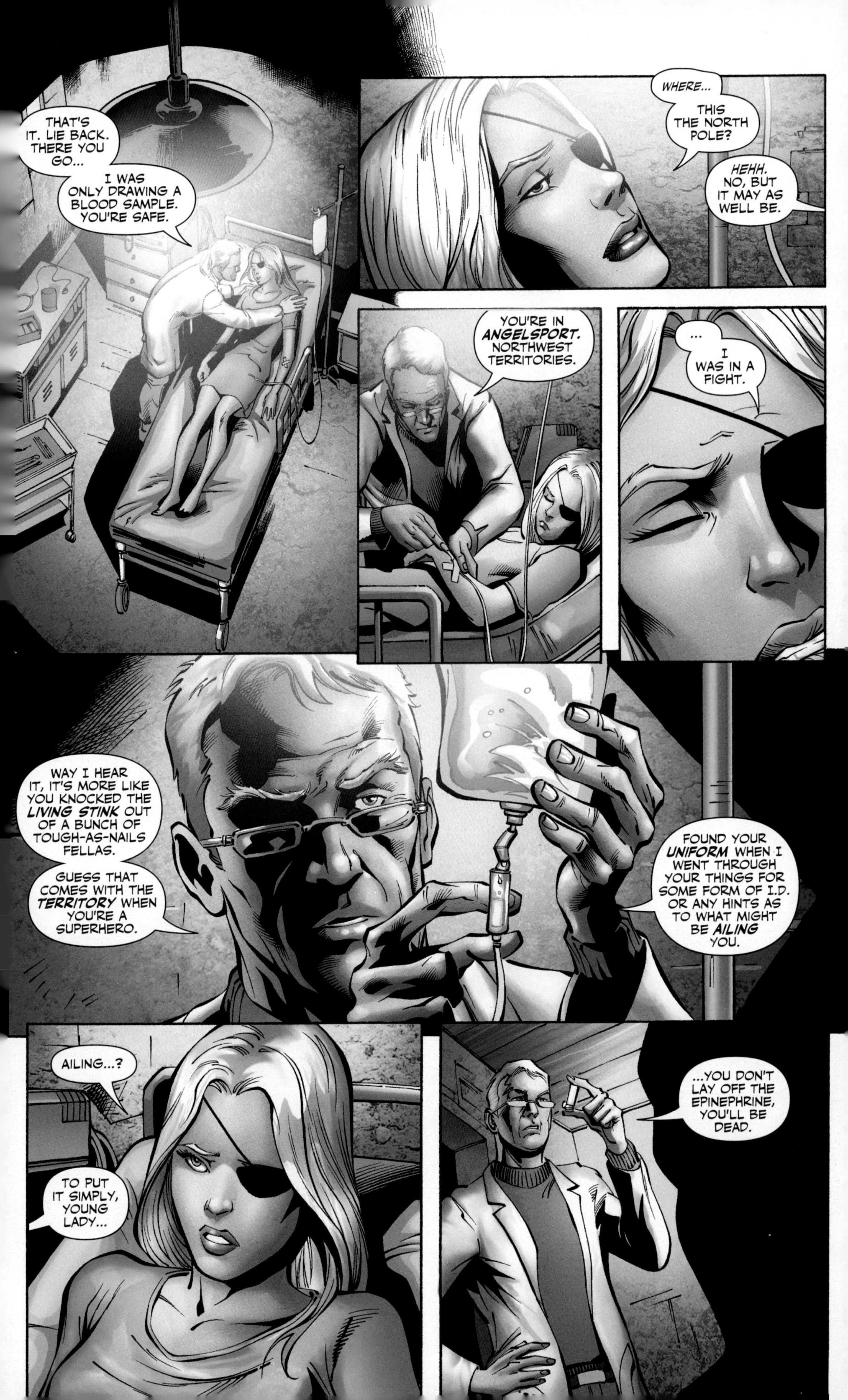
THAT'S IT. LIE BACK. THERE YOU GO...
I WAS ONLY DRAWING A BLOOD SAMPLE. YOU'RE SAFE.
WHERE...
THIS THE NORTH POLE?
HEHH. NO, BUT IT MAY AS WELL BE.
YOU'RE IN ANGELSPORT. NORTHWEST TERRITORIES.
...
I WAS IN A FIGHT.
WAY I HEAR IT, IT'S MORE LIKE YOU KNOCKED THE LIVING STINK OUT OF A BUNCH OF TOUGH-AS-NAILS FELLAS.
GUESS THAT COMES WITH THE TERRITORY WHEN YOU'RE A SUPERHERO.
FOUND YOUR UNIFORM WHEN I WENT THROUGH YOUR THINGS FOR SOME FORM OF I.D. OR ANY HINTS AS TO WHAT MIGHT BE AILING YOU.
AILING...?
TO PUT IT SIMPLY, YOUNG LADY...
...YOU DON'T LAY OFF THE EPINEPHRINE, YOU'LL BE DEAD.

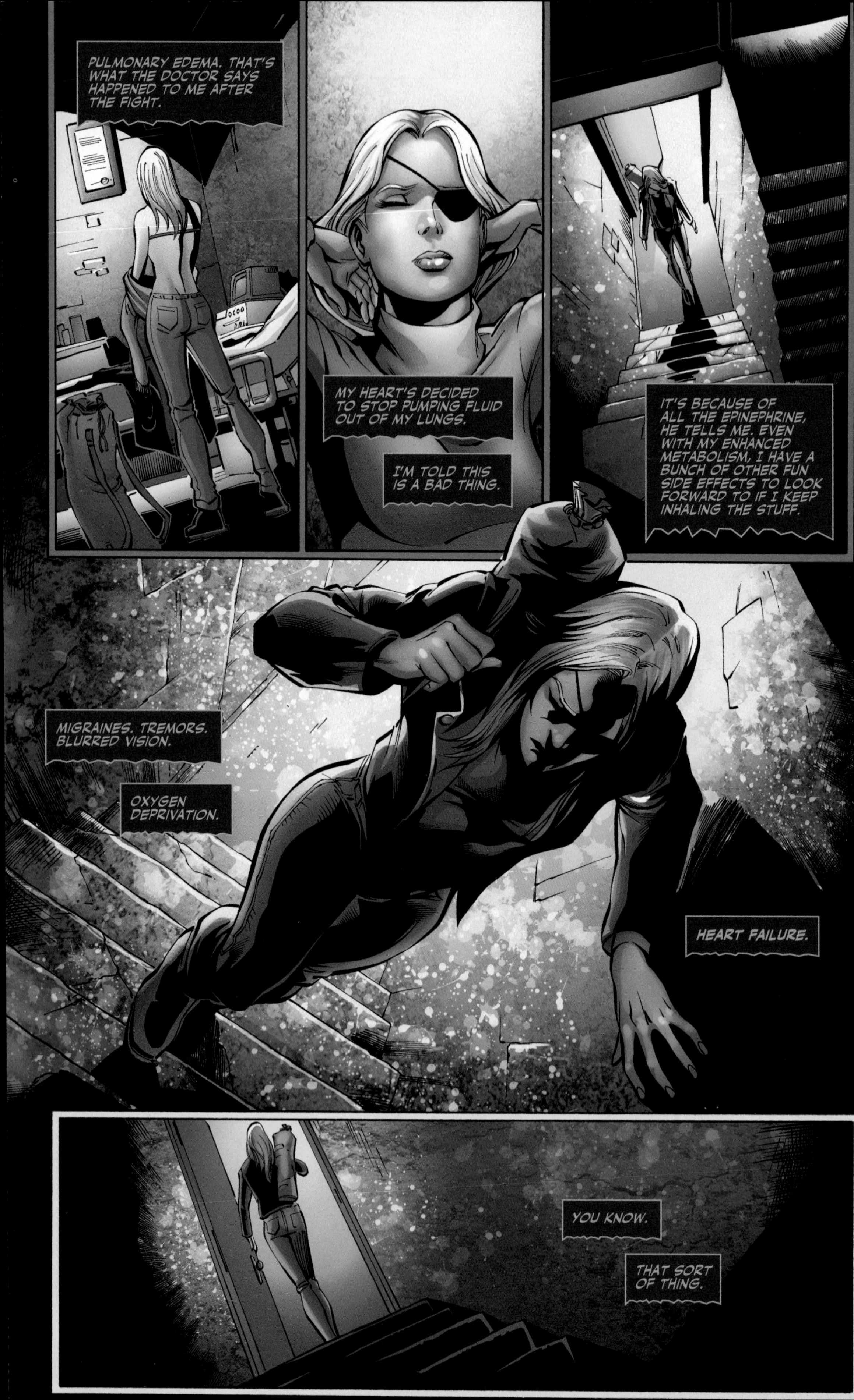
PULMONARY EDEMA. THAT'S WHAT THE DOCTOR SAYS HAPPENED TO ME AFTER THE FIGHT.
MY HEART'S DECIDED TO STOP PUMPING FLUID OUT OF MY LUNGS.
I'M TOLD THIS IS A BAD THING.
IT'S BECAUSE OF ALL THE EPINEPHRINE, HE TELLS ME. EVEN WITH MY ENHANCED METABOLISM, I HAVE A BUNCH OF OTHER FUN SIDE EFFECTS TO LOOK FORWARD TO IF I KEEP INHALING THE STUFF.
MIGRAINES. TREMORS. BLURRED VISION.
OXYGEN DEPRIVATION.
HEART FAILURE.
YOU KNOW.
THAT SORT OF THING.

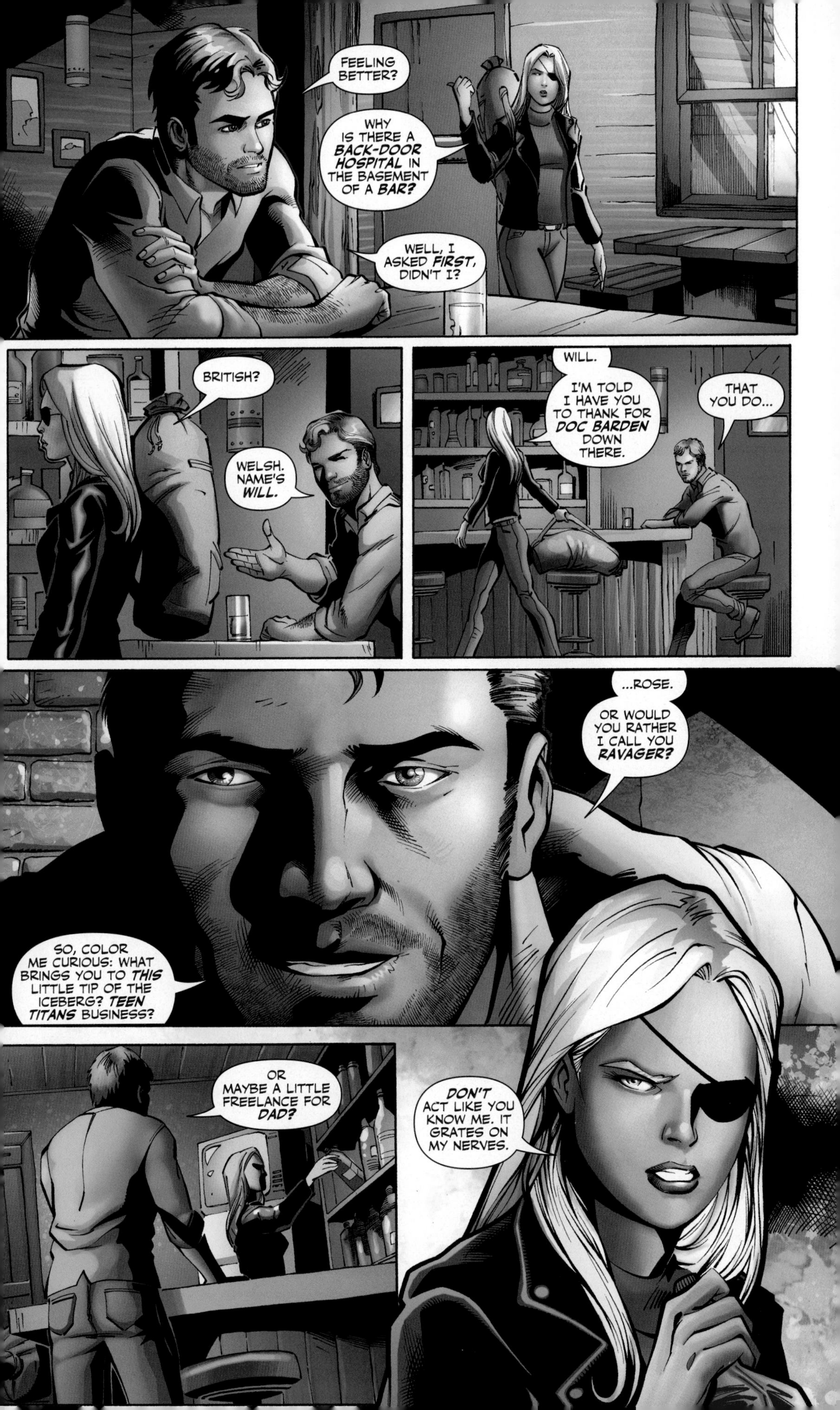

FEELING BETTER?
WHY IS THERE A BACK-DOOR HOSPITAL IN THE BASEMENT OF A BAR?
WELL, I ASKED FIRST, DIDN'T I?
BRITISH?
WELSH. NAME'S WILL.
WILL.
I'M TOLD I HAVE YOU TO THANK FOR DOC BARDEN DOWN THERE.
THAT YOU DO...
...ROSE.
OR WOULD YOU RATHER I CALL YOU RAVAGER?
SO, COLOR ME CURIOUS: WHAT BRINGS YOU TO THIS LITTLE TIP OF THE ICEBERG? TEEN TITANS BUSINESS?
OR MAYBE A LITTLE FREELANCE FOR DAD?
DON'T ACT LIKE YOU KNOW ME. IT GRATES ON MY NERVES.

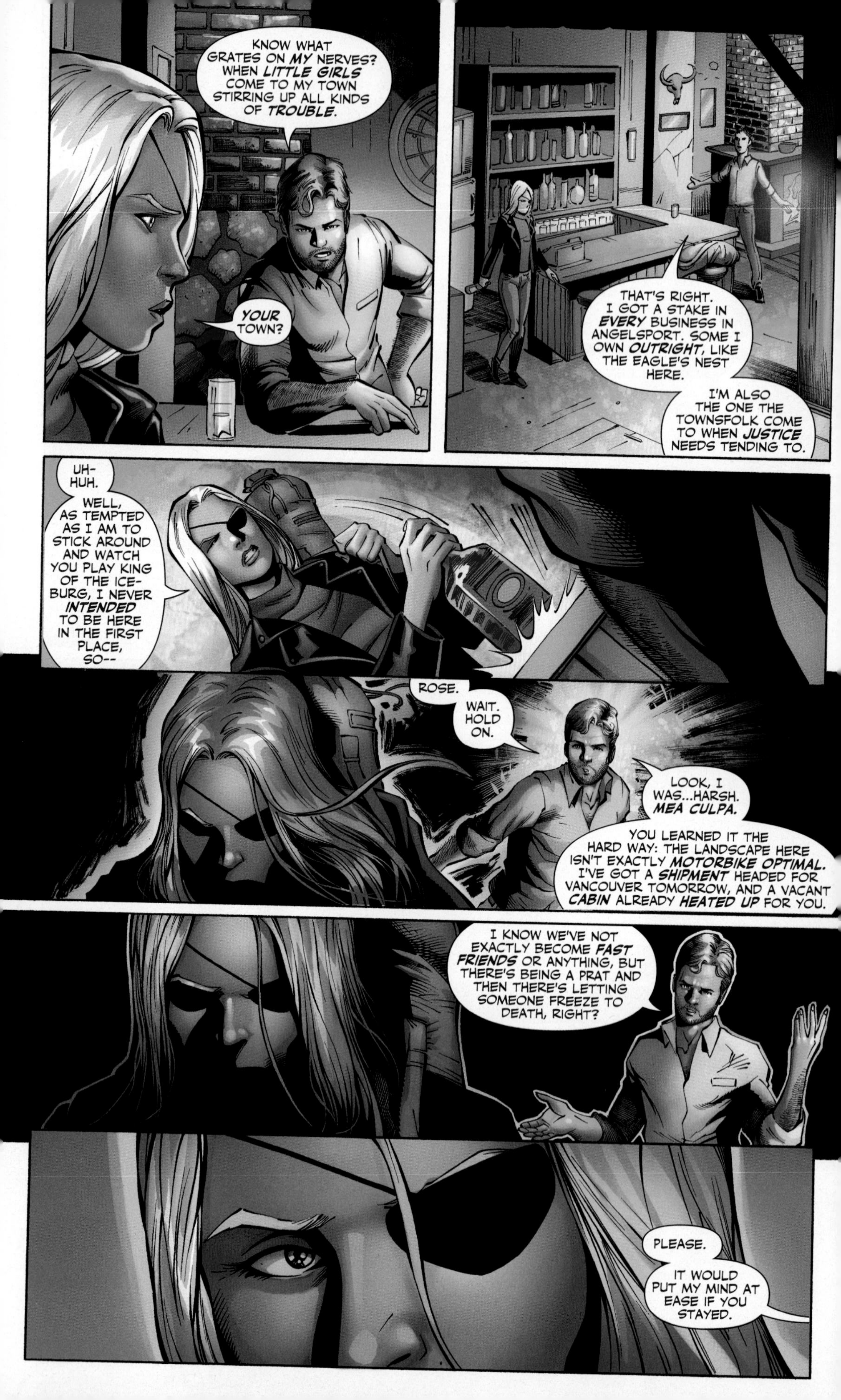
KNOW WHAT GRATES ON MY NERVES? WHEN LITTLE GIRLS COME TO MY TOWN STIRRING UP ALL KINDS OF TROUBLE.
YOUR TOWN?
THAT'S RIGHT. I GOT A STAKE IN EVERY BUSINESS IN ANGELSPORT. SOME I OWN OUTRIGHT, LIKE THE EAGLE'S NEST HERE.
I'M ALSO THE ONE THE TOWNSFOLK COME TO WHEN JUSTICE NEEDS TENDING TO.
UH-HUH.
WELL, AS TEMPTED AS I AM TO STICK AROUND AND WATCH YOU PLAY KING OF THE ICE-BURG, I NEVER INTENDED TO BE HERE IN THE FIRST PLACE, SO--
ROSE.
WAIT. HOLD ON.
LOOK, I WAS...HARSH. MEA CULPA.
YOU LEARNED IT THE HARD WAY: THE LANDSCAPE HERE ISN'T EXACTLY MOTORBIKE OPTIMAL. I'VE GOT A SHIPMENT HEADED FOR VANCOUVER TOMORROW, AND A VACANT CABIN ALREADY HEATED UP FOR YOU.
I KNOW WE'VE NOT EXACTLY BECOME FAST FRIENDS OR ANYTHING, BUT THERE'S BEING A PRAT AND THEN THERE'S LETTING SOMEONE FREEZE TO DEATH, RIGHT?
PLEASE.
IT WOULD PUT MY MIND AT EASE IF YOU STAYED.

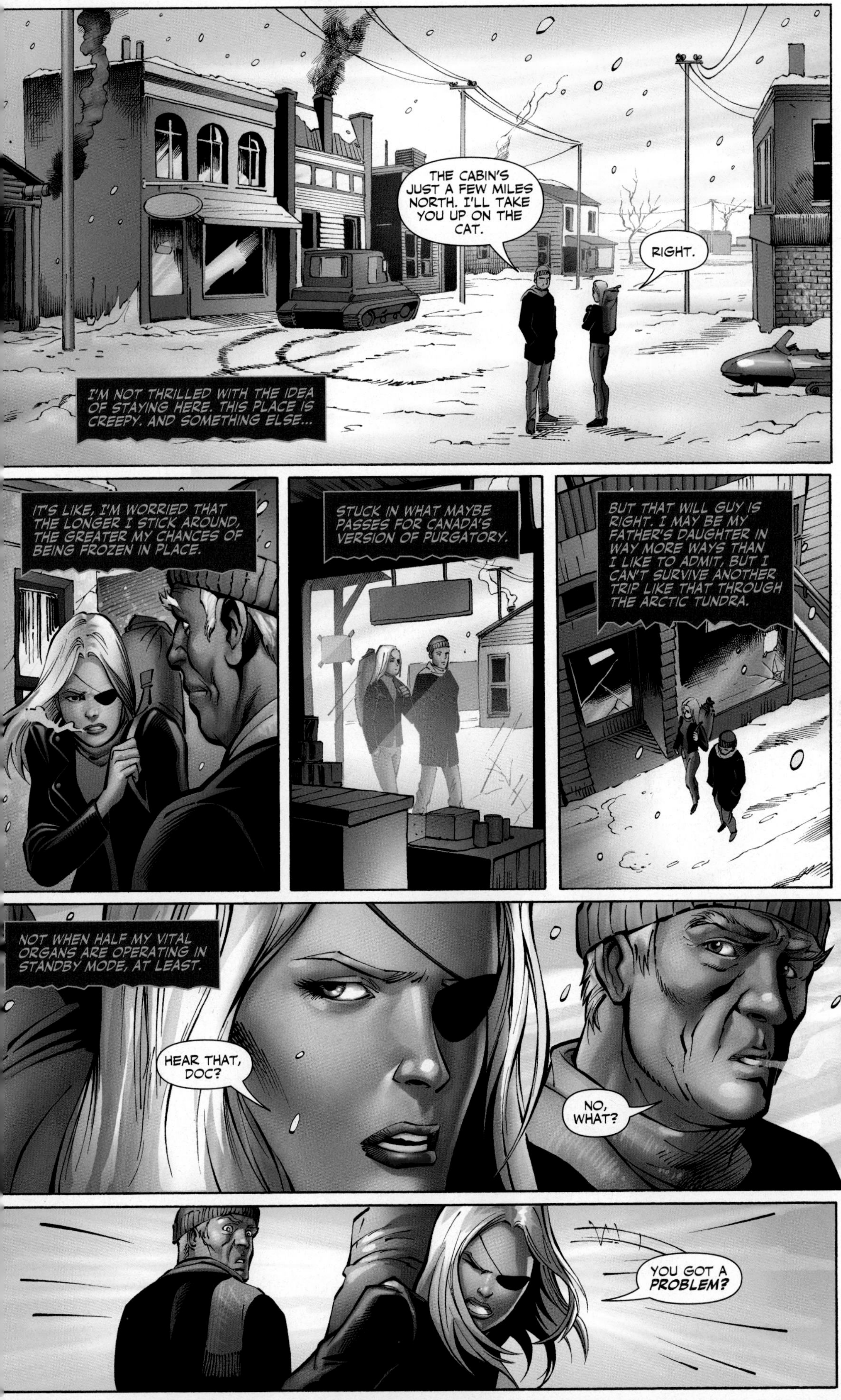
THE CABIN'S JUST A FEW MILES NORTH. I'LL TAKE YOU UP ON THE CAT.
RIGHT.
I'M NOT THRILLED WITH THE IDEA OF STAYING HERE. THIS PLACE IS CREEPY. AND SOMETHING ELSE...
IT'S LIKE, I'M WORRIED THAT THE LONGER I STICK AROUND, THE GREATER MY CHANCES OF BEING FROZEN IN PLACE.
STUCK IN WHAT MAYBE PASSES FOR CANADA'S VERSION OF PURGATORY.
BUT THAT WILL GUY IS RIGHT. I MAY BE MY FATHER'S DAUGHTER IN WAY MORE WAYS THAN I LIKE TO ADMIT, BUT I CAN'T SURVIVE ANOTHER TRIP LIKE THAT THROUGH THE ARCTIC TUNDRA.
NOT WHEN HALF MY VITAL ORGANS ARE OPERATING IN STANDBY MODE, AT LEAST.
HEAR THAT, DOC?
NO, WHAT?
YOU GOT A PROBLEM?

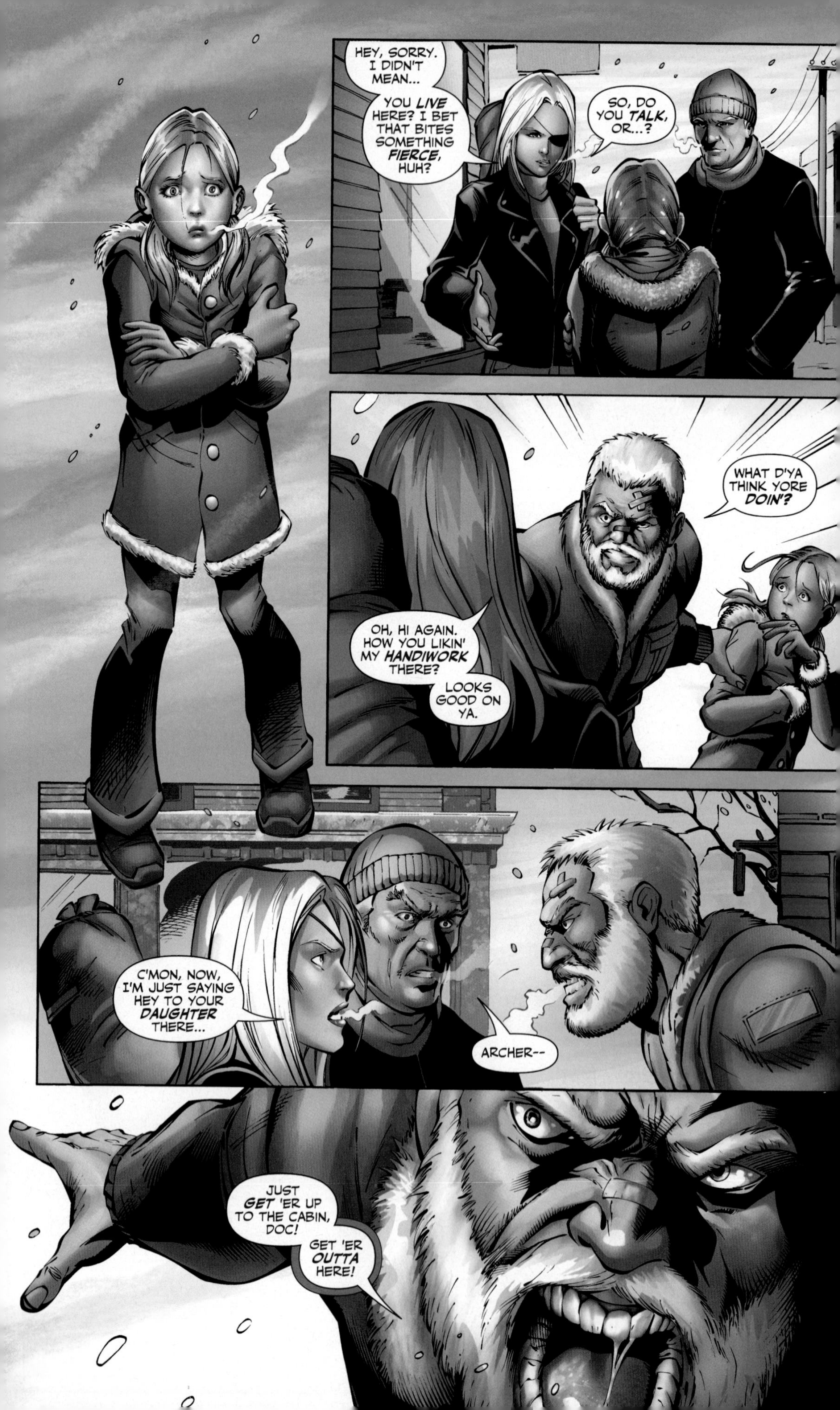
HEY, SORRY. I DIDN'T MEAN...
YOU LIVE HERE? I BET THAT BITES SOMETHING FIERCE, HUH?
SO, DO YOU TALK, OR...?
WHAT D'YA THINK YORE DOIN'?
OH, HI AGAIN. HOW YOU LIKIN' MY HANDIWORK THERE?
LOOKS GOOD ON YA.
C'MON, NOW, I'M JUST SAYING HEY TO YOUR DAUGHTER THERE...
ARCHER--
JUST GET 'ER UP TO THE CABIN, DOC!
GET 'ER OUTTA HERE!

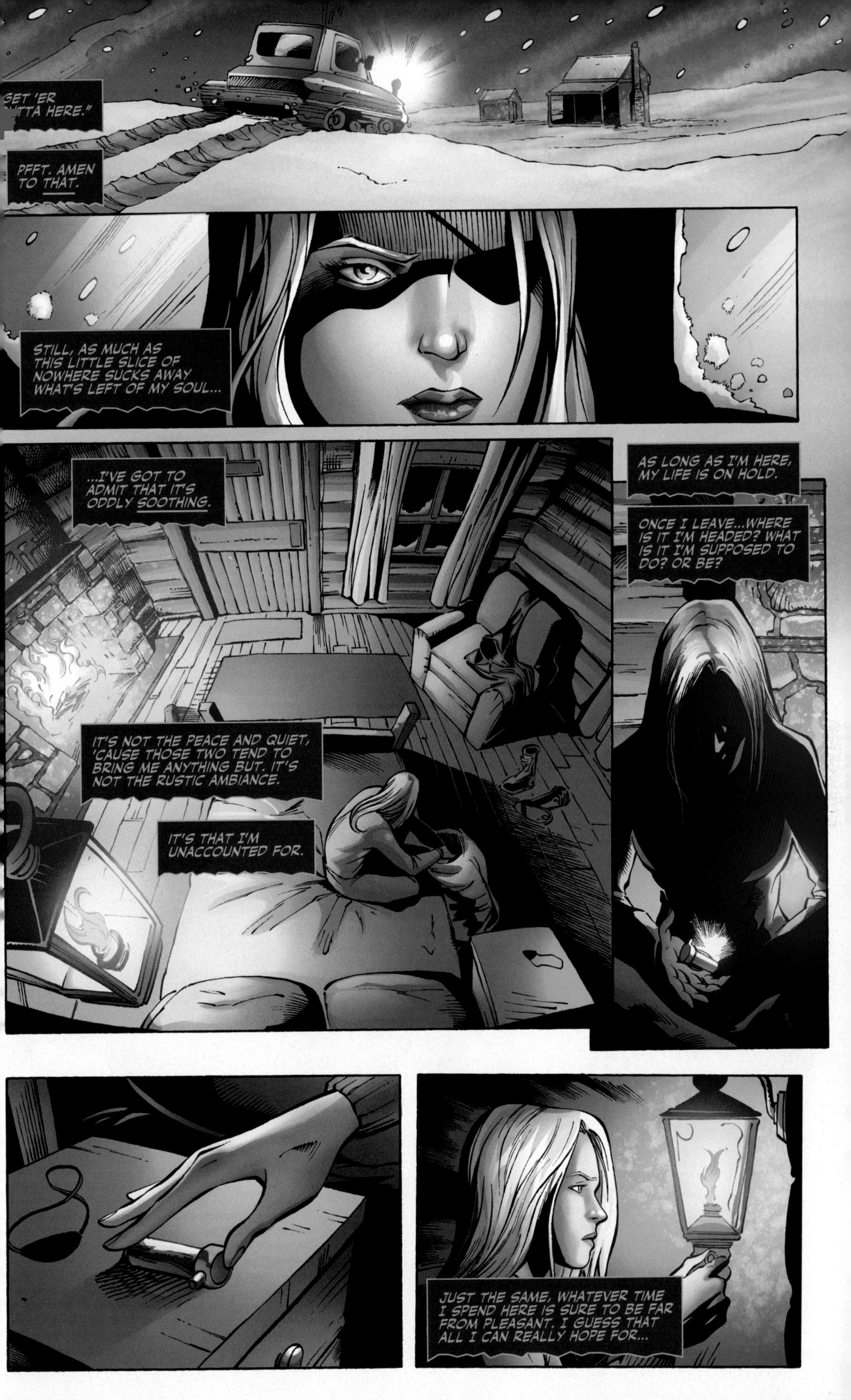

GET 'ER
...TTA HERE."
PFFT. AMEN TO THAT.
STILL, AS MUCH AS THIS LITTLE SLICE OF NOWHERE SUCKS AWAY WHAT'S LEFT OF MY SOUL...
...I'VE GOT TO ADMIT THAT IT'S ODDLY SOOTHING.
IT'S NOT THE PEACE AND QUIET, 'CAUSE THOSE TWO TEND TO BRING ME ANYTHING BUT. IT'S NOT THE RUSTIC AMBIANCE.
IT'S THAT I'M UNACCOUNTED FOR.
AS LONG AS I'M HERE, MY LIFE IS ON HOLD.
ONCE I LEAVE...WHERE IS IT I'M HEADED? WHAT IS IT I'M SUPPOSED TO DO? OR BE?
JUST THE SAME, WHATEVER TIME I SPEND HERE IS SURE TO BE FAR FROM PLEASANT. I GUESS THAT ALL I CAN REALLY HOPE FOR...

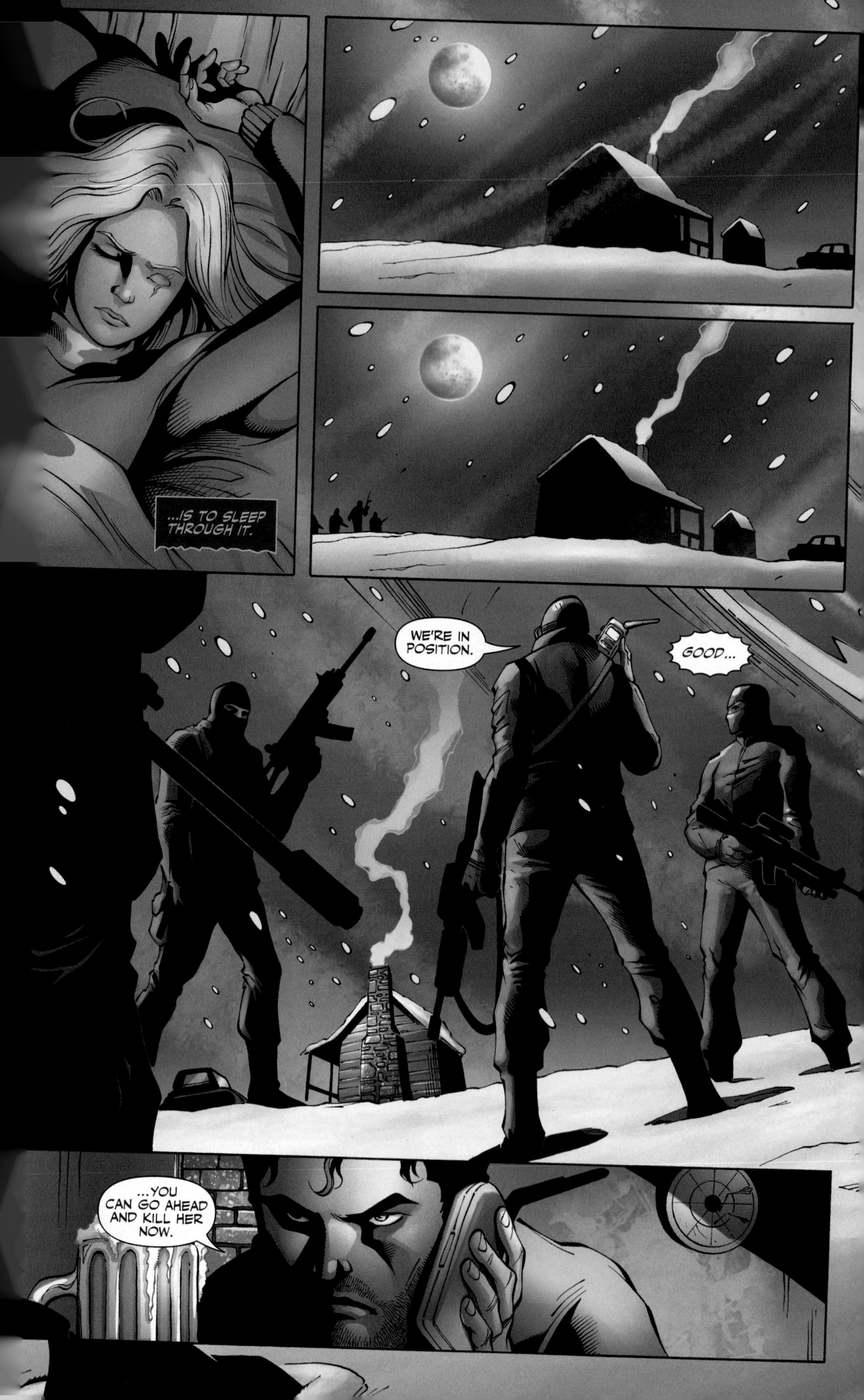
...IS TO SLEEP THROUGH IT.
WE'RE IN POSITION.
GOOD...
...YOU CAN GO AHEAD AND KILL HER NOW.

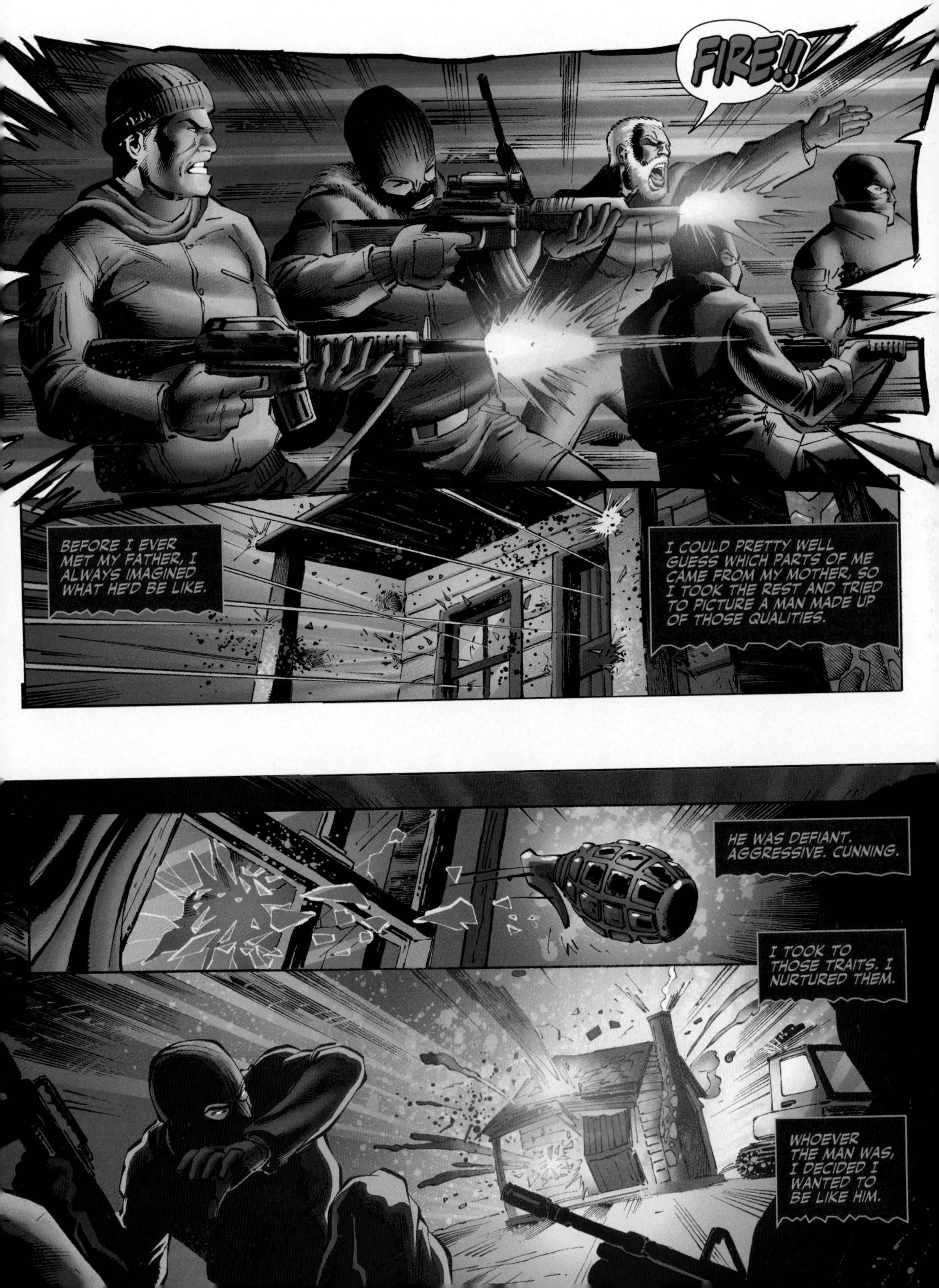

FIRE!!
BEFORE I EVER MET MY FATHER, I ALWAYS IMAGINED WHAT HE'D BE LIKE.
I COULD PRETTY WELL GUESS WHICH PARTS OF ME CAME FROM MY MOTHER, SO I TOOK THE REST AND TRIED TO PICTURE A MAN MADE UP OF THOSE QUALITIES.
HE WAS DEFIANT. AGGRESSIVE. CUNNING.
I TOOK TO THOSE TRAITS. I NURTURED THEM.
WHOEVER THE MAN WAS, I DECIDED I WANTED TO BE LIKE HIM.

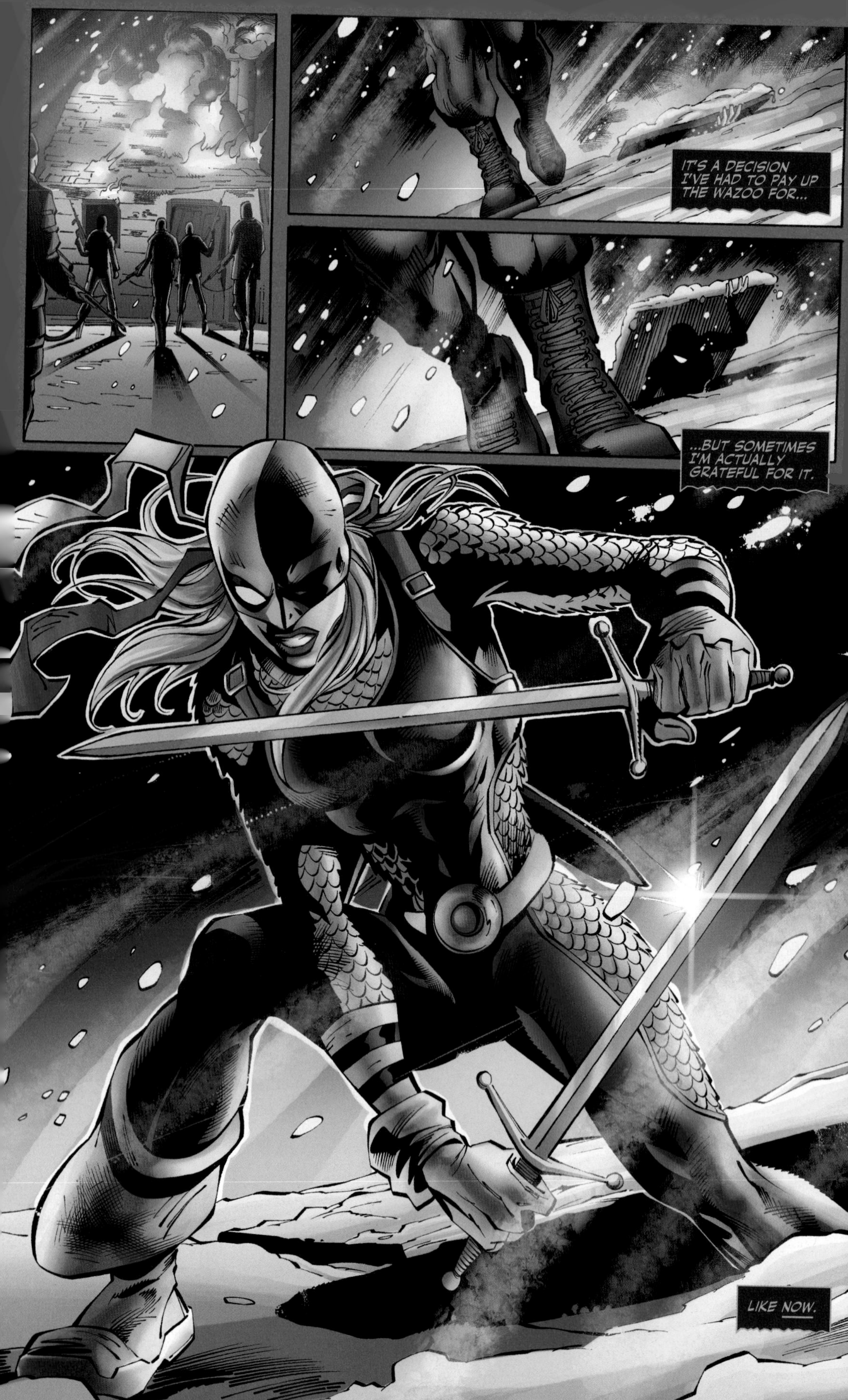
IT'S A DECISION I'VE HAD TO PAY UP THE WAZOO FOR...
...BUT SOMETIMES I'M ACTUALLY GRATEFUL FOR IT.
LIKE NOW.

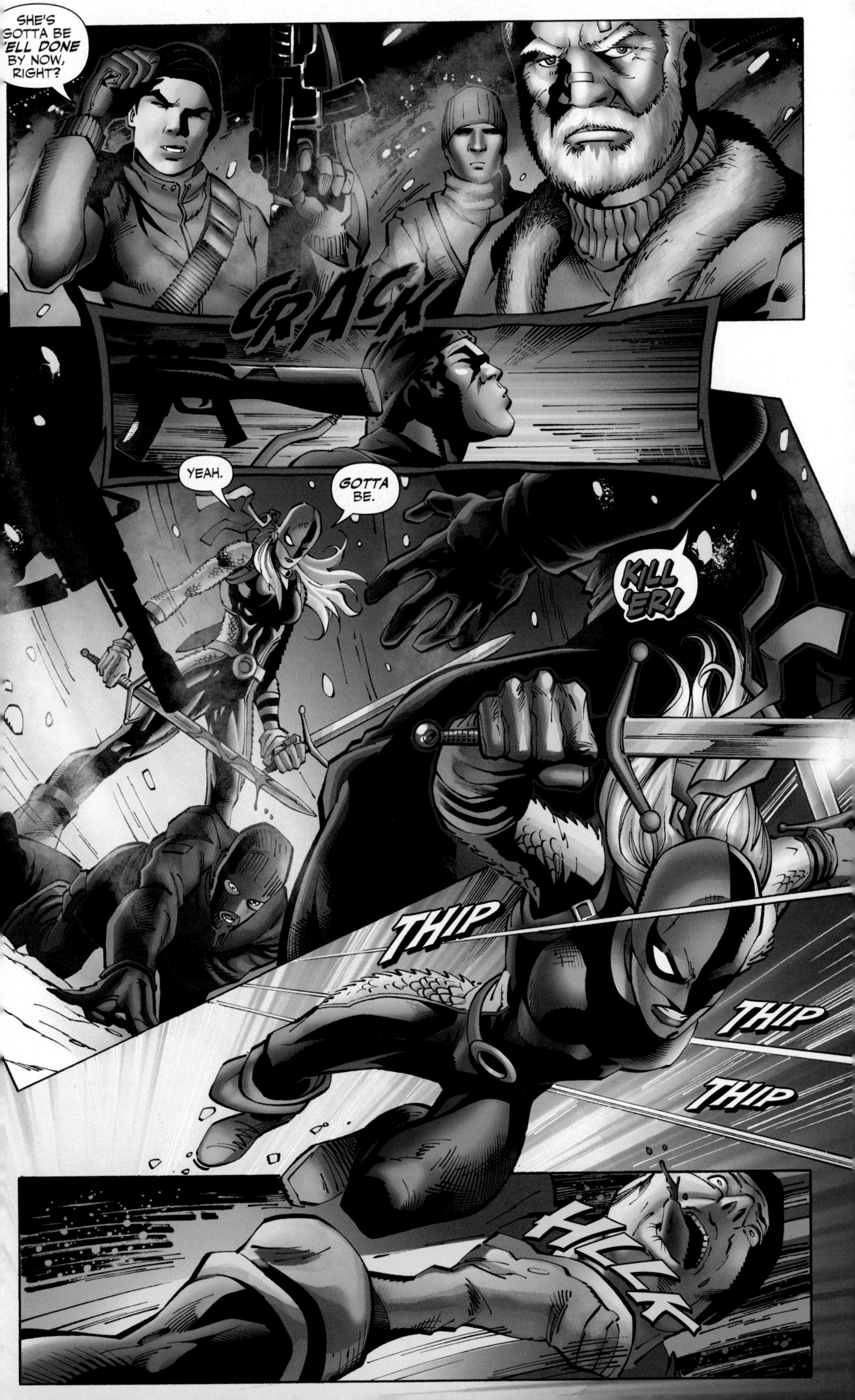

SHE'S GOTTA BE 'ELL DONE BY NOW, RIGHT?
CRACK
YEAH.
GOTTA BE.
KILL 'ER!
THIP
THIP
THIP
HLLK

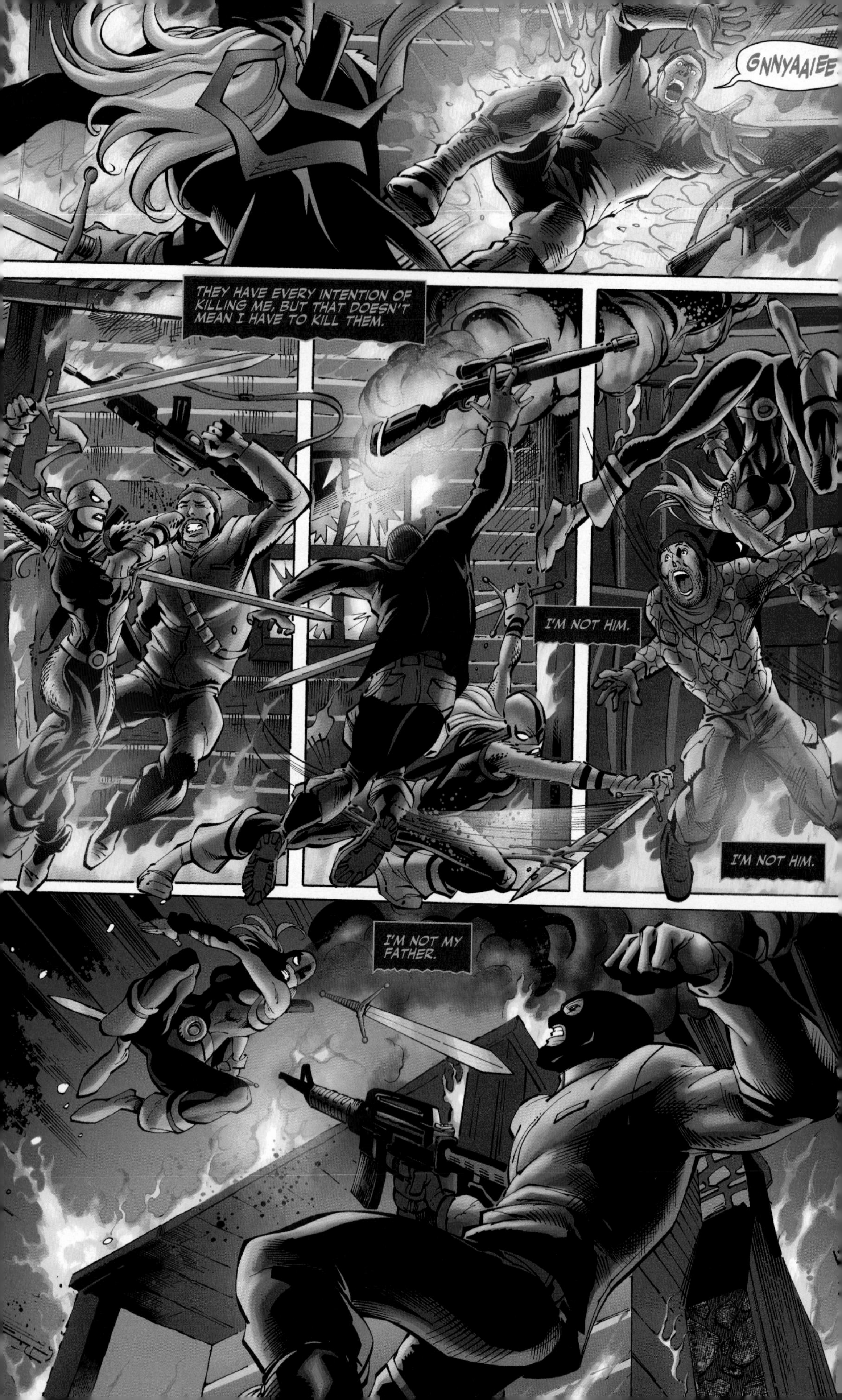

GNNYAAIEE
THEY HAVE EVERY INTENTION OF KILLING ME, BUT THAT DOESN'T MEAN I HAVE TO KILL THEM.
I'M NOT HIM.
I'M NOT HIM.
I'M NOT MY FATHER.

AAAAGH!

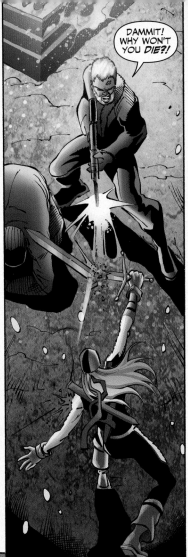

DAMMIT! WHY WON'T YOU *DIE?!*

DON'T *FEEL* LIKE IT.

GNAAH!

IT WAS *WILL* WHO SENT YOU, WASN'T IT?

WHY'S HE WANT ME DEAD? WHAT'S HE *HIDING?*

HEHH...

YER ALREADY DEAD AN' YOU DON' *EVEN* KNOW IT...

OH, COME *ON...*

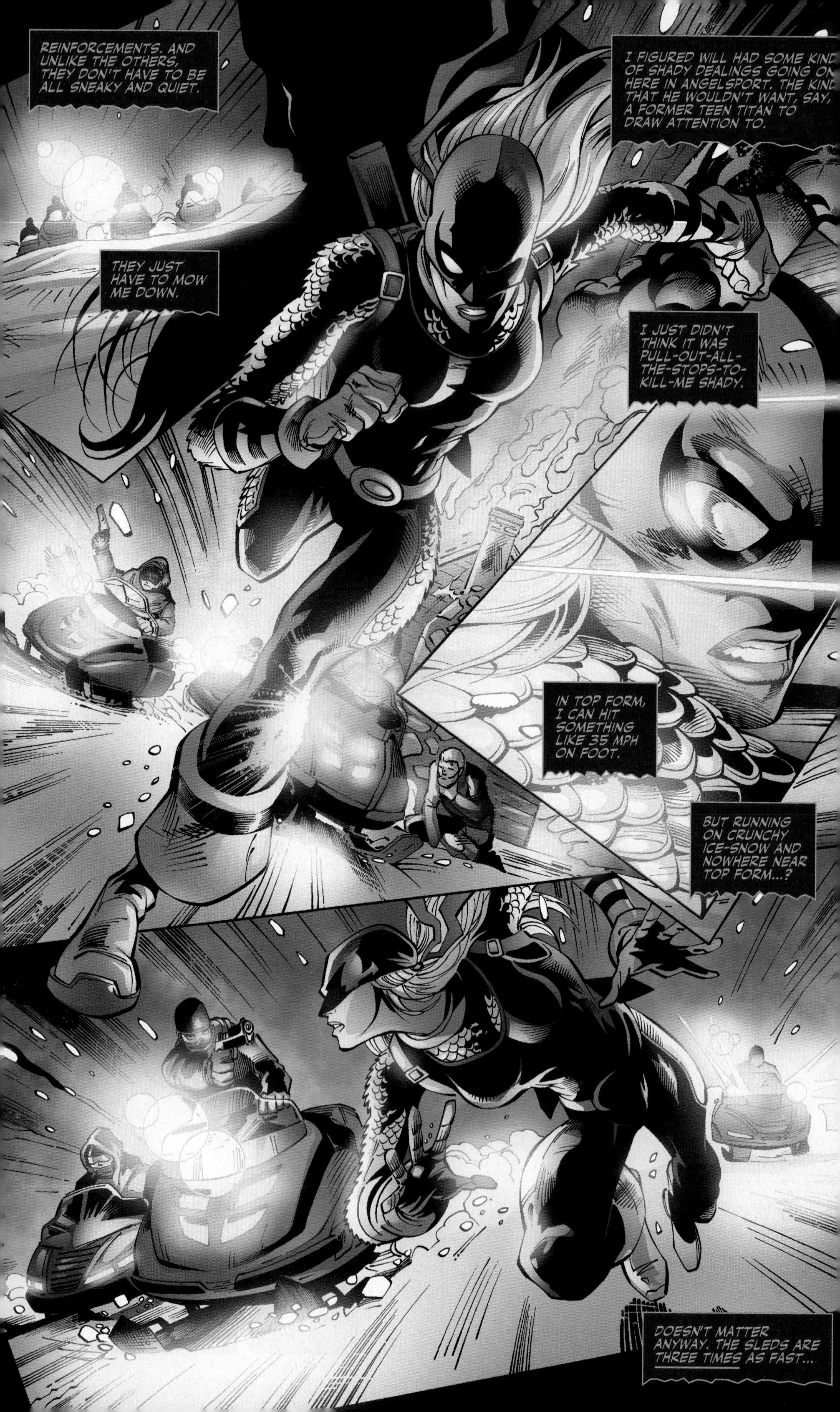
REINFORCEMENTS. AND UNLIKE THE OTHERS, THEY DON'T HAVE TO BE ALL SNEAKY AND QUIET.
I FIGURED WILL HAD SOME KIND OF SHADY DEALINGS GOING ON HERE IN ANGELSPORT. THE KIND THAT HE WOULDN'T WANT, SAY, A FORMER TEEN TITAN TO DRAW ATTENTION TO.
THEY JUST HAVE TO MOW ME DOWN.
I JUST DIDN'T THINK IT WAS PULL-OUT-ALL-THE-STOPS-TO-KILL-ME SHADY.
IN TOP FORM, I CAN HIT SOMETHING LIKE 35 MPH ON FOOT.
BUT RUNNING ON CRUNCHY ICE-SNOW AND NOWHERE NEAR TOP FORM...?
DOESN'T MATTER ANYWAY. THE SLEDS ARE THREE TIMES AS FAST...

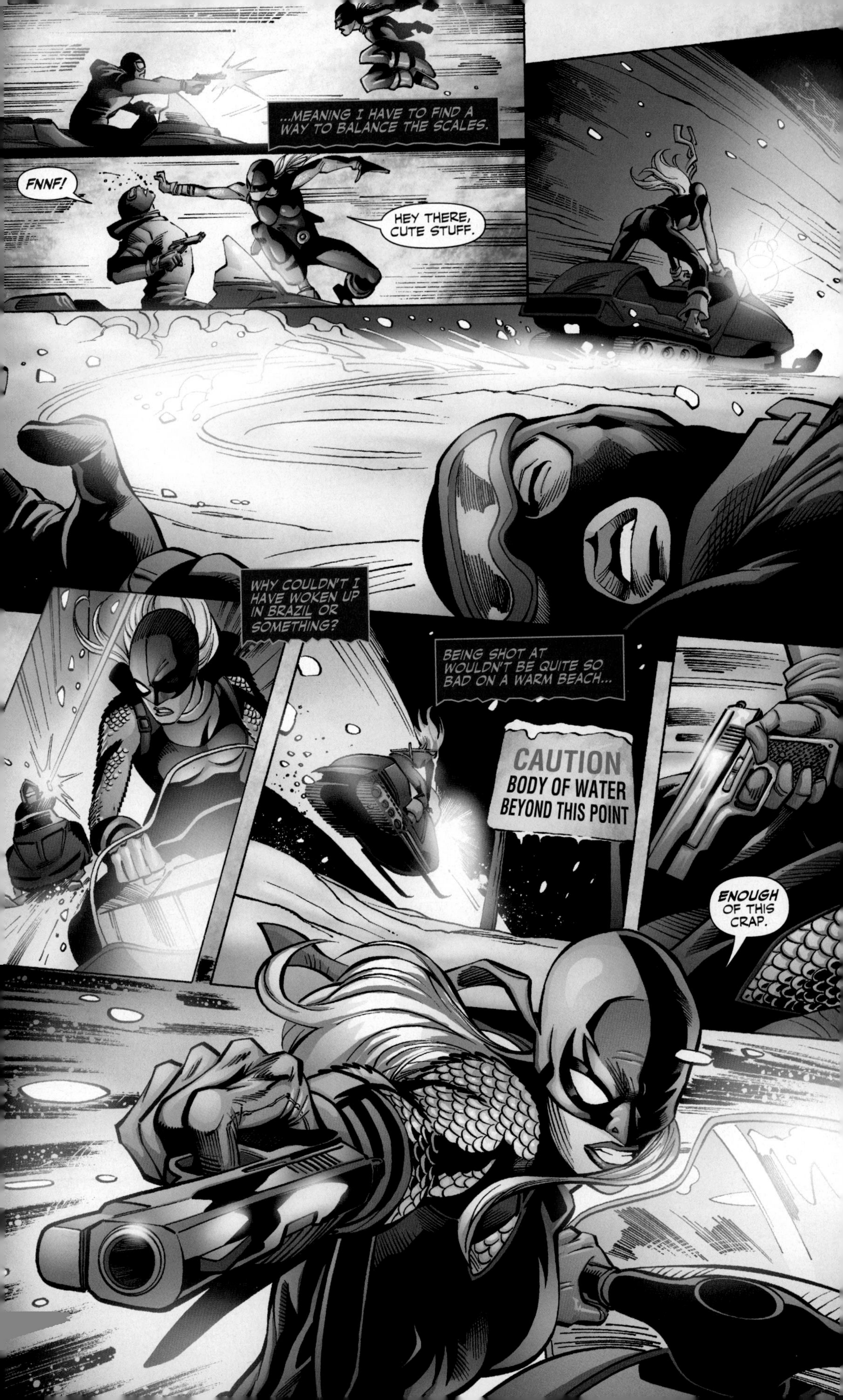
...MEANING I HAVE TO FIND A WAY TO BALANCE THE SCALES.
FNNF!
HEY THERE, CUTE STUFF.
WHY COULDN'T I HAVE WOKEN UP IN BRAZIL OR SOMETHING?
BEING SHOT AT WOULDN'T BE QUITE SO BAD ON A WARM BEACH...
CAUTION
BODY OF WATER
BEYOND THIS POINT
ENOUGH OF THIS CRAP.

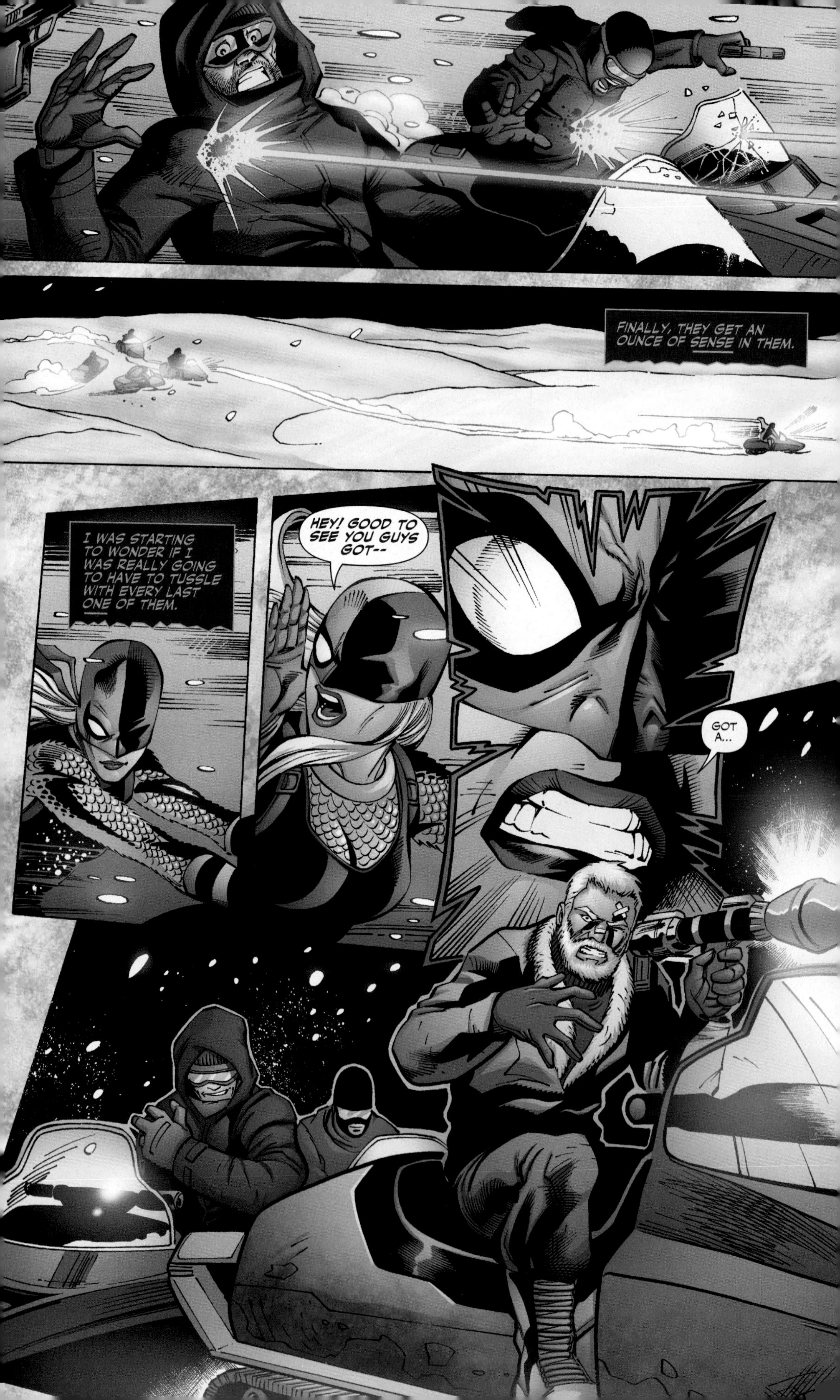

FINALLY, THEY GET AN OUNCE OF SENSE IN THEM.
I WAS STARTING TO WONDER IF I WAS REALLY GOING TO HAVE TO TUSSLE WITH EVERY LAST ONE OF THEM.
HEY! GOOD TO SEE YOU GUYS GOT--
GOT A...

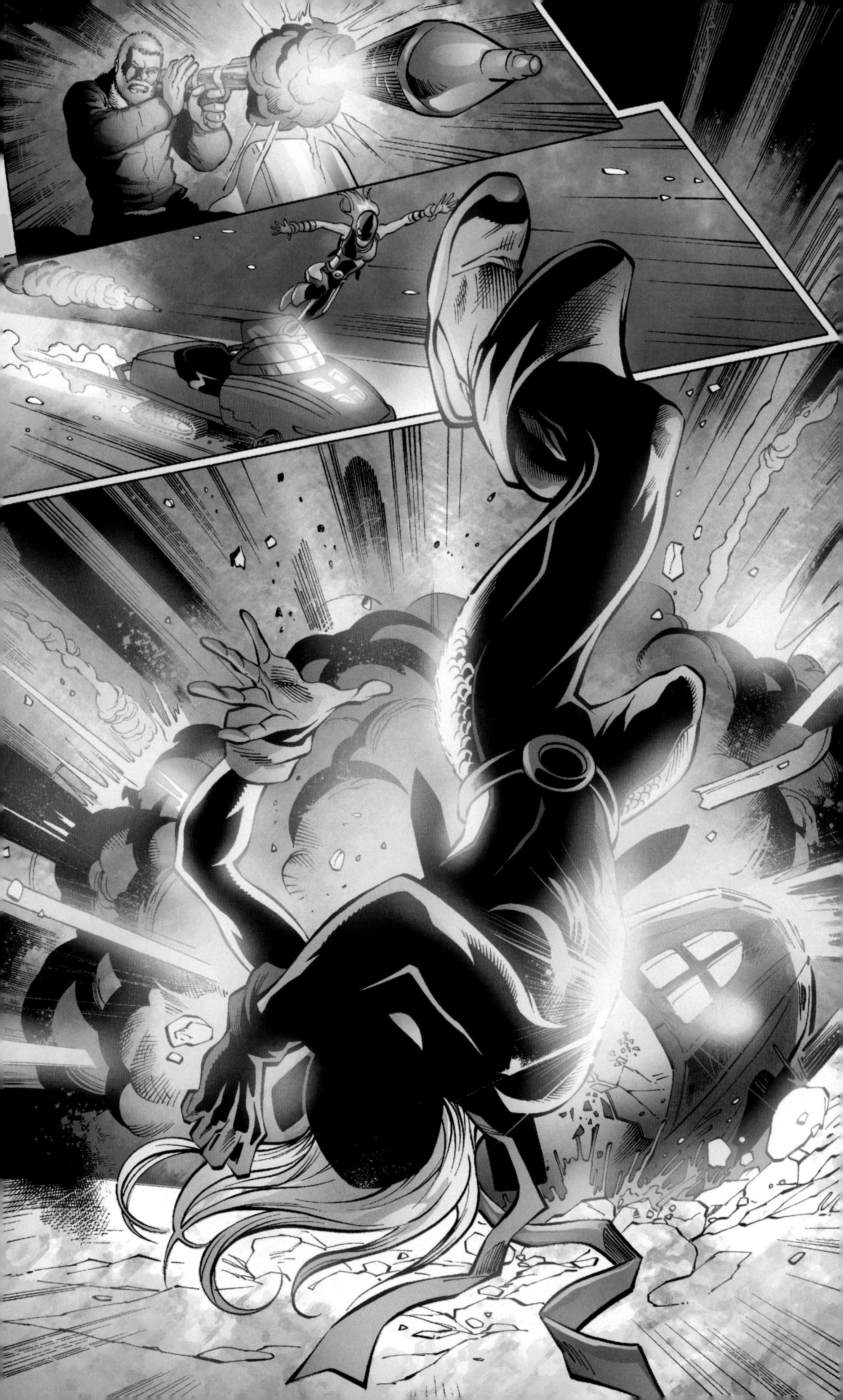

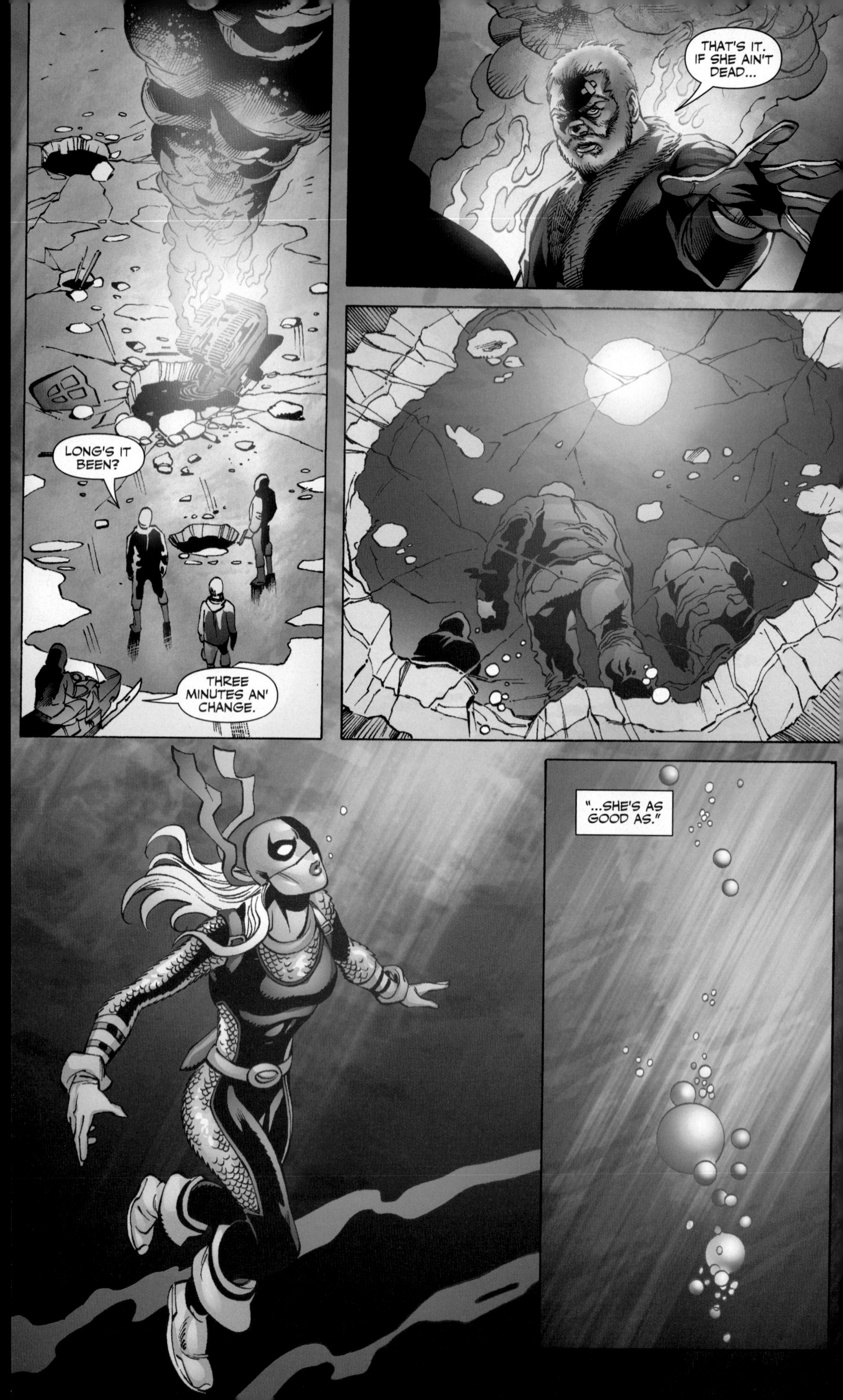
LONG'S IT BEEN?
THREE MINUTES AN' CHANGE.
THAT'S IT. IF SHE AIN'T DEAD...
"...SHE'S AS GOOD AS."

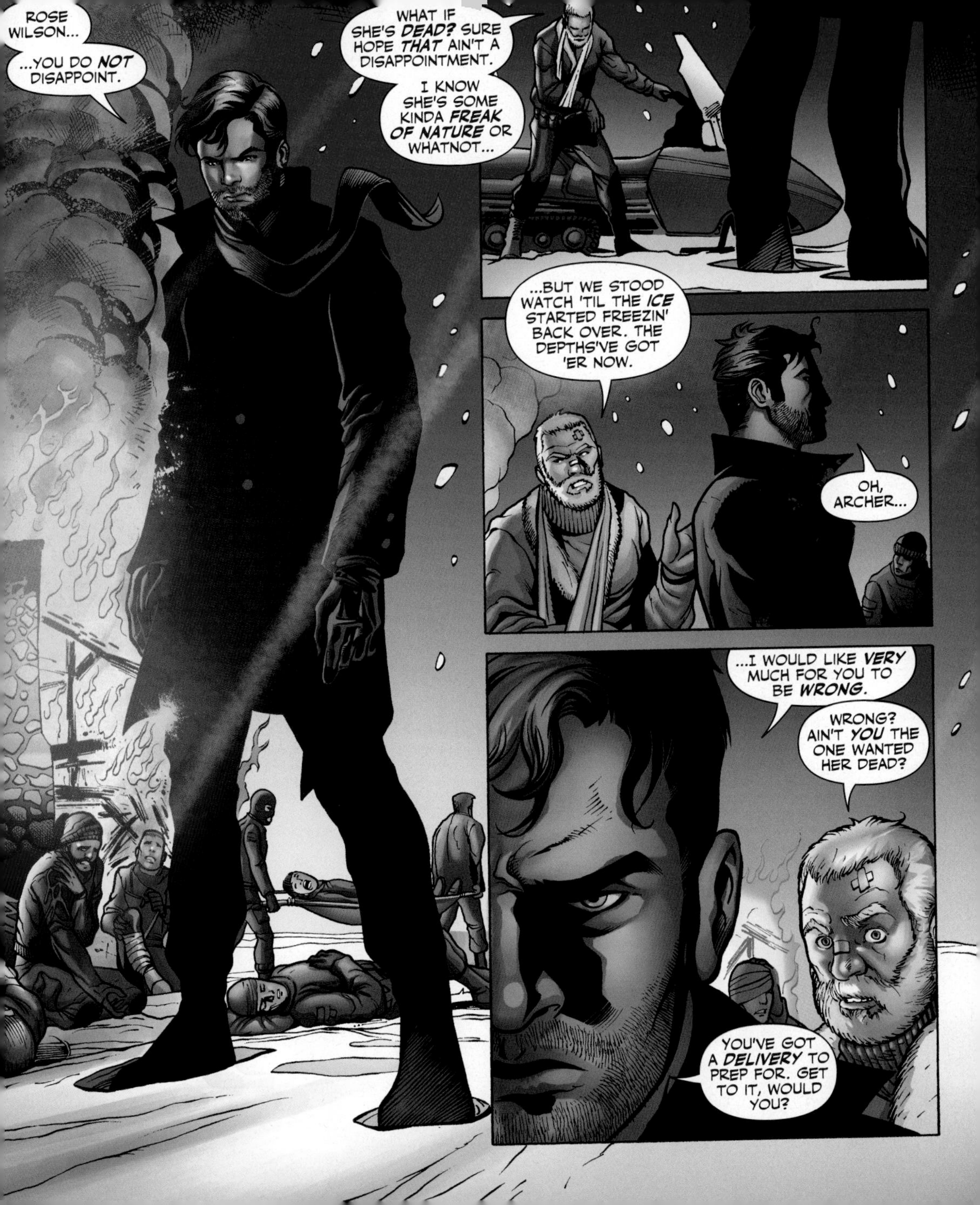
ROSE WILSON...
...YOU DO NOT DISAPPOINT.
WHAT IF SHE'S DEAD? SURE HOPE THAT AIN'T A DISAPPOINTMENT.
I KNOW SHE'S SOME KINDA FREAK OF NATURE OR WHATNOT...
...BUT WE STOOD WATCH 'TIL THE ICE STARTED FREEZIN' BACK OVER. THE DEPTHS'VE GOT 'ER NOW.
OH, ARCHER...
...I WOULD LIKE VERY MUCH FOR YOU TO BE WRONG.
WRONG? AIN'T YOU THE ONE WANTED HER DEAD?
YOU'VE GOT A DELIVERY TO PREP FOR. GET TO IT, WOULD YOU?

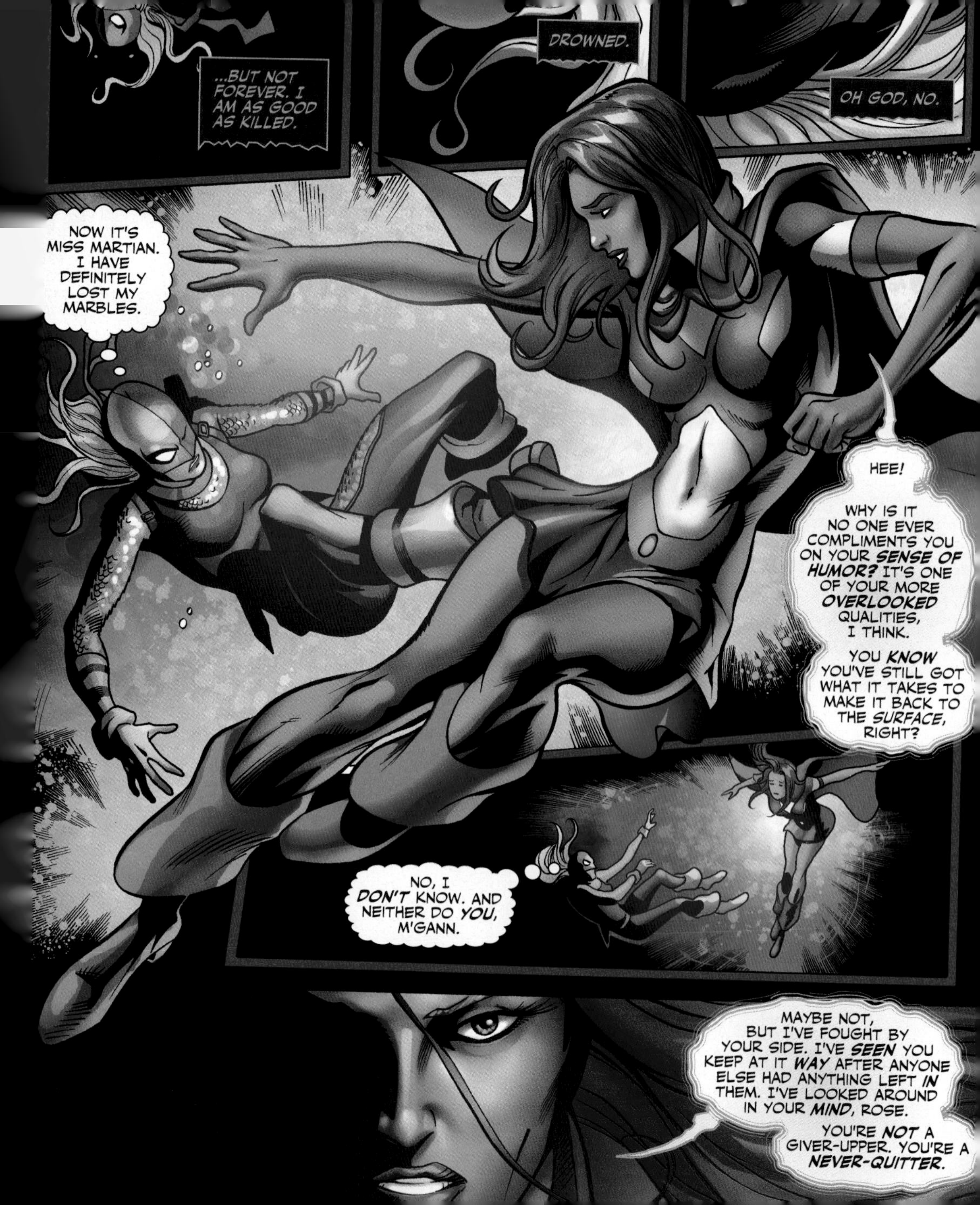
...BUT NOT FOREVER. I AM AS GOOD AS KILLED.
DROWNED.
OH GOD, NO.
NOW IT'S MISS MARTIAN. I HAVE DEFINITELY LOST MY MARBLES.
HEE!
WHY IS IT NO ONE EVER COMPLIMENTS YOU ON YOUR SENSE OF HUMOR? IT'S ONE OF YOUR MORE OVERLOOKED QUALITIES, I THINK.
YOU KNOW YOU'VE STILL GOT WHAT IT TAKES TO MAKE IT BACK TO THE SURFACE, RIGHT?
NO, I DON'T KNOW. AND NEITHER DO YOU, M'GANN.
MAYBE NOT, BUT I'VE FOUGHT BY YOUR SIDE. I'VE SEEN YOU KEEP AT IT WAY AFTER ANYONE ELSE HAD ANYTHING LEFT IN THEM. I'VE LOOKED AROUND IN YOUR MIND, ROSE.
YOU'RE NOT A GIVER-UPPER. YOU'RE A NEVER-QUITTER.

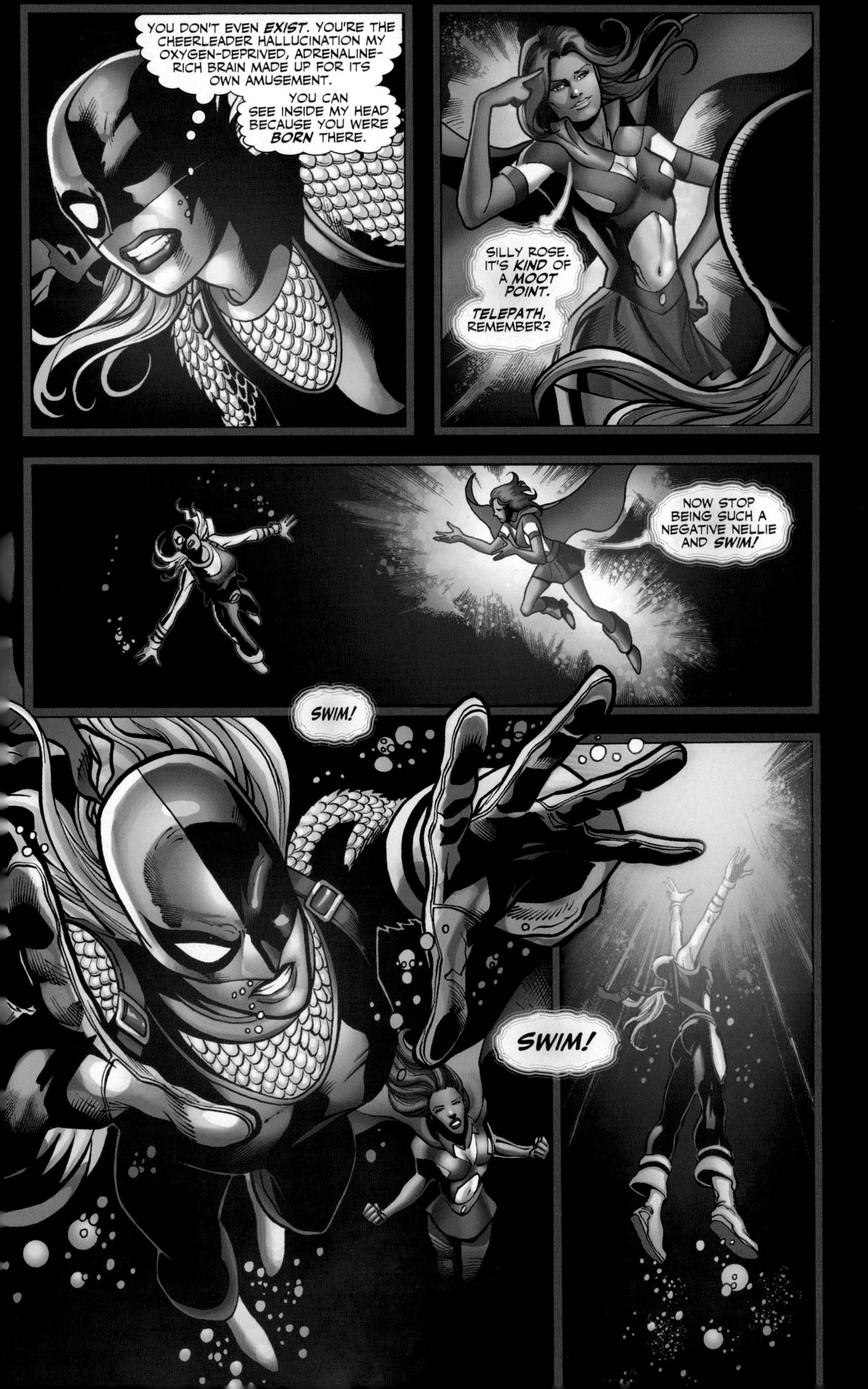
YOU DON'T EVEN EXIST. YOU'RE THE CHEERLEADER HALLUCINATION MY OXYGEN-DEPRIVED, ADRENALINE-RICH BRAIN MADE UP FOR ITS OWN AMUSEMENT.
YOU CAN SEE INSIDE MY HEAD BECAUSE YOU WERE BORN THERE.
SILLY ROSE. IT'S KIND OF A MOOT POINT.
TELEPATH, REMEMBER?
NOW STOP BEING SUCH A NEGATIVE NELLIE AND SWIM!
SWIM!
SWIM!

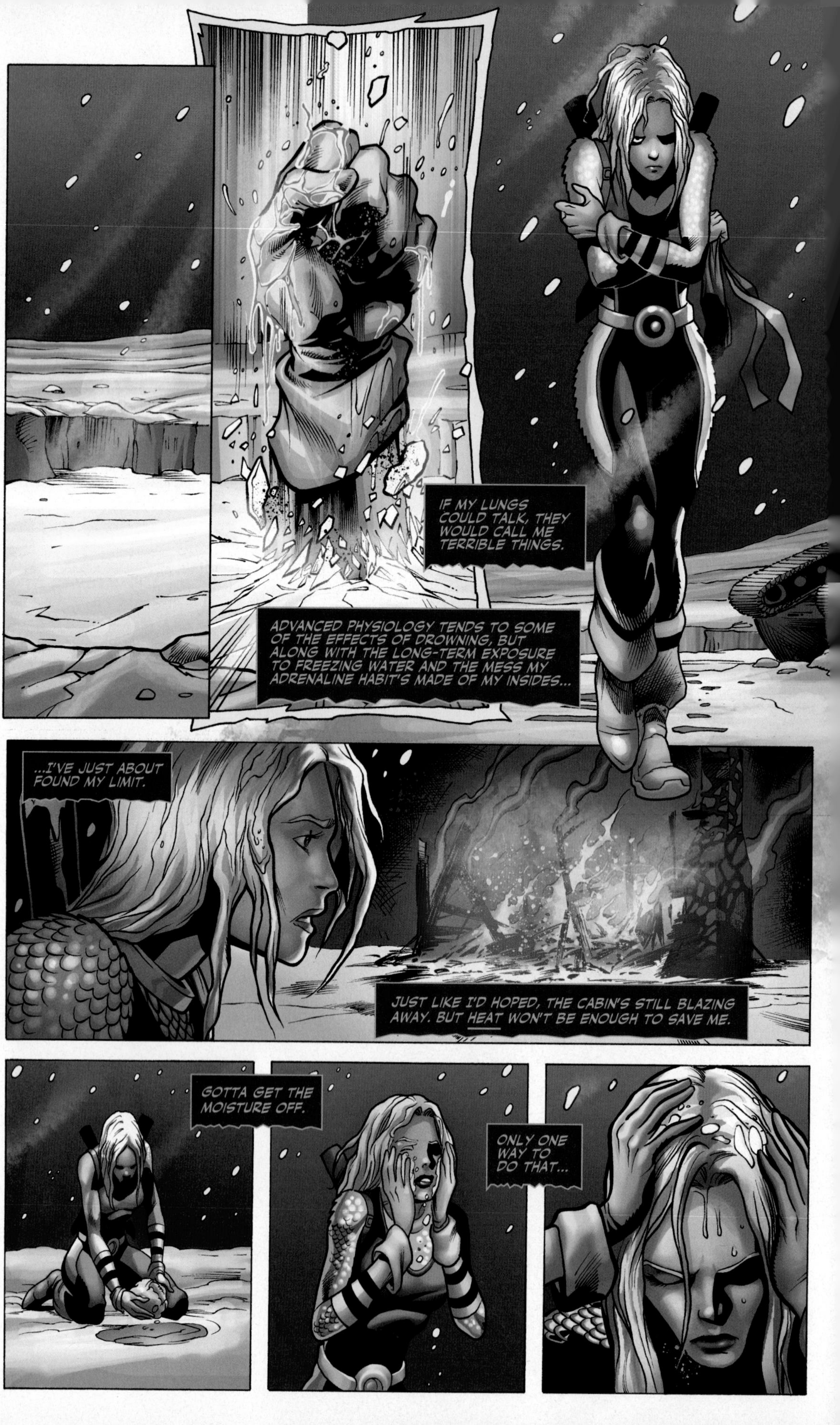
IF MY LUNGS COULD TALK, THEY WOULD CALL ME TERRIBLE THINGS.
ADVANCED PHYSIOLOGY TENDS TO SOME OF THE EFFECTS OF DROWNING, BUT ALONG WITH THE LONG-TERM EXPOSURE TO FREEZING WATER AND THE MESS MY ADRENALINE HABIT'S MADE OF MY INSIDES...
...I'VE JUST ABOUT FOUND MY LIMIT.
JUST LIKE I'D HOPED, THE CABIN'S STILL BLAZING AWAY. BUT HEAT WON'T BE ENOUGH TO SAVE ME.
GOTTA GET THE MOISTURE OFF.
ONLY ONE WAY TO DO THAT...

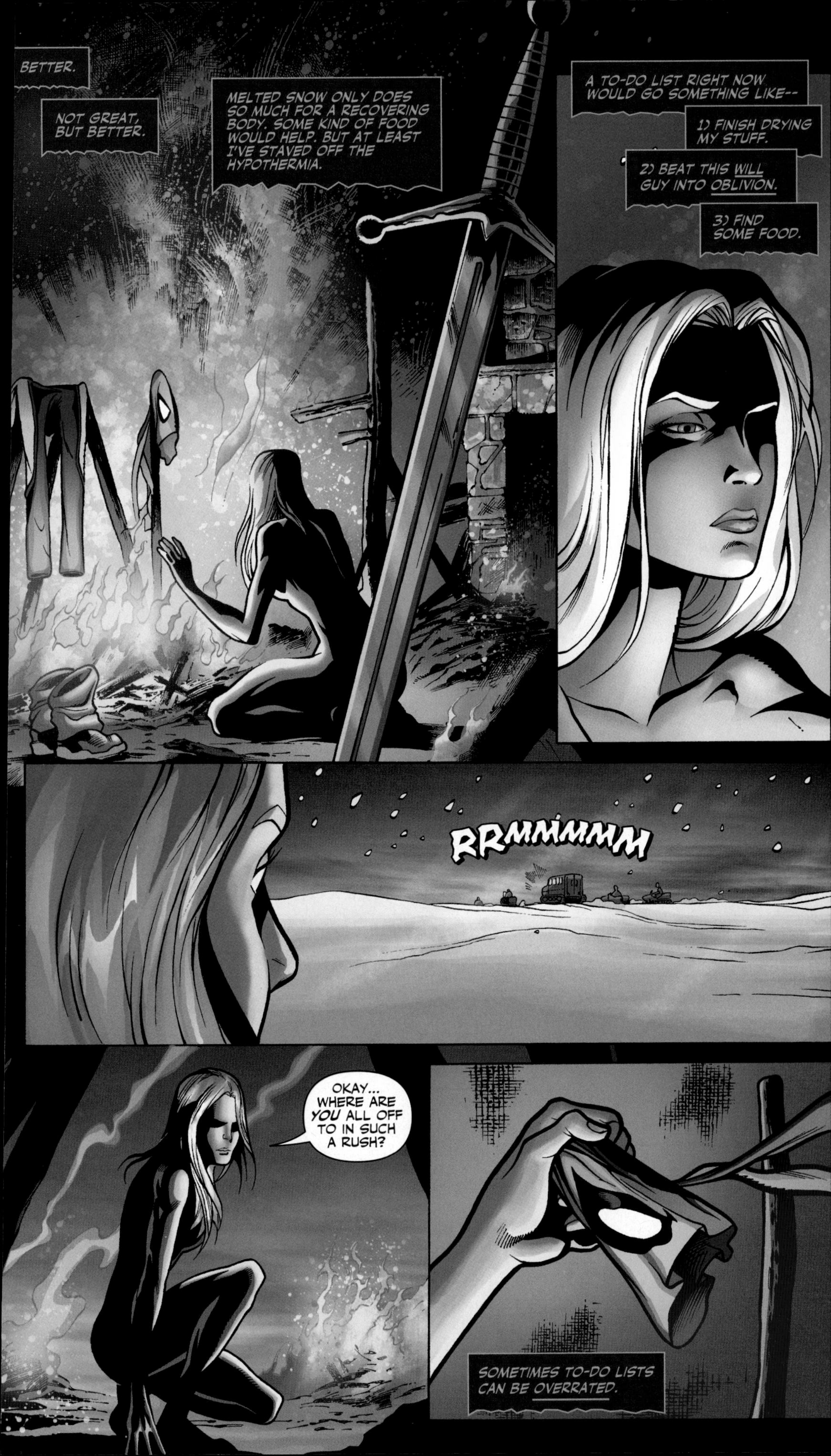
BETTER.
NOT GREAT, BUT BETTER.
MELTED SNOW ONLY DOES SO MUCH FOR A RECOVERING BODY. SOME KIND OF FOOD WOULD HELP. BUT AT LEAST I'VE STAVED OFF THE HYPOTHERMIA.
A TO-DO LIST RIGHT NOW WOULD GO SOMETHING LIKE--
1) FINISH DRYING MY STUFF.
2) BEAT THIS WILL GUY INTO OBLIVION.
3) FIND SOME FOOD.
RRMMMMMM
OKAY... WHERE ARE YOU ALL OFF TO IN SUCH A RUSH?
SOMETIMES TO-DO LISTS CAN BE OVERRATED.

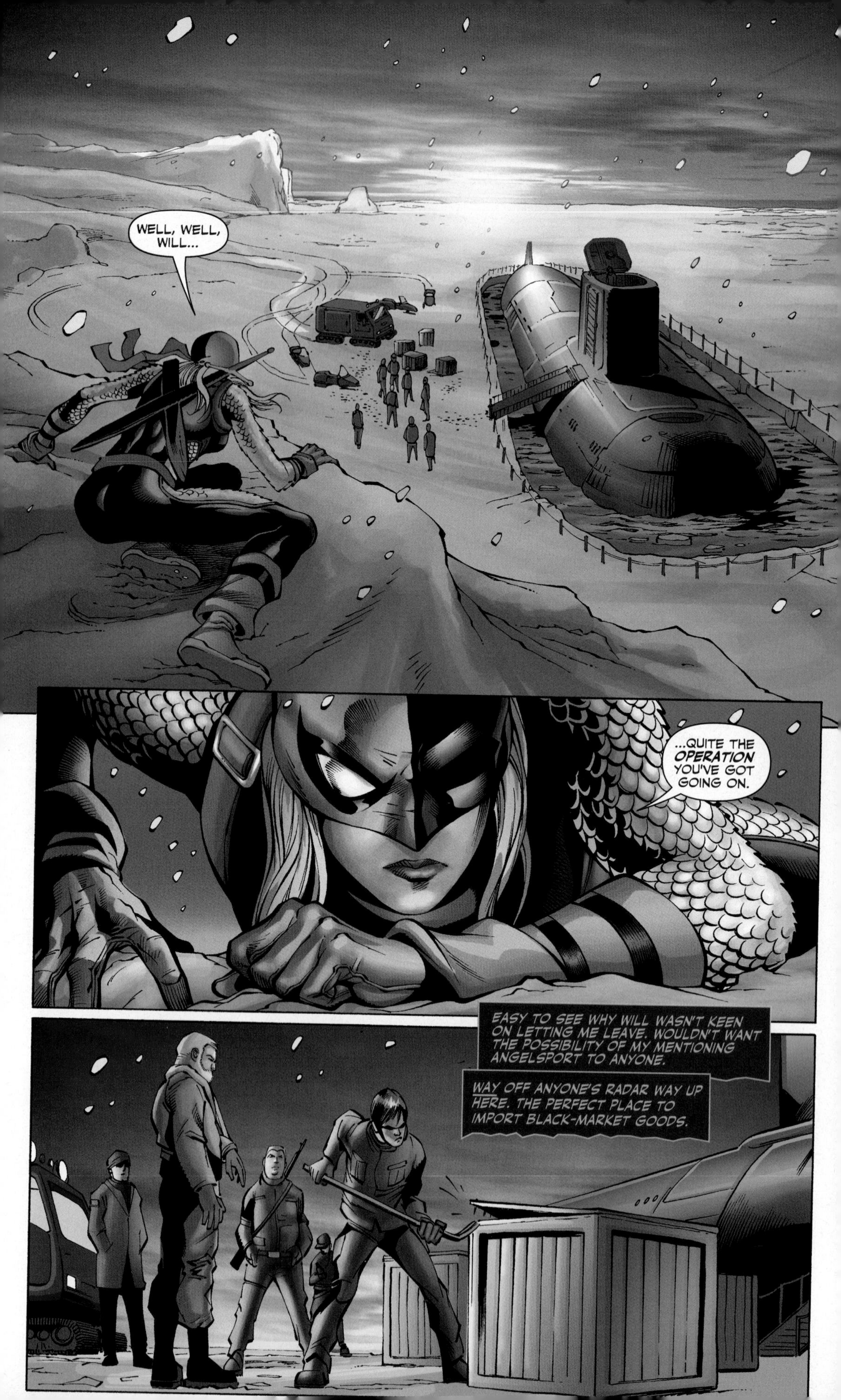
WELL, WELL, WILL...
...QUITE THE OPERATION YOU'VE GOT GOING ON.
EASY TO SEE WHY WILL WASN'T KEEN ON LETTING ME LEAVE. WOULDN'T WANT THE POSSIBILITY OF MY MENTIONING ANGELSPORT TO ANYONE.
WAY OFF ANYONE'S RADAR WAY UP HERE. THE PERFECT PLACE TO IMPORT BLACK-MARKET GOODS.

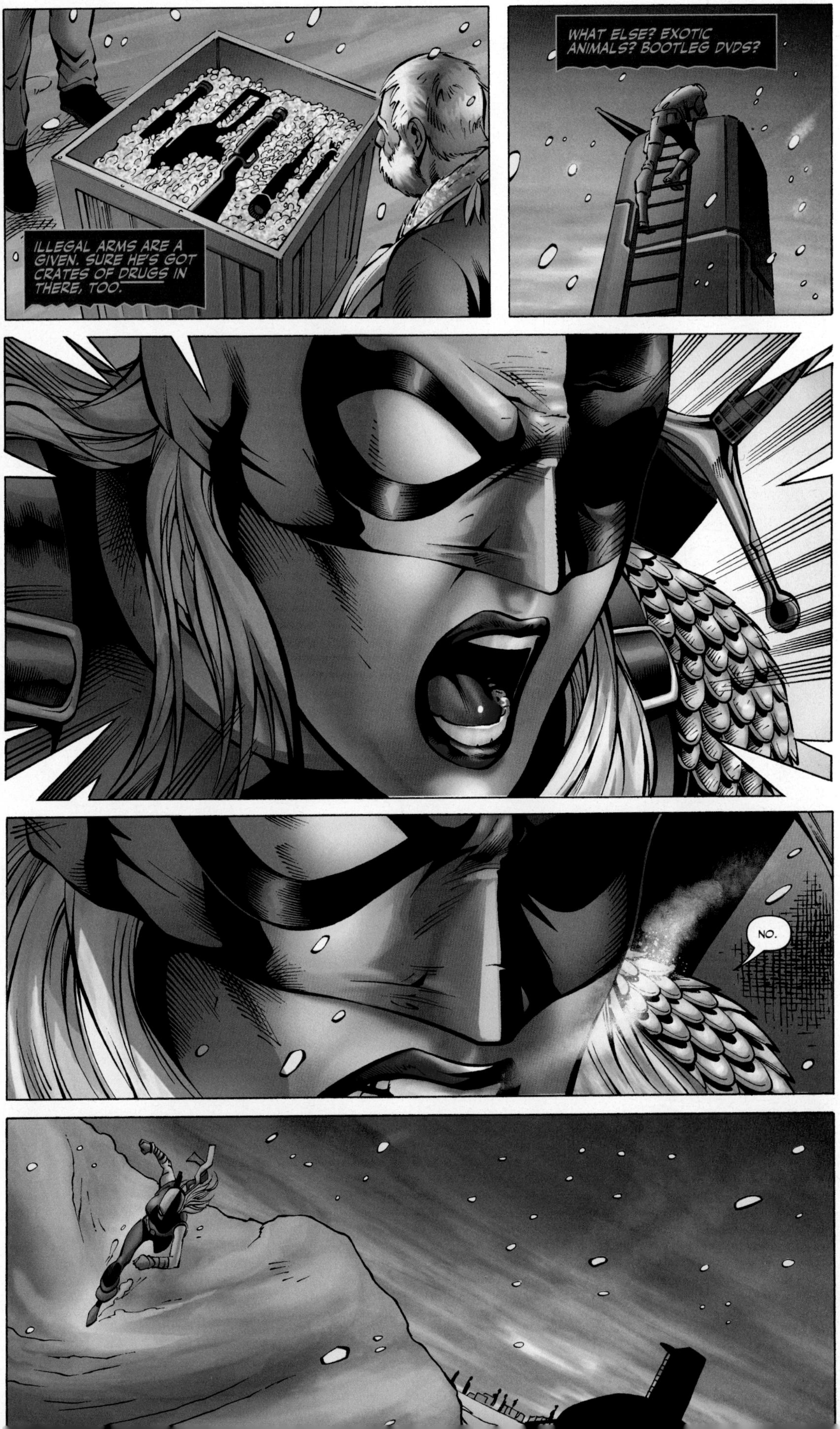
ILLEGAL ARMS ARE A GIVEN. SURE HE'S GOT CRATES OF DRUGS IN THERE, TOO.
WHAT ELSE? EXOTIC ANIMALS? BOOTLEG DVDS?
NO.

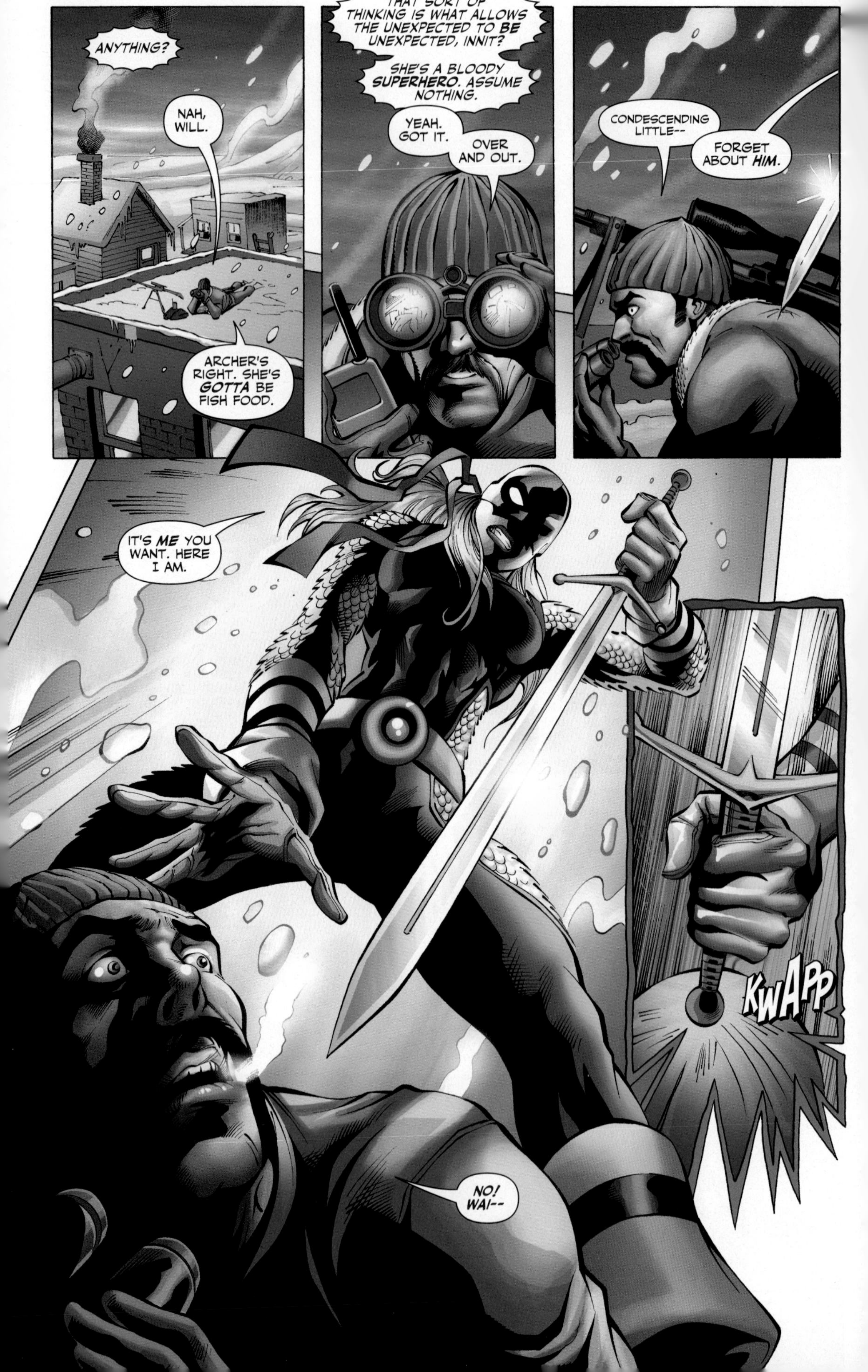
ANYTHING?
NAH, WILL.
ARCHER'S RIGHT. SHE'S *GOTTA* BE FISH FOOD.
THAT SORT OF THINKING IS WHAT ALLOWS THE UNEXPECTED TO *BE* UNEXPECTED, INNIT?
SHE'S A BLOODY *SUPERHERO*. ASSUME NOTHING.
YEAH. GOT IT.
OVER AND OUT.
CONDESCENDING LITTLE--
FORGET ABOUT *HIM*.
IT'S *ME* YOU WANT. HERE I AM.
KWAPP
NO! WAI--

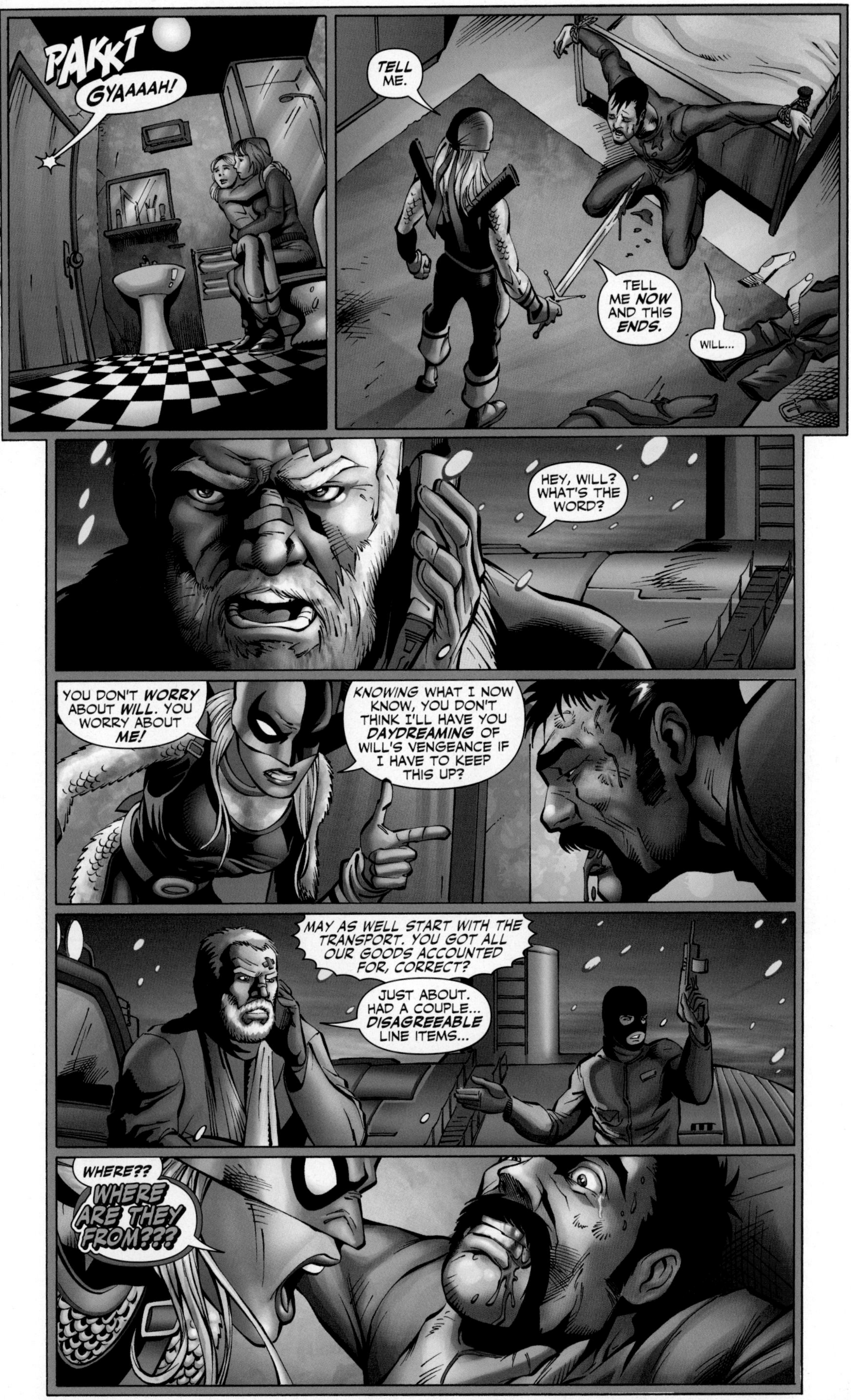
PAKKT
GYAAAAH!
TELL ME.
TELL ME NOW AND THIS ENDS.
WILL...
HEY, WILL? WHAT'S THE WORD?
YOU DON'T WORRY ABOUT WILL. YOU WORRY ABOUT ME!
KNOWING WHAT I NOW KNOW, YOU DON'T THINK I'LL HAVE YOU DAYDREAMING OF WILL'S VENGEANCE IF I HAVE TO KEEP THIS UP?
MAY AS WELL START WITH THE TRANSPORT. YOU GOT ALL OUR GOODS ACCOUNTED FOR, CORRECT?
JUST ABOUT. HAD A COUPLE... DISAGREEABLE LINE ITEMS...
WHERE??
WHERE ARE THEY FROM???

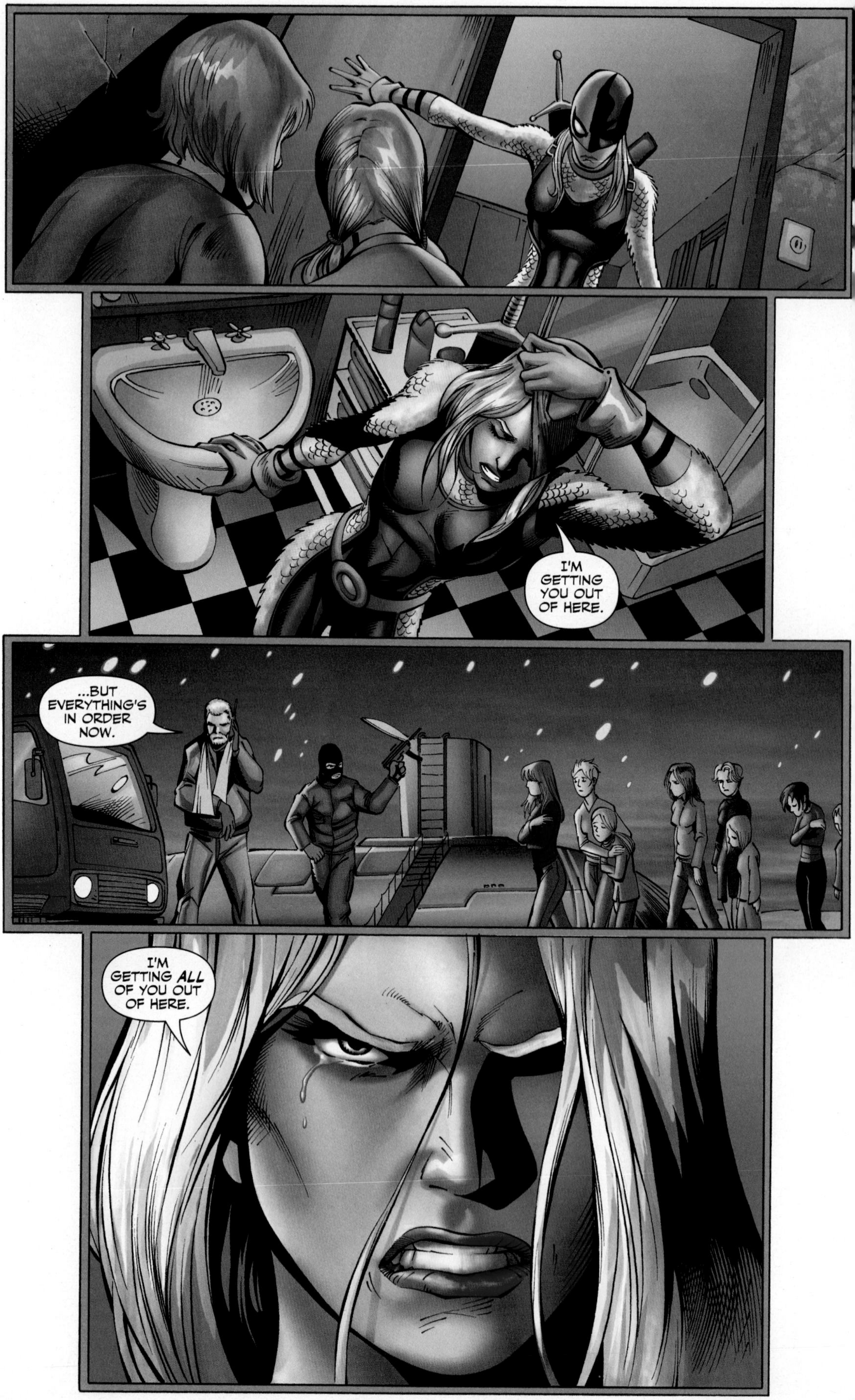
I'M GETTING YOU OUT OF HERE.
...BUT EVERYTHING'S IN ORDER NOW.
I'M GETTING *ALL* OF YOU OUT OF HERE.

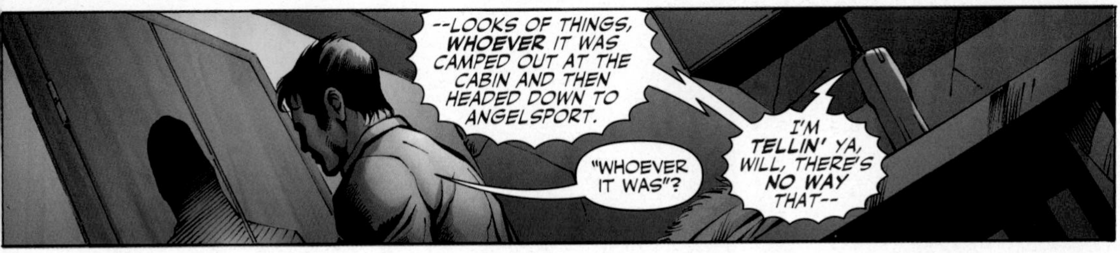
--LOOKS OF THINGS, WHOEVER IT WAS CAMPED OUT AT THE CABIN AND THEN HEADED DOWN TO ANGELSPORT.
"WHOEVER IT WAS"?
I'M TELLIN' YA, WILL, THERE'S NO WAY THAT--

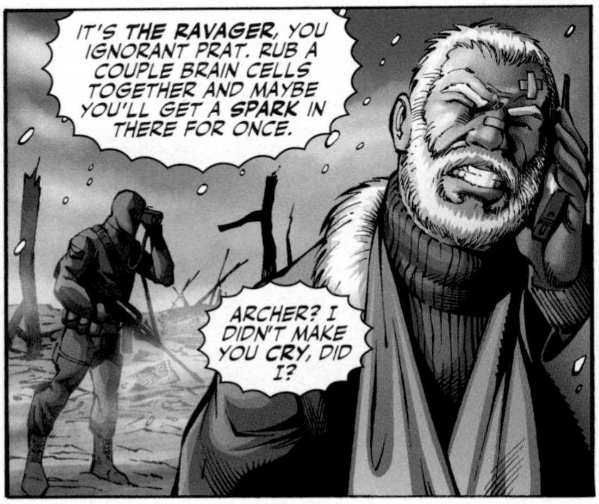
IT'S THE RAVAGER, YOU IGNORANT PRAT. RUB A COUPLE BRAIN CELLS TOGETHER AND MAYBE YOU'LL GET A SPARK IN THERE FOR ONCE.
ARCHER? I DIDN'T MAKE YOU CRY, DID I?

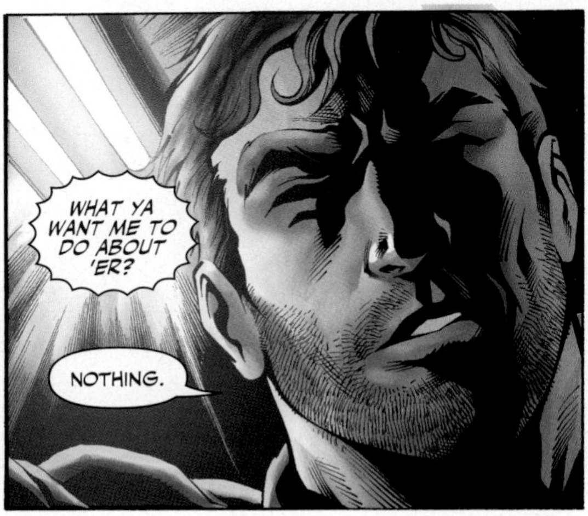
WHAT YA WANT ME TO DO ABOUT 'ER?
NOTHING.

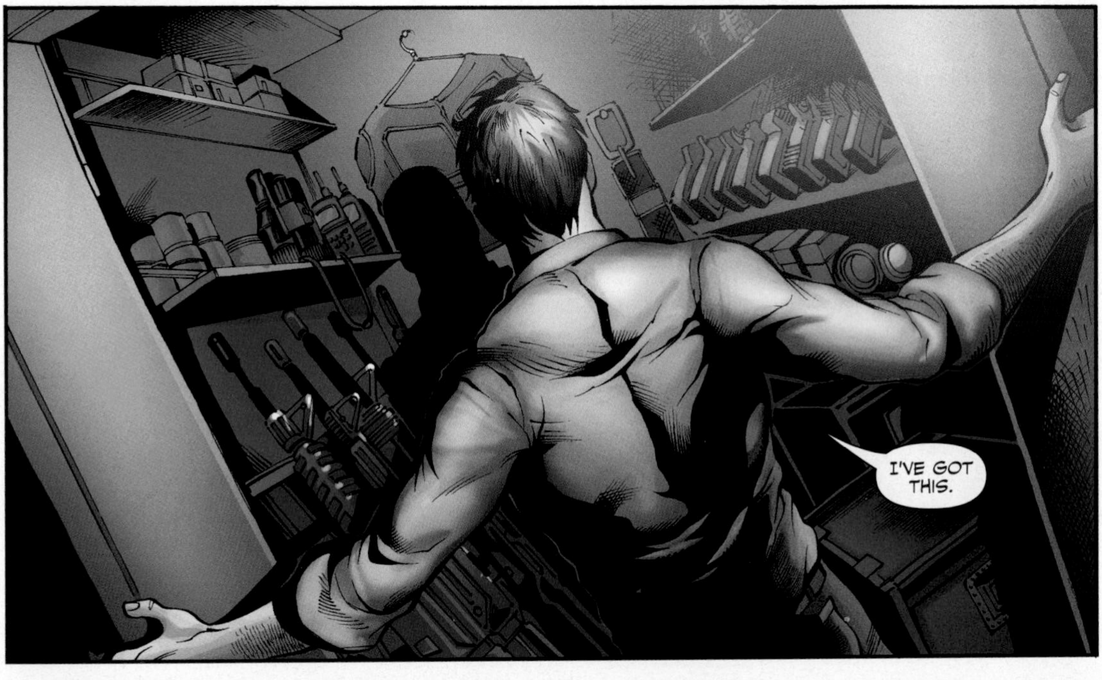
I'VE GOT THIS.

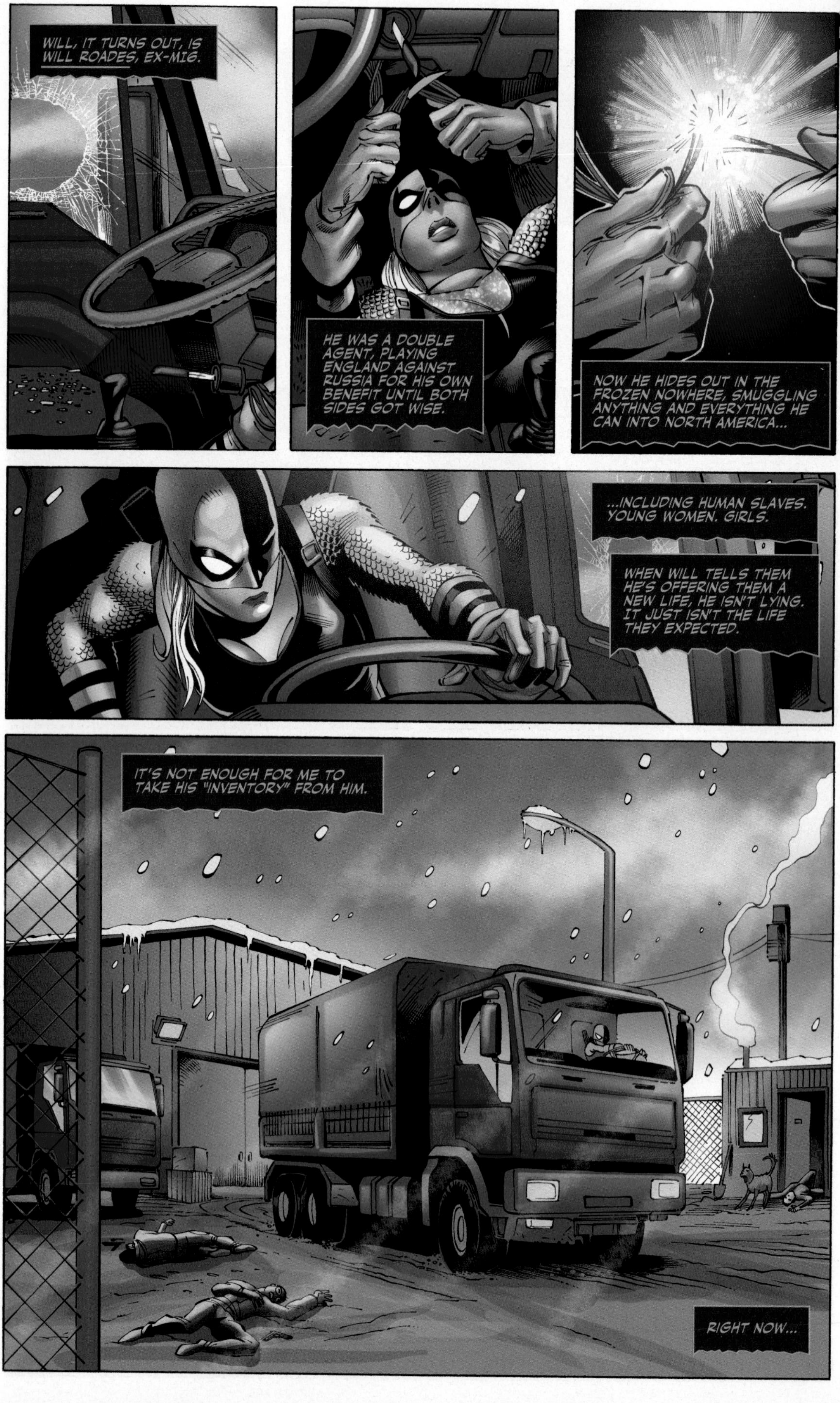
WILL, IT TURNS OUT, IS WILL ROADES, EX-MI6.
HE WAS A DOUBLE AGENT, PLAYING ENGLAND AGAINST RUSSIA FOR HIS OWN BENEFIT UNTIL BOTH SIDES GOT WISE.
NOW HE HIDES OUT IN THE FROZEN NOWHERE, SMUGGLING ANYTHING AND EVERYTHING HE CAN INTO NORTH AMERICA...
...INCLUDING HUMAN SLAVES. YOUNG WOMEN. GIRLS.
WHEN WILL TELLS THEM HE'S OFFERING THEM A NEW LIFE, HE ISN'T LYING. IT JUST ISN'T THE LIFE THEY EXPECTED.
IT'S NOT ENOUGH FOR ME TO TAKE HIS "INVENTORY" FROM HIM.
RIGHT NOW...

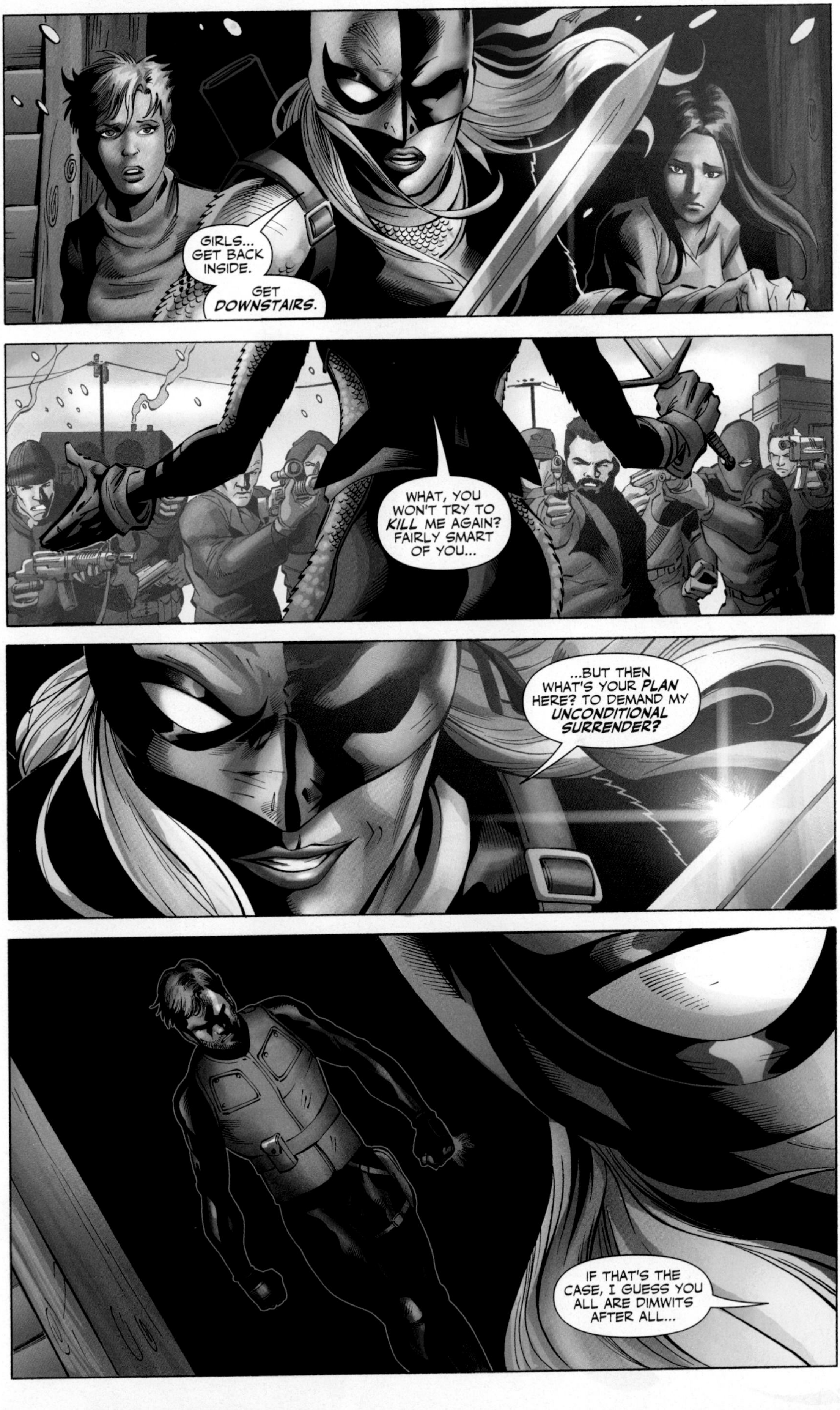
GIRLS... GET BACK INSIDE.
GET DOWNSTAIRS.
WHAT, YOU WON'T TRY TO KILL ME AGAIN? FAIRLY SMART OF YOU...
...BUT THEN WHAT'S YOUR PLAN HERE? TO DEMAND MY UNCONDITIONAL SURRENDER?
IF THAT'S THE CASE, I GUESS YOU ALL ARE DIMWITS AFTER ALL...

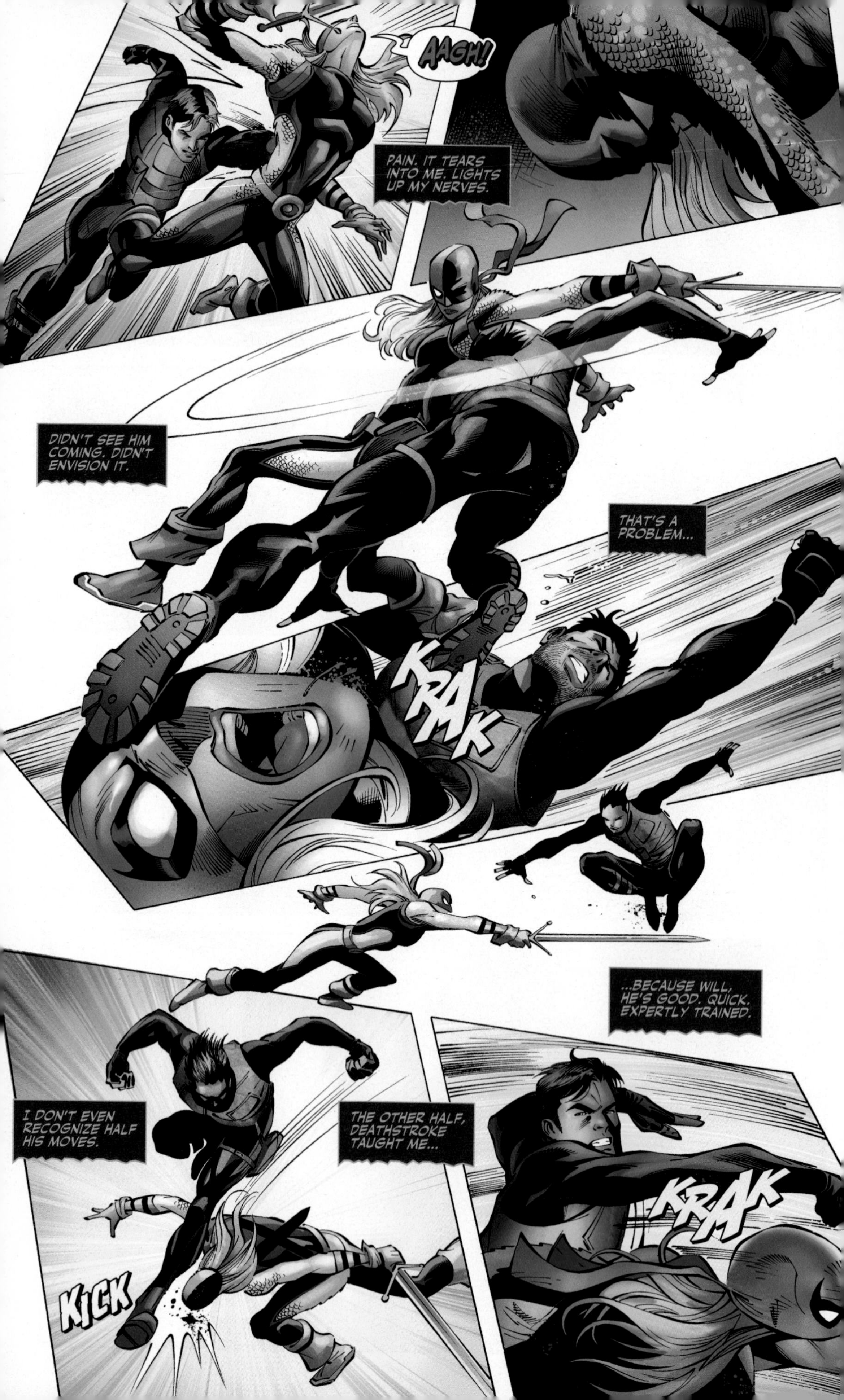
AAGH!
PAIN. IT TEARS INTO ME. LIGHTS UP MY NERVES.
DIDN'T SEE HIM COMING. DIDN'T ENVISION IT.
THAT'S A PROBLEM...
KRAK
...BECAUSE WILL, HE'S GOOD. QUICK. EXPERTLY TRAINED.
I DON'T EVEN RECOGNIZE HALF HIS MOVES.
THE OTHER HALF, DEATHSTROKE TAUGHT ME...
KICK
KRAK

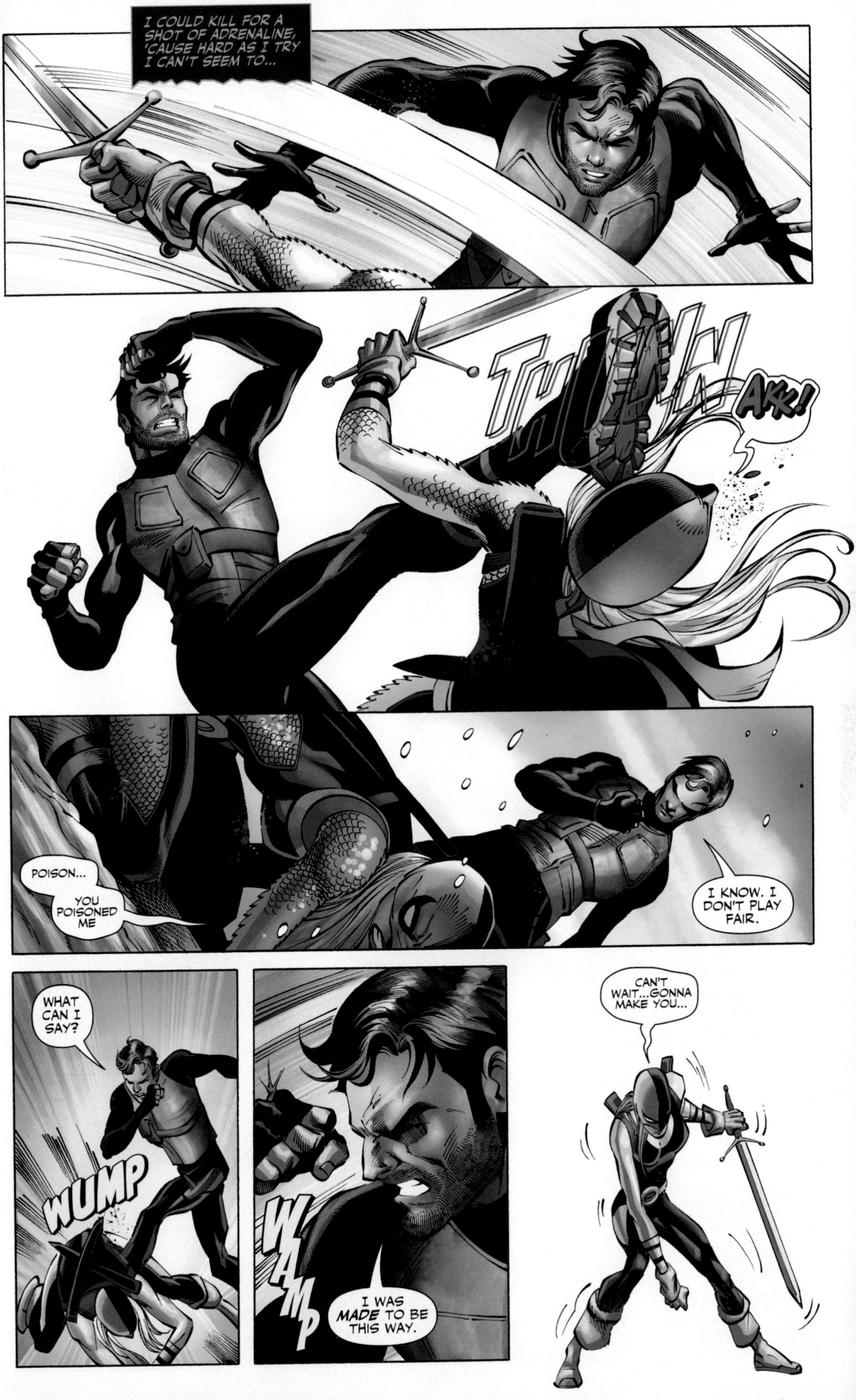
I COULD KILL FOR A SHOT OF ADRENALINE, 'CAUSE HARD AS I TRY I CAN'T SEEM TO...
AKK!
POISON...
YOU POISONED ME
I KNOW. I DON'T PLAY FAIR.
WHAT CAN I SAY?
WUMP
WAMP
I WAS *MADE* TO BE THIS WAY.
CAN'T WAIT...GONNA MAKE YOU...

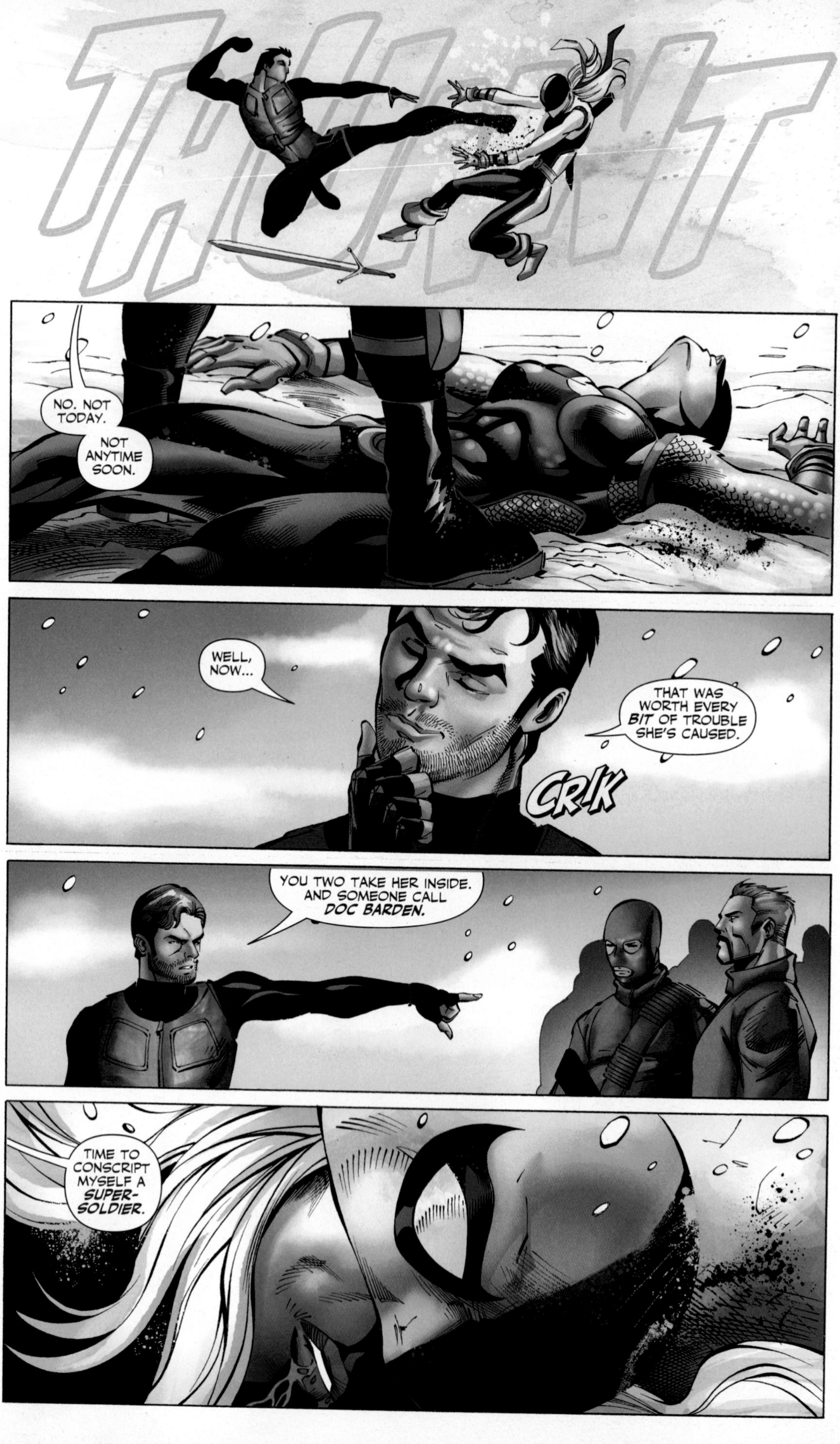
THOOM
NO. NOT TODAY.
NOT ANYTIME SOON.
WELL, NOW...
THAT WAS WORTH EVERY *BIT* OF TROUBLE SHE'S CAUSED.
CRIK
YOU TWO TAKE HER INSIDE. AND SOMEONE CALL *DOC BARDEN.*
TIME TO CONSCRIPT MYSELF A *SUPER-SOLDIER.*

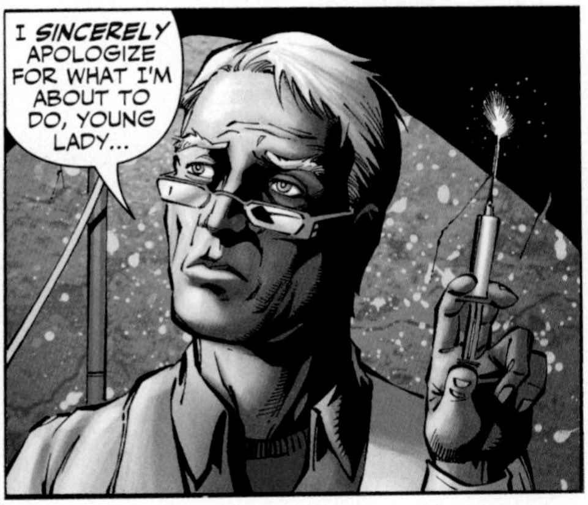
I SINCERELY APOLOGIZE FOR WHAT I'M ABOUT TO DO, YOUNG LADY...

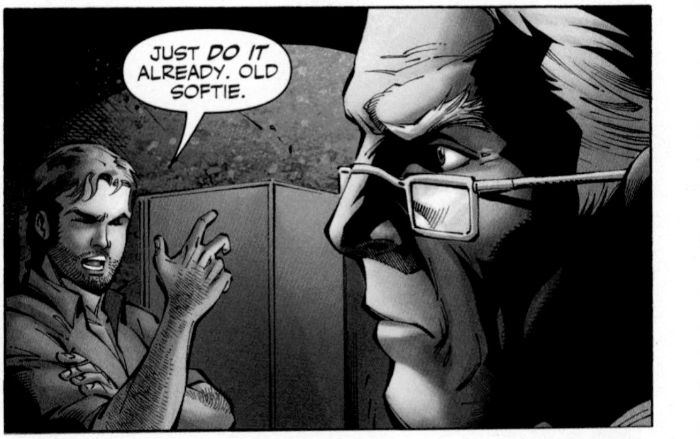
JUST DO IT ALREADY. OLD SOFTIE.

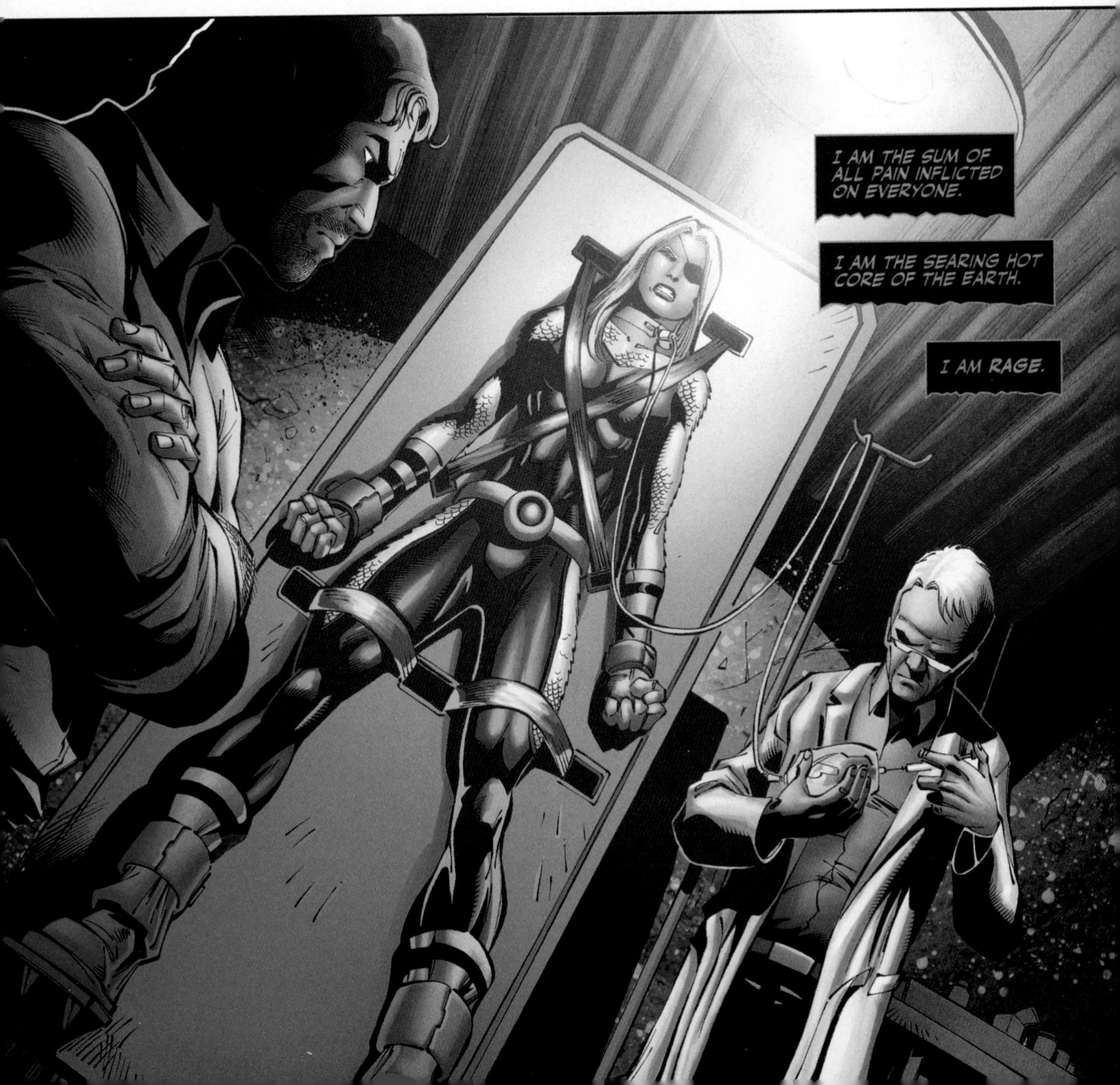
I AM THE SUM OF ALL PAIN INFLICTED ON EVERYONE.
I AM THE SEARING HOT CORE OF THE EARTH.
I AM RAGE.

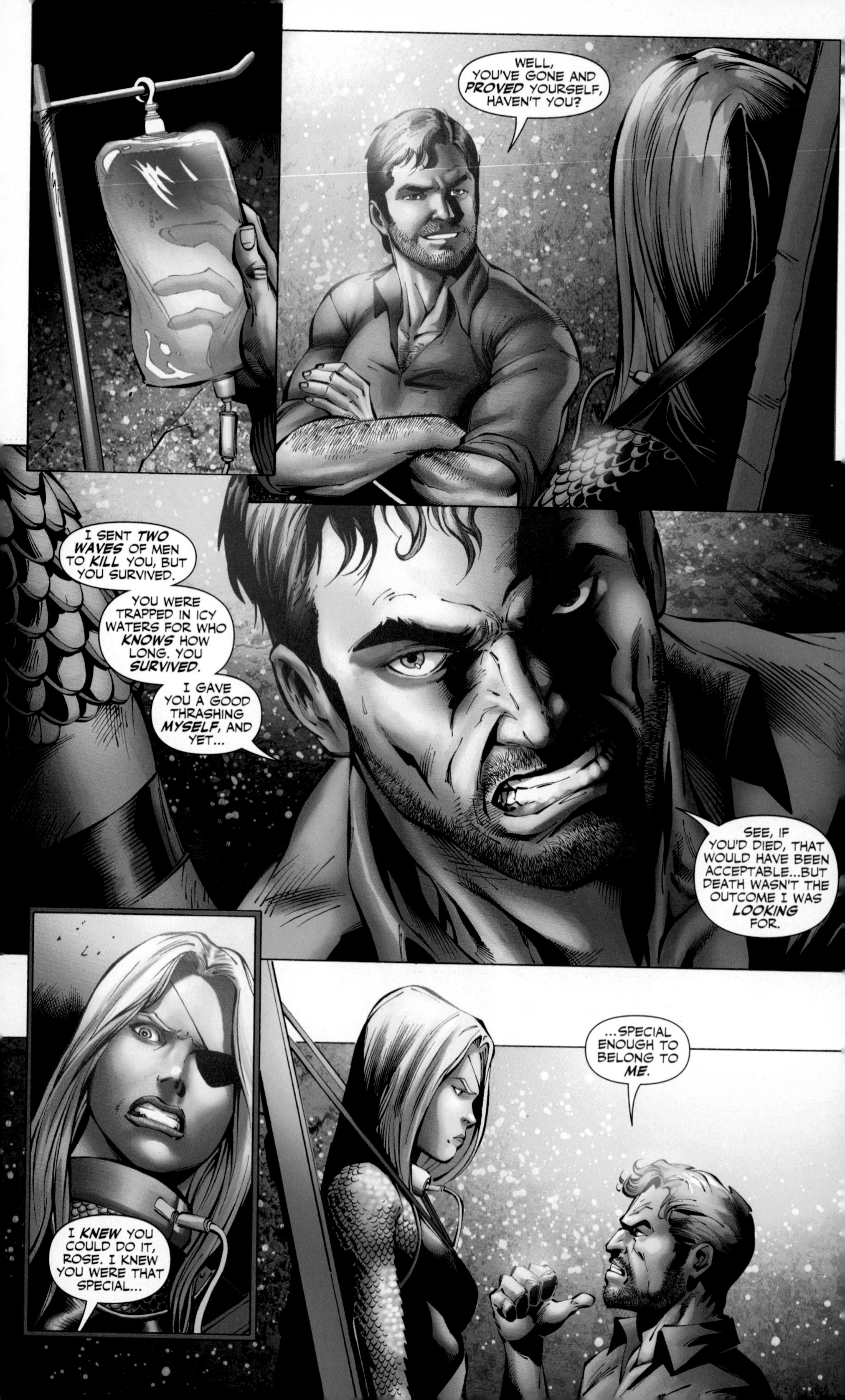
WELL, YOU'VE GONE AND PROVED YOURSELF, HAVEN'T YOU?
I SENT TWO WAVES OF MEN TO KILL YOU, BUT YOU SURVIVED.
YOU WERE TRAPPED IN ICY WATERS FOR WHO KNOWS HOW LONG. YOU SURVIVED.
I GAVE YOU A GOOD THRASHING MYSELF, AND YET...
SEE, IF YOU'D DIED, THAT WOULD HAVE BEEN ACCEPTABLE...BUT DEATH WASN'T THE OUTCOME I WAS LOOKING FOR.
I KNEW YOU COULD DO IT, ROSE. I KNEW YOU WERE THAT SPECIAL...
...SPECIAL ENOUGH TO BELONG TO ME.

WELL?

IT'S IN HER SYSTEM NOW...

...BUT HER UNIQUE METABOLISM MEANS WE DON'T KNOW FOR SURE IF IT'S **ENOUGH**. IT'LL TAKE **TIME** TO FIND THE RIGHT LEVELS.

THAT'S FINE. WE'VE NOTHING **BUT**, HAVEN'T WE?

WHAT ARE YOU **DOSING** ME WITH, YOU WASTE OF FLESH?

IT'S A SORT OF... **CONDITIONER**, I SUPPOSE YOU COULD SAY.

WHEN ALL IS SAID AND DONE, YOU'LL BE MY GREATEST PRIZE. MY PERSONAL BODYGUARD. MY ONE-GIRL ARMY. MY **ASSASSIN**.

NOTHING TO SAY? NO PITHY COMEBACKS? NO VICIOUS RANTS?

NO CALLS FOR MERCY?

PTOO

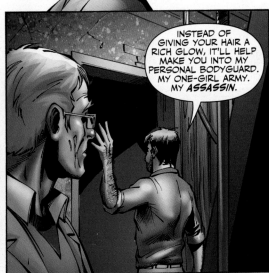

INSTEAD OF GIVING YOUR HAIR A RICH GLOW, IT'LL HELP MAKE YOU INTO MY PERSONAL BODYGUARD. MY ONE-GIRL ARMY. MY **ASSASSIN**.

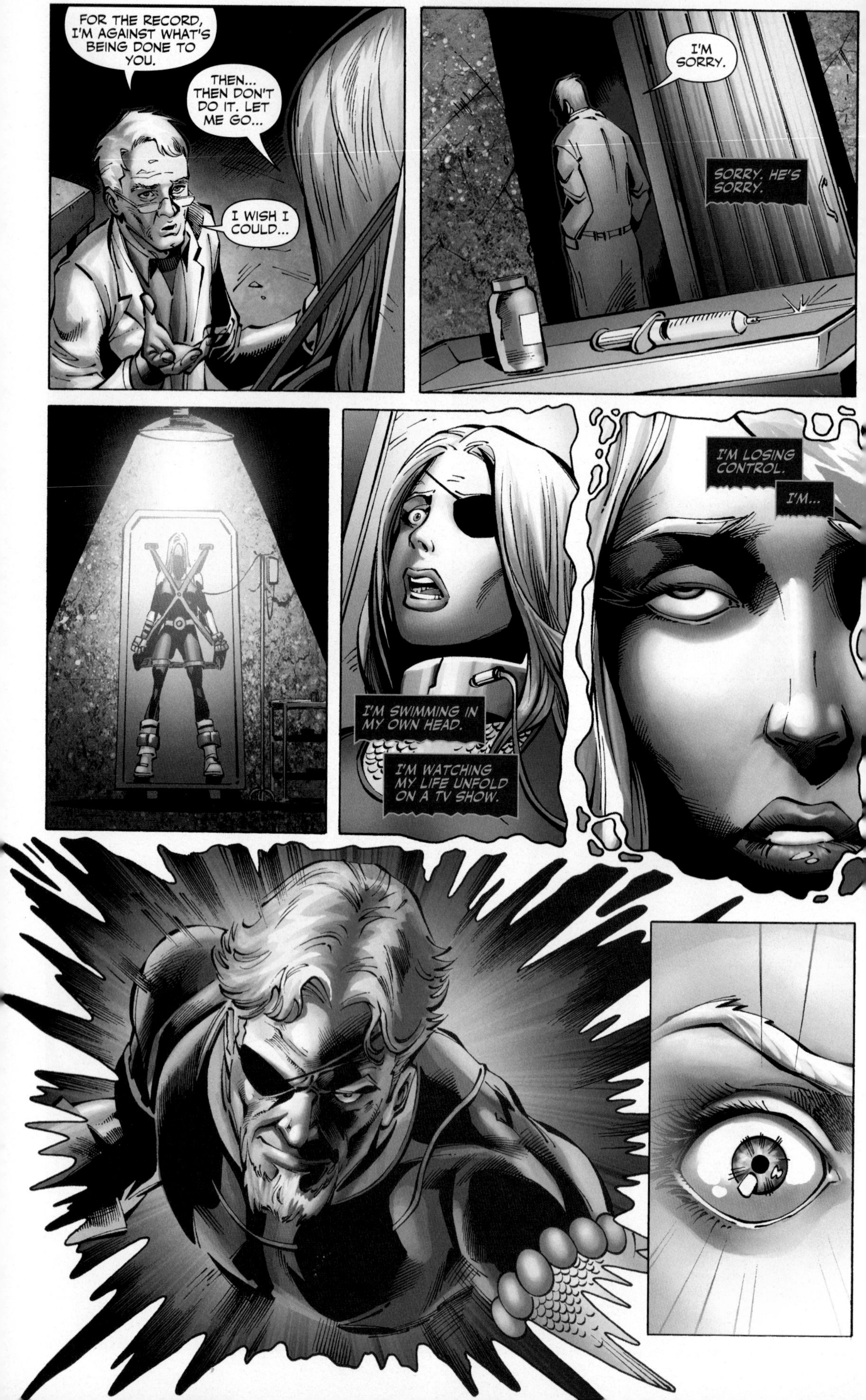
FOR THE RECORD, I'M AGAINST WHAT'S BEING DONE TO YOU.
THEN... THEN DON'T DO IT. LET ME GO...
I WISH I COULD...
I'M SORRY.
SORRY. HE'S SORRY.
I'M SWIMMING IN MY OWN HEAD.
I'M WATCHING MY LIFE UNFOLD ON A TV SHOW.
I'M LOSING CONTROL.
I'M...

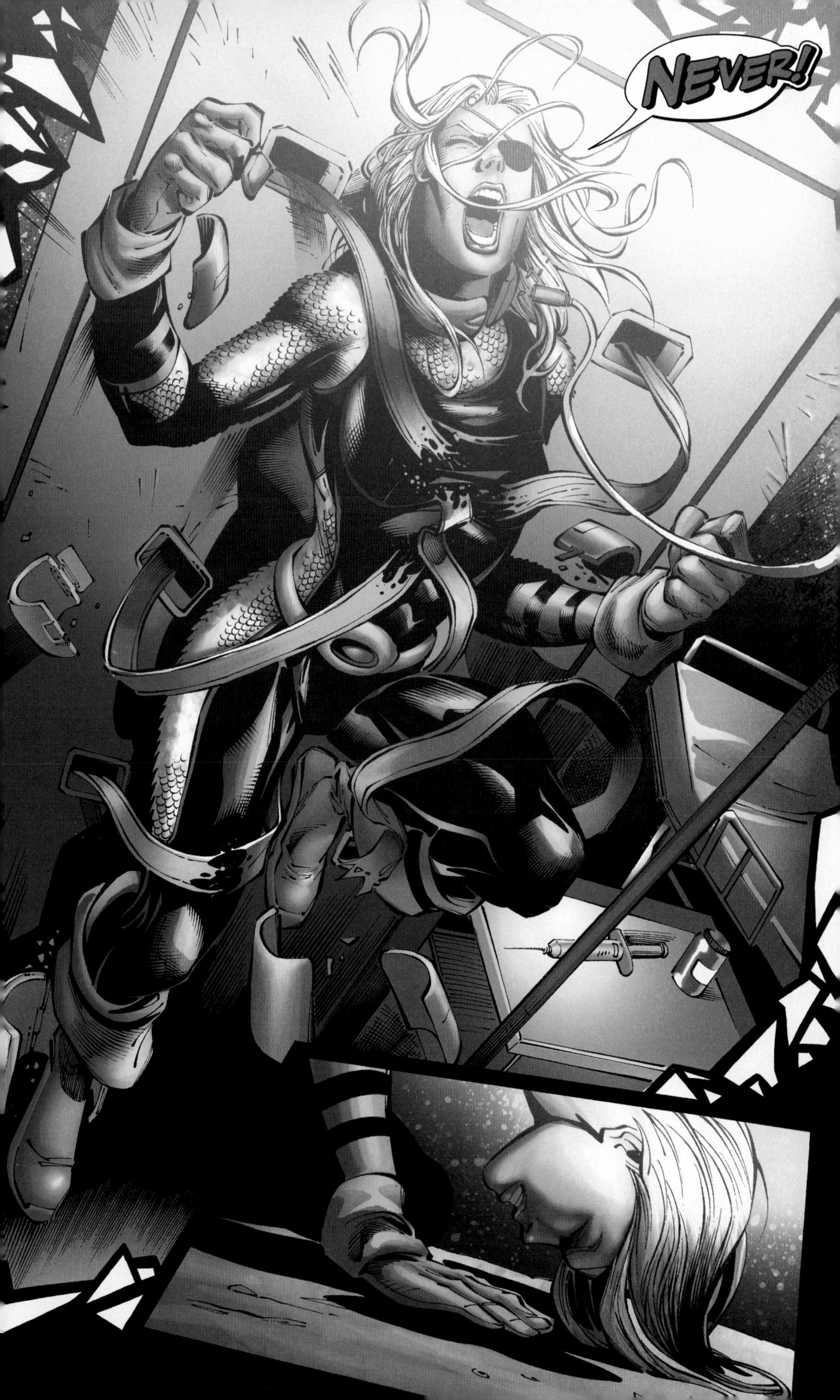
NEVER!

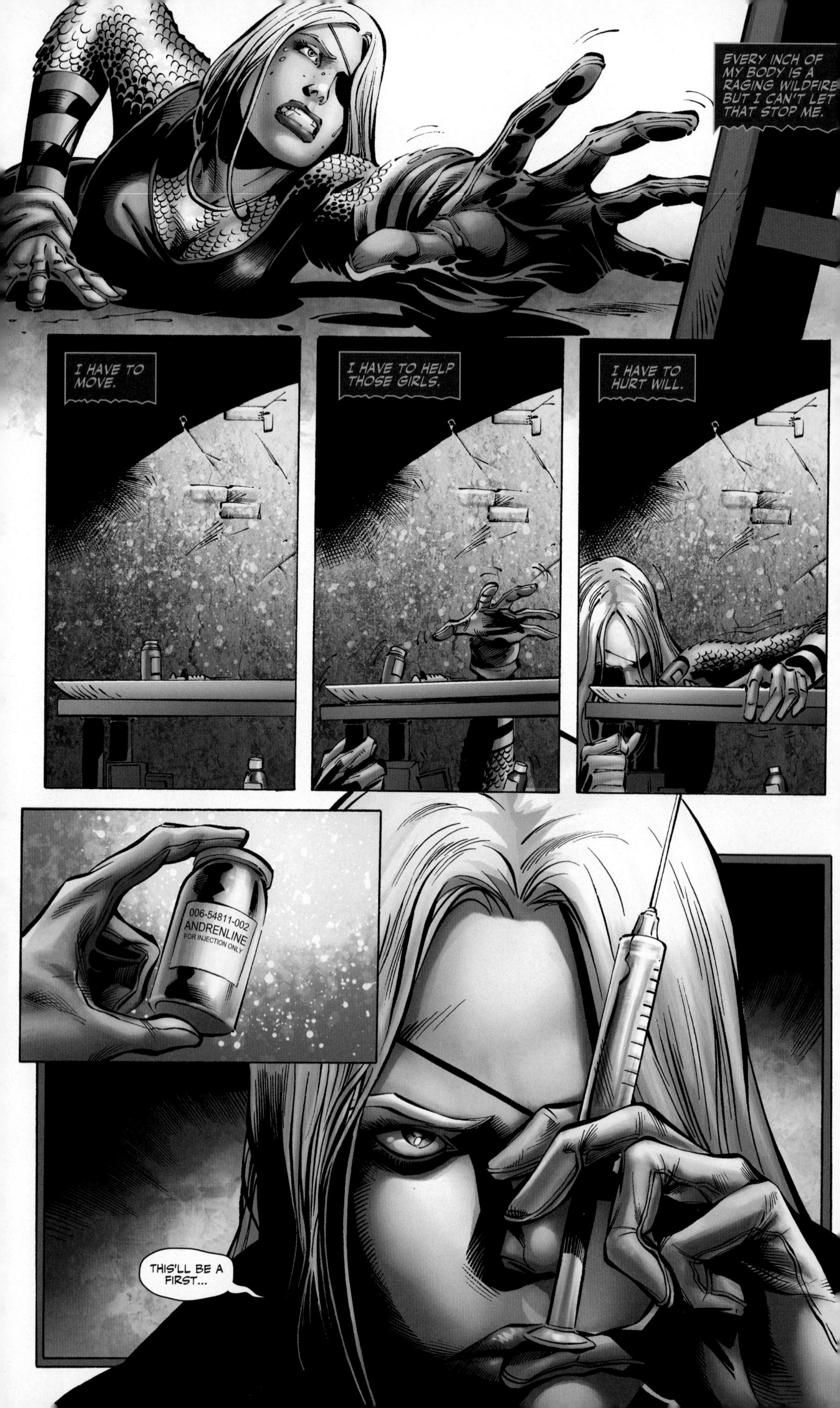
EVERY INCH OF MY BODY IS A RAGING WILDFIRE BUT I CAN'T LET THAT STOP ME.
I HAVE TO MOVE.
I HAVE TO HELP THOSE GIRLS.
I HAVE TO HURT WILL.
006-54811-002
ANDRENLINE
FOR INJECTION ONLY
THIS'LL BE A FIRST...

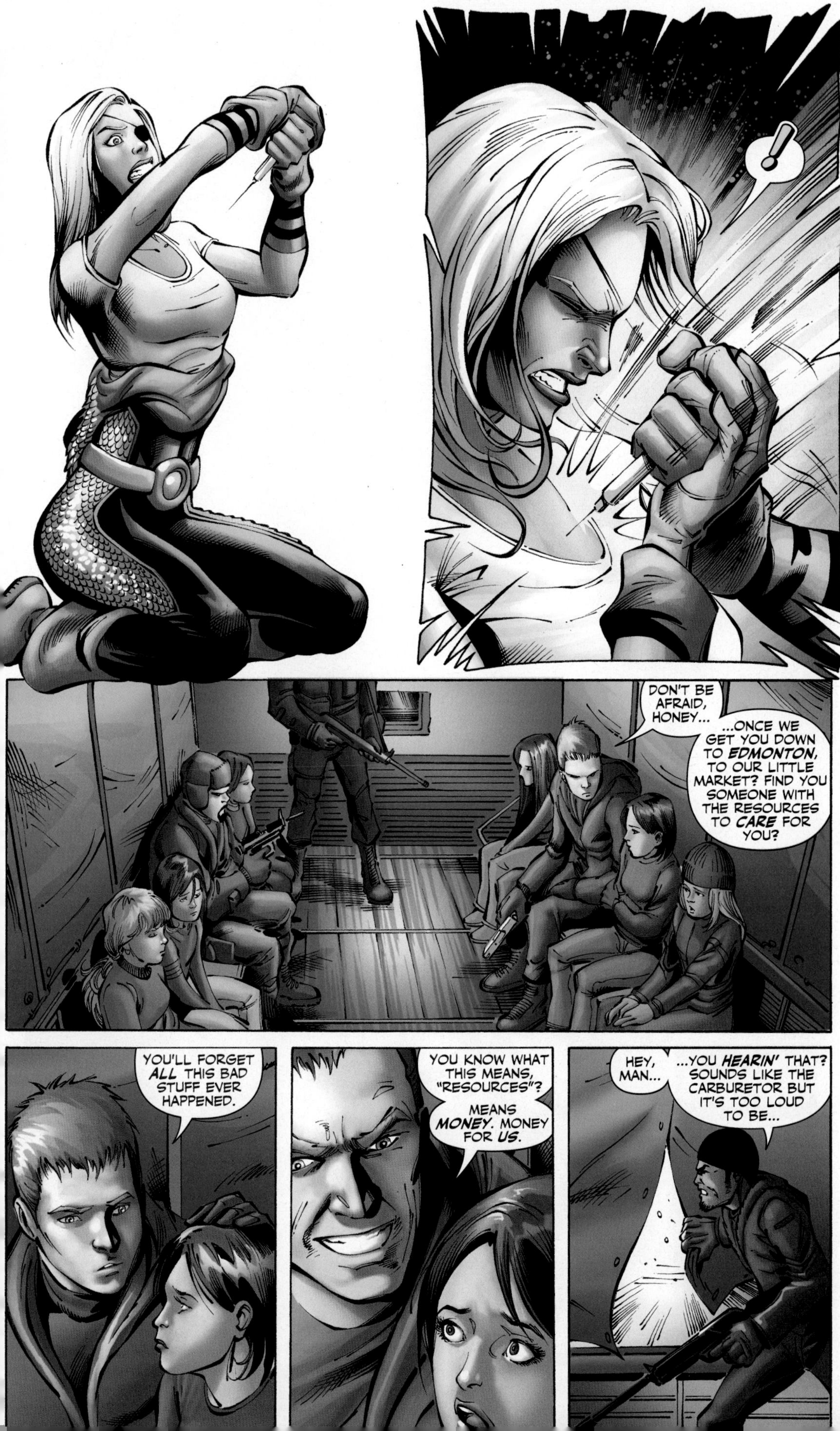

!
DON'T BE AFRAID, HONEY...
...ONCE WE GET YOU DOWN TO EDMONTON, TO OUR LITTLE MARKET? FIND YOU SOMEONE WITH THE RESOURCES TO CARE FOR YOU?
YOU'LL FORGET ALL THIS BAD STUFF EVER HAPPENED.
YOU KNOW WHAT THIS MEANS, "RESOURCES"?
MEANS MONEY. MONEY FOR US.
HEY, MAN...
...YOU HEARIN' THAT? SOUNDS LIKE THE CARBURETOR BUT IT'S TOO LOUD TO BE...

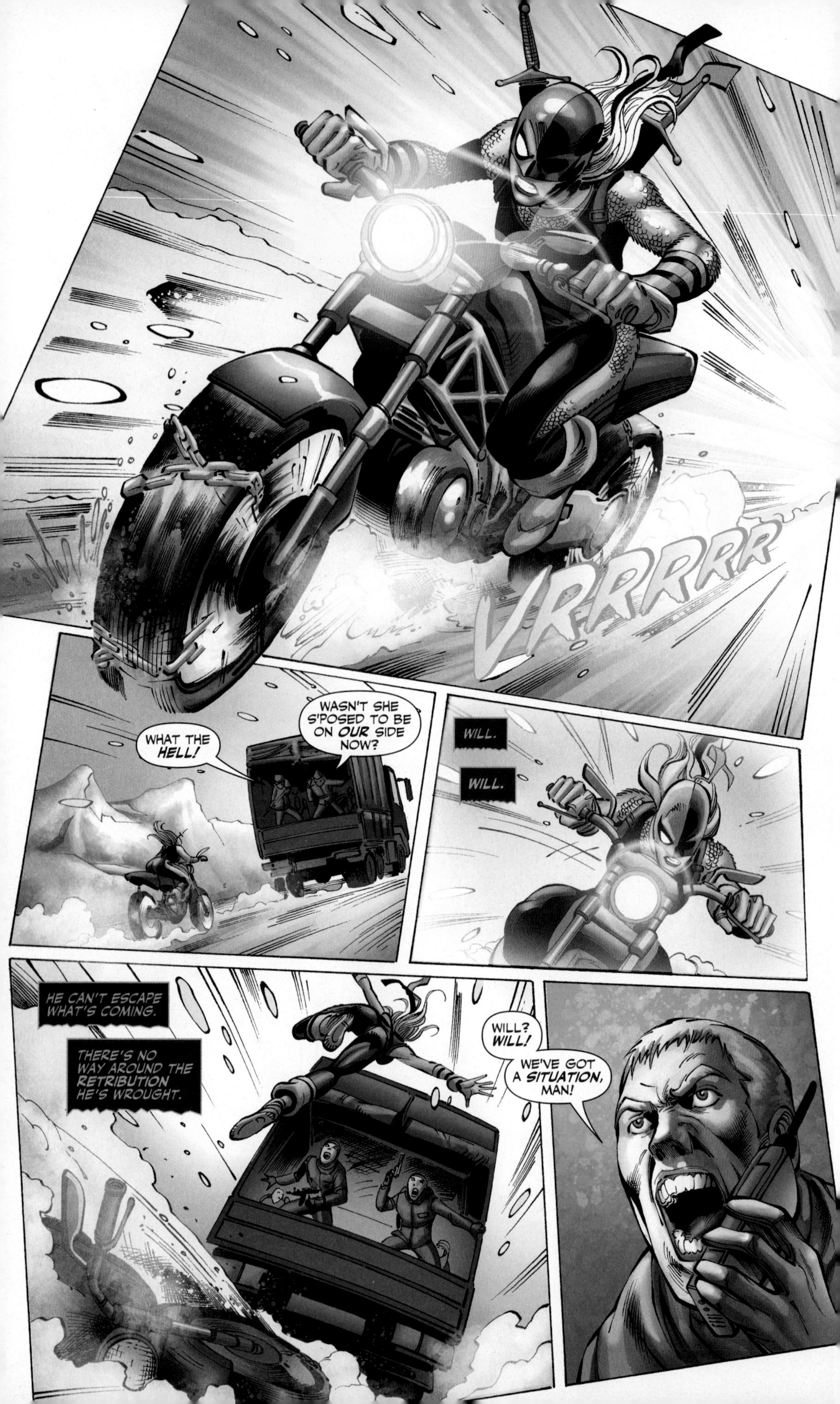
VRRRRRR
WHAT THE HELL!
WASN'T SHE S'POSED TO BE ON OUR SIDE NOW?
WILL.
WILL.
HE CAN'T ESCAPE WHAT'S COMING.
THERE'S NO WAY AROUND THE RETRIBUTION HE'S WROUGHT.
WILL? WILL!
WE'VE GOT A SITUATION, MAN!

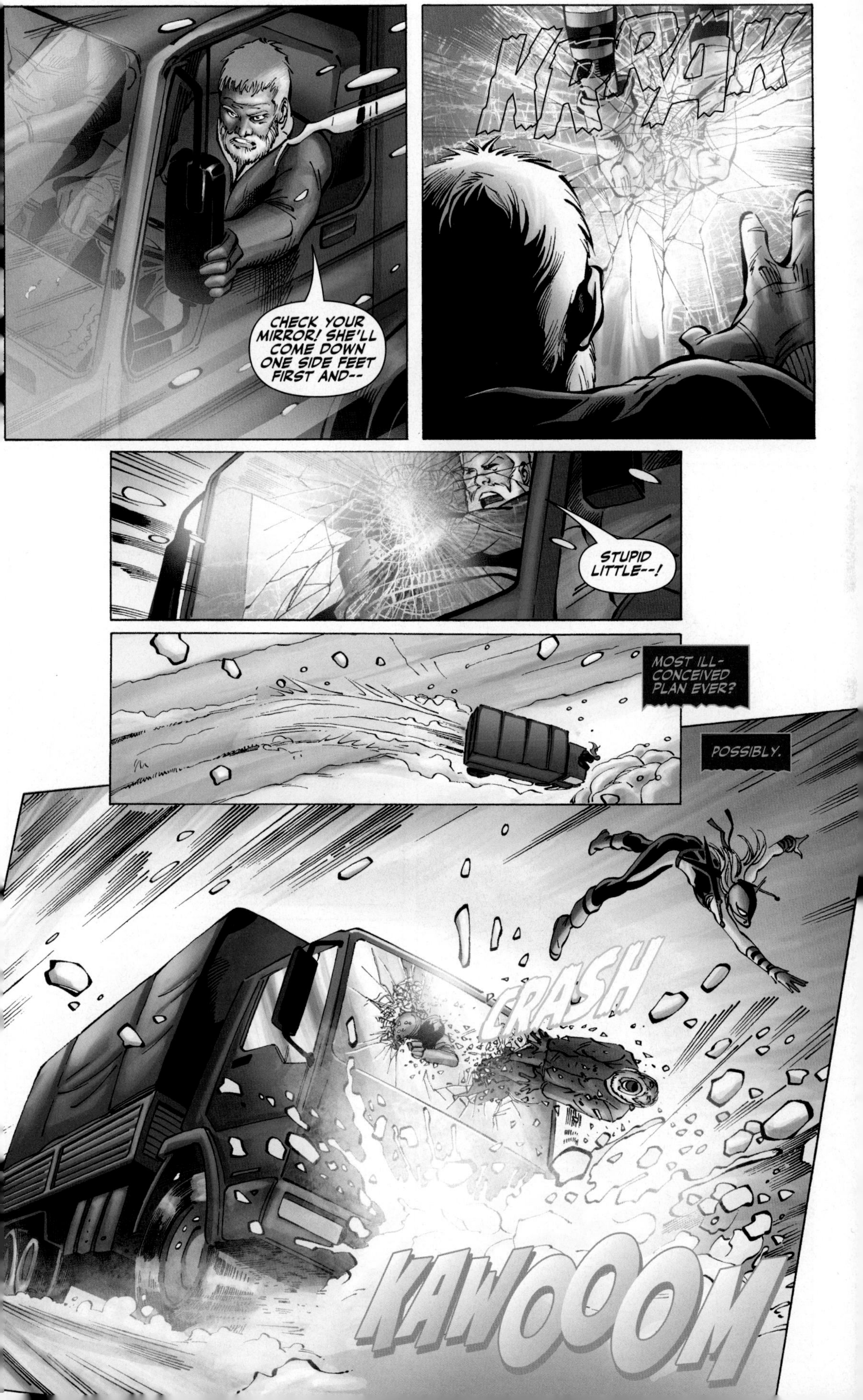
CHECK YOUR MIRROR! SHE'LL COME DOWN ONE SIDE FEET FIRST AND--
KRAKK
STUPID LITTLE--!
MOST ILL-CONCEIVED PLAN EVER?
POSSIBLY.
CRASH
KAWOOOM

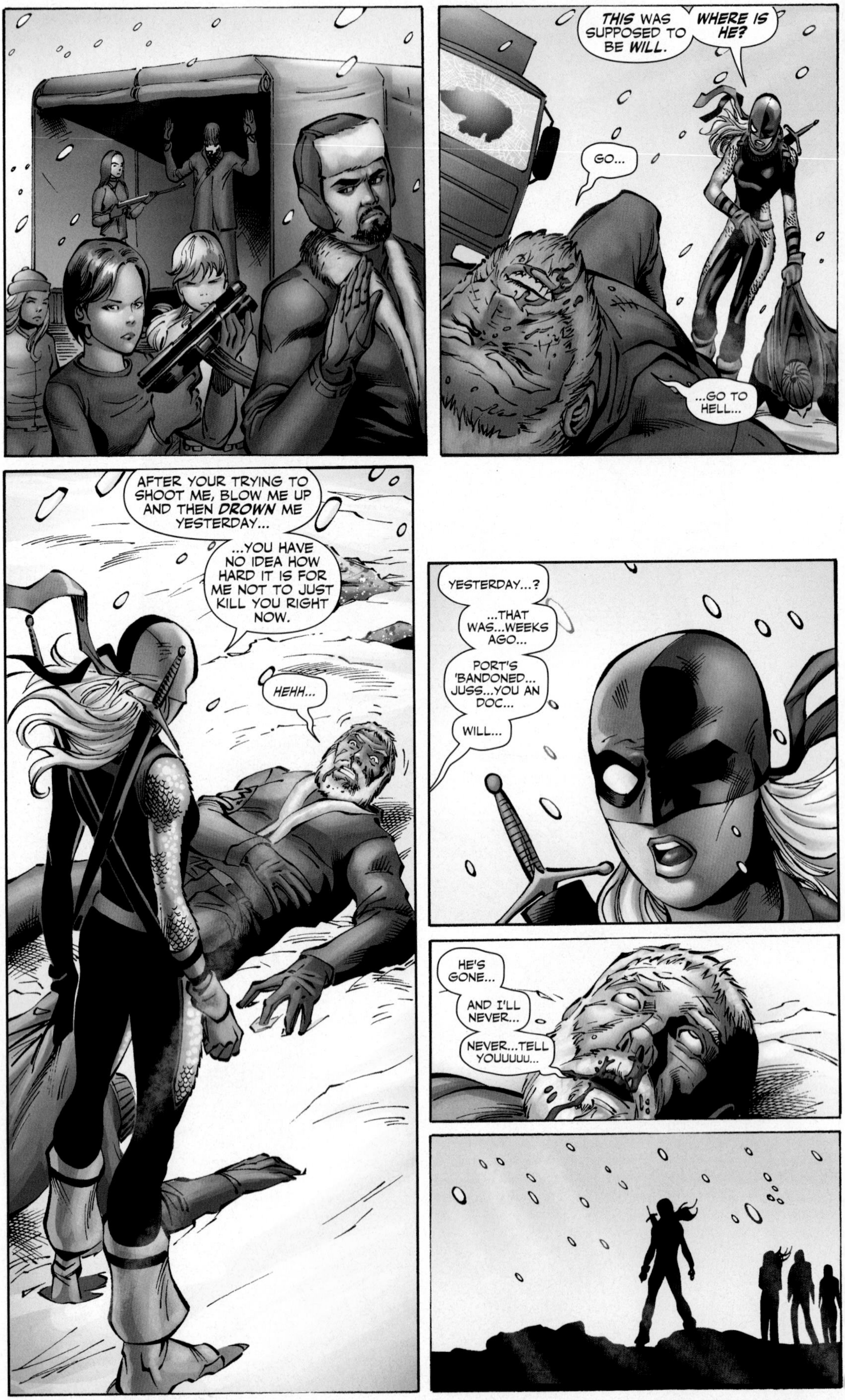
THIS WAS SUPPOSED TO BE WILL.
WHERE IS HE?
GO...
...GO TO HELL...
AFTER YOUR TRYING TO SHOOT ME, BLOW ME UP AND THEN DROWN ME YESTERDAY...
...YOU HAVE NO IDEA HOW HARD IT IS FOR ME NOT TO JUST KILL YOU RIGHT NOW.
HEHH...
YESTERDAY...?
...THAT WAS...WEEKS AGO...
PORT'S 'BANDONED... JUSS...YOU AN DOC...
WILL...
HE'S GONE...
AND I'LL NEVER...
NEVER...TELL YOUUUUU...

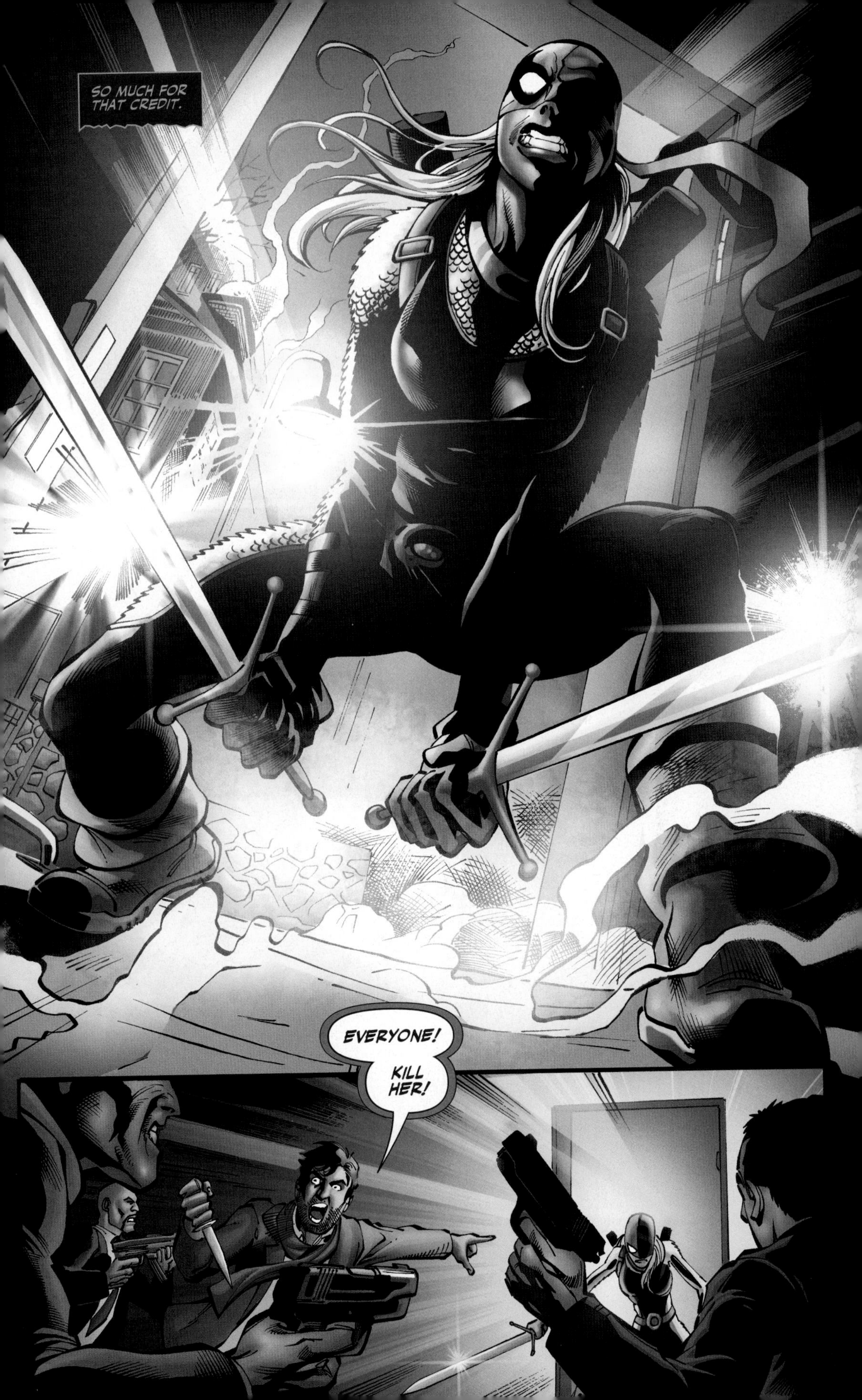
SO MUCH FOR THAT CREDIT.
EVERYONE!
KILL HER!

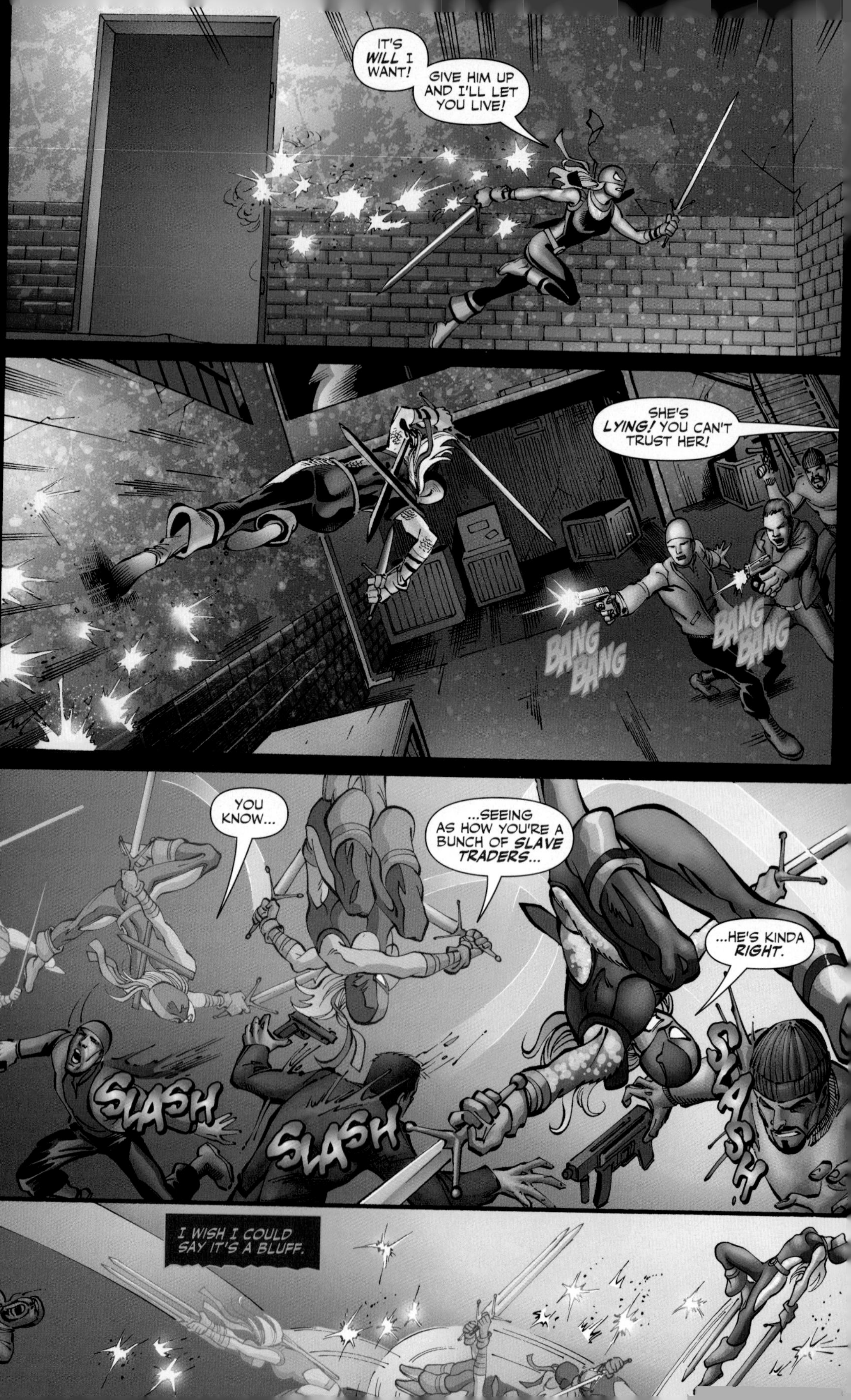
IT'S WILL I WANT!
GIVE HIM UP AND I'LL LET YOU LIVE!
SHE'S LYING! YOU CAN'T TRUST HER!
BANG BANG
BANG BANG
YOU KNOW...
...SEEING AS HOW YOU'RE A BUNCH OF SLAVE TRADERS...
...HE'S KINDA RIGHT.
SLASH
SLASH
SLASH
I WISH I COULD SAY IT'S A BLUFF.

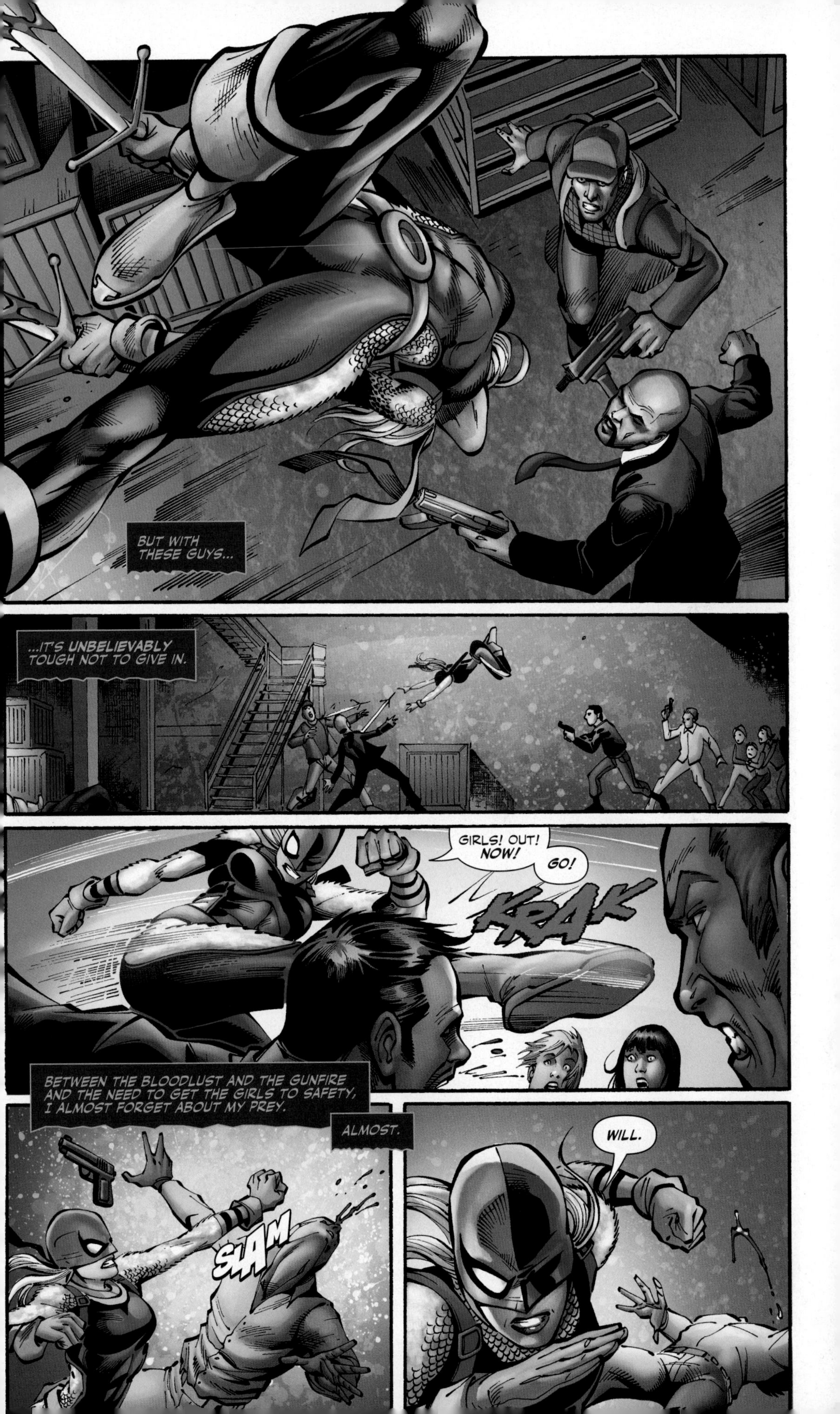
BUT WITH THESE GUYS...
...IT'S UNBELIEVABLY TOUGH NOT TO GIVE IN.
GIRLS! OUT! NOW!
GO!
KRAK
BETWEEN THE BLOODLUST AND THE GUNFIRE AND THE NEED TO GET THE GIRLS TO SAFETY, I ALMOST FORGET ABOUT MY PREY.
ALMOST.
SLAM
WILL.

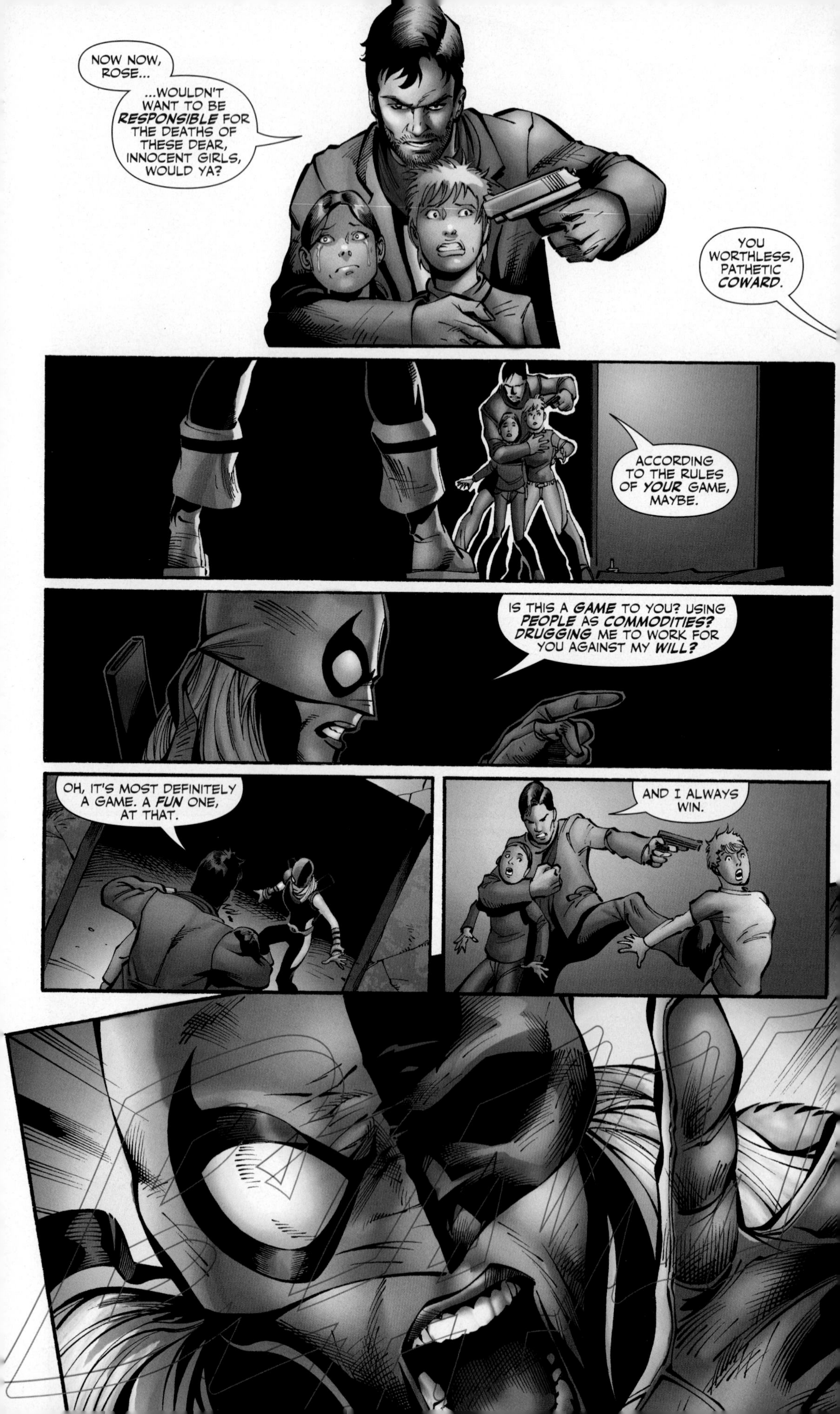
NOW NOW, ROSE...
...WOULDN'T WANT TO BE RESPONSIBLE FOR THE DEATHS OF THESE DEAR, INNOCENT GIRLS, WOULD YA?
YOU WORTHLESS, PATHETIC COWARD.
ACCORDING TO THE RULES OF YOUR GAME, MAYBE.
IS THIS A GAME TO YOU? USING PEOPLE AS COMMODITIES? DRUGGING ME TO WORK FOR YOU AGAINST MY WILL?
OH, IT'S MOST DEFINITELY A GAME. A FUN ONE, AT THAT.
AND I ALWAYS WIN.

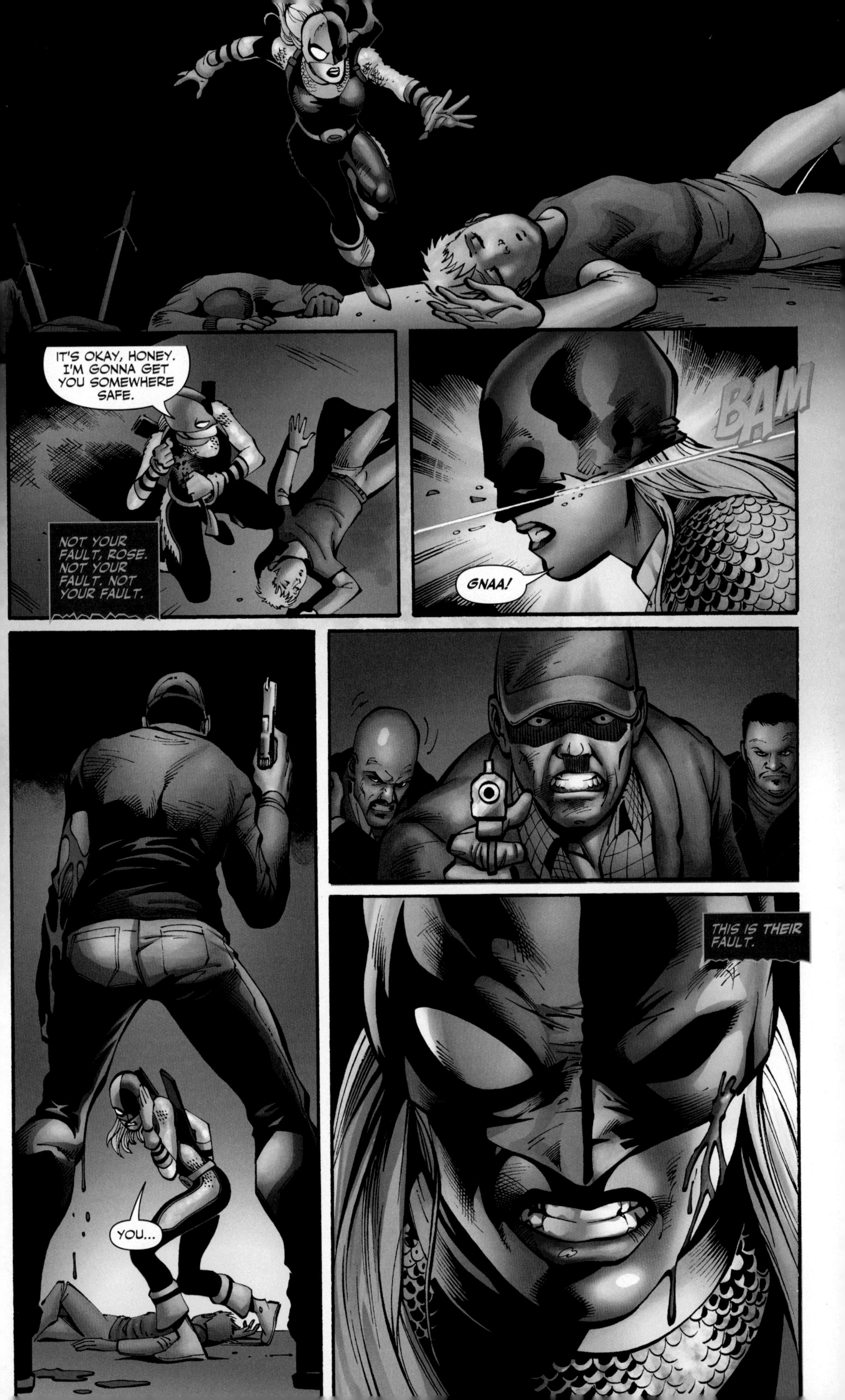
IT'S OKAY, HONEY. I'M GONNA GET YOU SOMEWHERE SAFE.
NOT YOUR FAULT, ROSE. NOT YOUR FAULT. NOT YOUR FAULT.
BAM
GNAA!
YOU...
THIS IS THEIR FAULT.

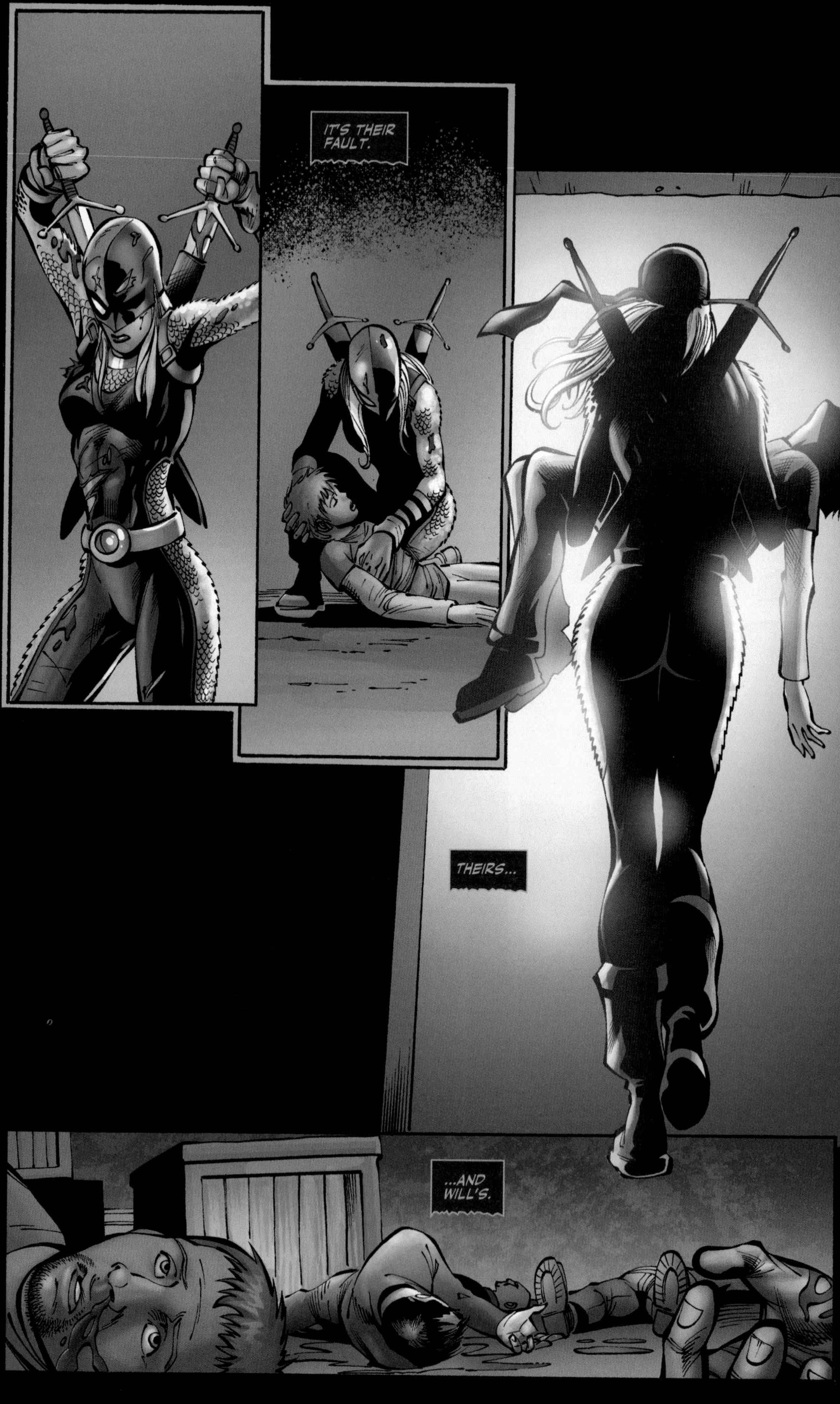
IT'S THEIR FAULT.
THEIRS...
...AND WILL'S.

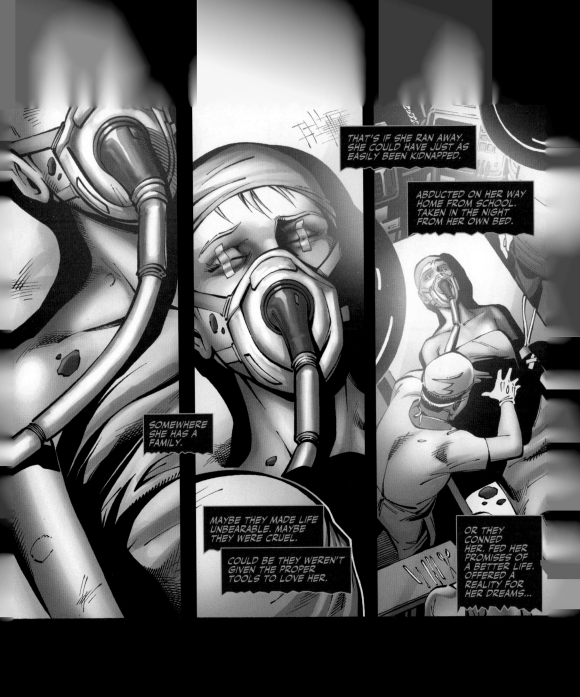

THAT'S IF SHE RAN AWAY. SHE COULD HAVE JUST AS EASILY BEEN KIDNAPPED.

ABDUCTED ON HER WAY HOME FROM SCHOOL. TAKEN IN THE NIGHT FROM HER OWN BED.

SOMEWHERE SHE HAS A FAMILY.

MAYBE THEY MADE LIFE UNBEARABLE. MAYBE THEY WERE CRUEL.

COULD BE THEY WEREN'T GIVEN THE PROPER TOOLS TO LOVE HER.

OR THEY CONNED HER. FED HER PROMISES OF A BETTER LIFE. OFFERED A REALITY FOR HER DREAMS...

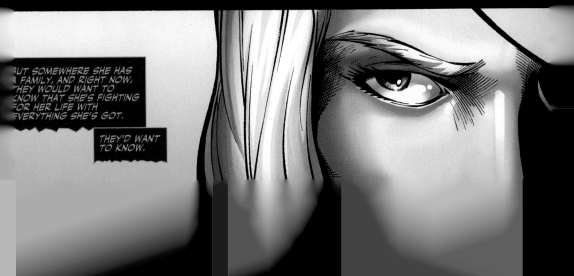

BUT SOMEWHERE SHE HAS A FAMILY, AND RIGHT NOW, THEY WOULD WANT TO KNOW THAT SHE'S FIGHTING FOR HER LIFE WITH EVERYTHING SHE'S GOT.

THEY'D WANT TO KNOW.

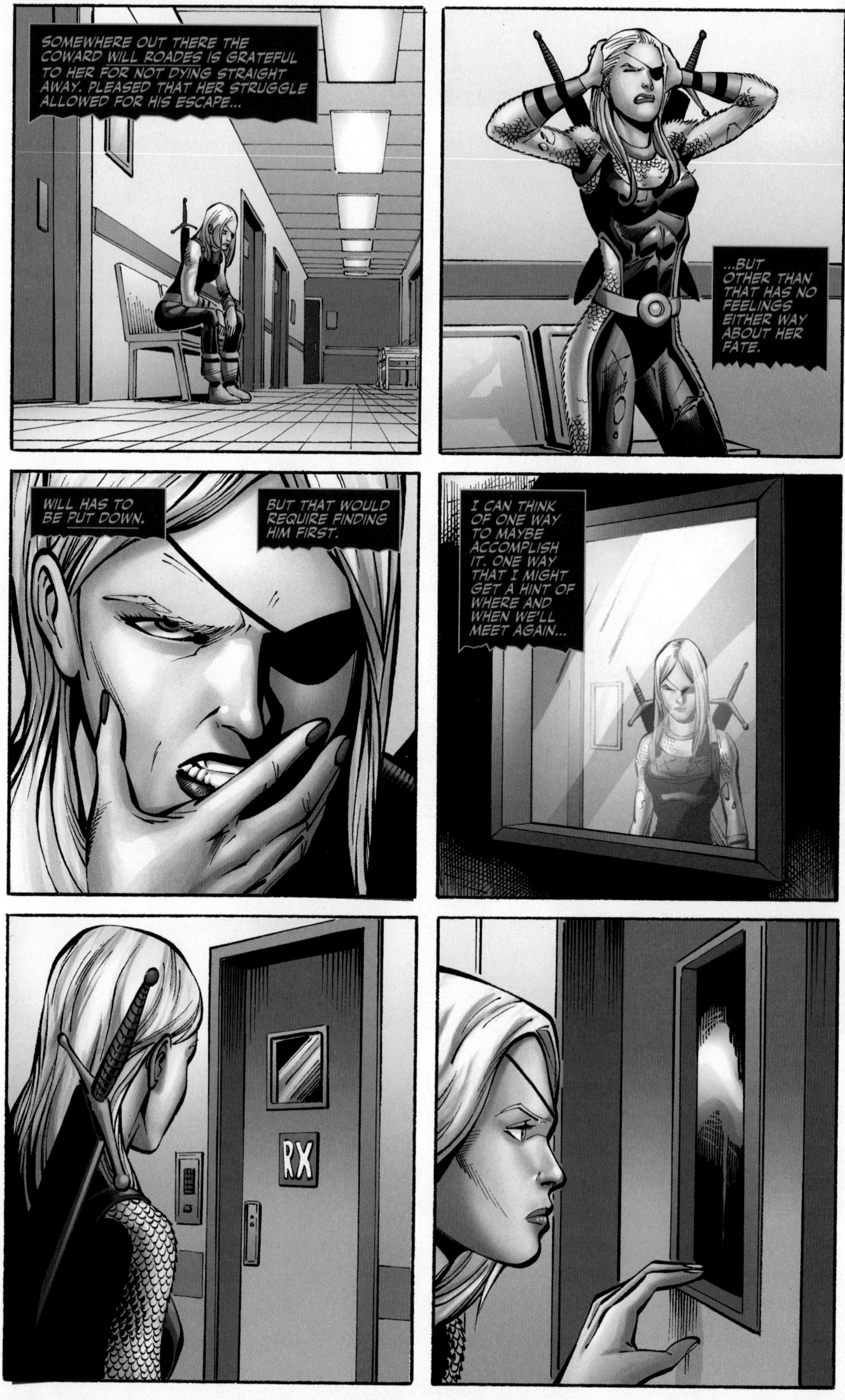
SOMEWHERE OUT THERE THE COWARD WILL ROADES IS GRATEFUL TO HER FOR NOT DYING STRAIGHT AWAY. PLEASED THAT HER STRUGGLE ALLOWED FOR HIS ESCAPE...
...BUT OTHER THAN THAT HAS NO FEELINGS EITHER WAY ABOUT HER FATE.
WILL HAS TO BE PUT DOWN.
BUT THAT WOULD REQUIRE FINDING HIM FIRST.
I CAN THINK OF ONE WAY TO MAYBE ACCOMPLISH IT. ONE WAY THAT I MIGHT GET A HINT OF WHERE AND WHEN WE'LL MEET AGAIN...
RX

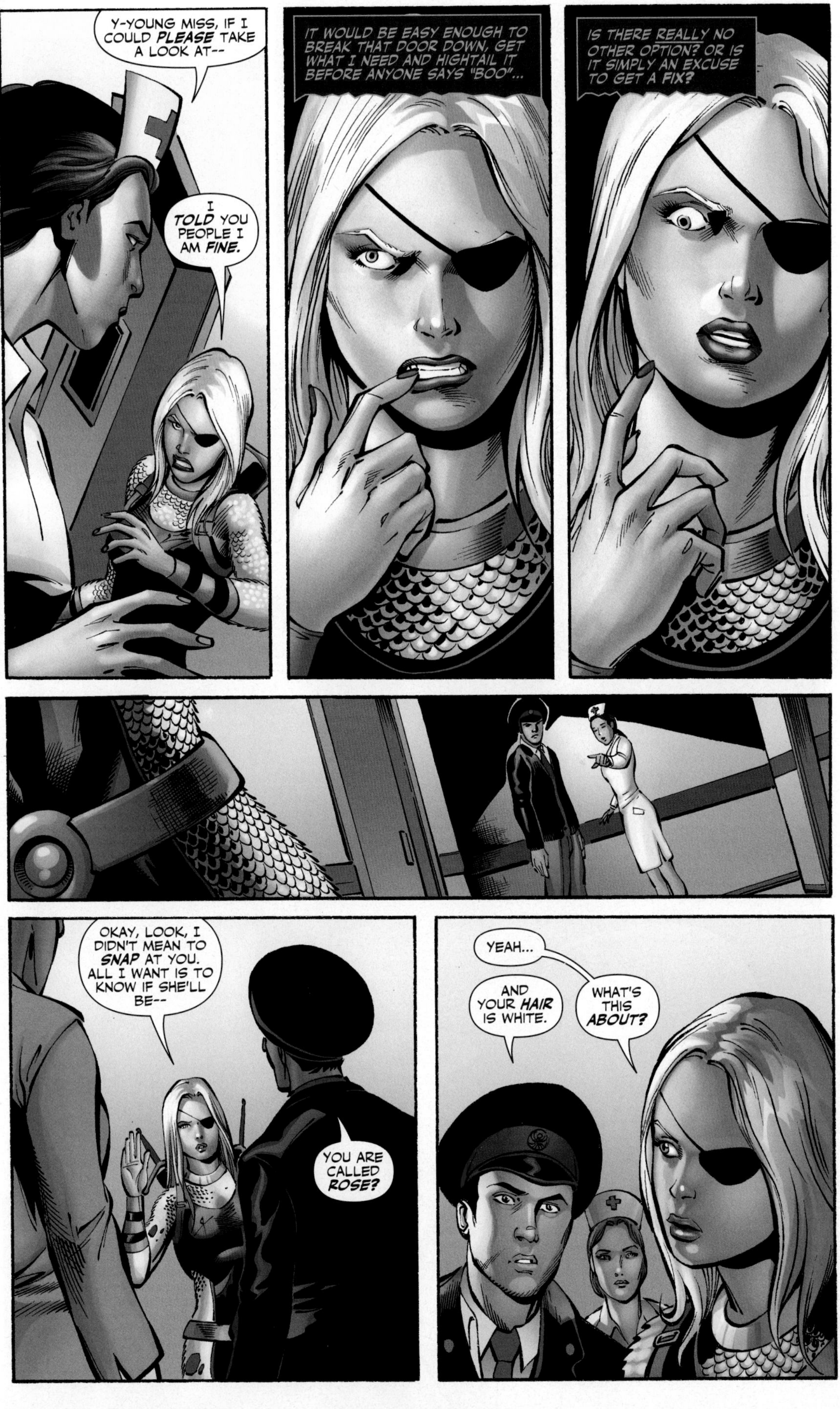
Y-YOUNG MISS, IF I COULD PLEASE TAKE A LOOK AT--
I TOLD YOU PEOPLE I AM FINE.
IT WOULD BE EASY ENOUGH TO BREAK THAT DOOR DOWN, GET WHAT I NEED AND HIGHTAIL IT BEFORE ANYONE SAYS "BOO"...
IS THERE REALLY NO OTHER OPTION? OR IS IT SIMPLY AN EXCUSE TO GET A FIX?
OKAY, LOOK, I DIDN'T MEAN TO SNAP AT YOU. ALL I WANT IS TO KNOW IF SHE'LL BE--
YOU ARE CALLED ROSE?
YEAH...
WHAT'S THIS ABOUT?
AND YOUR HAIR IS WHITE.

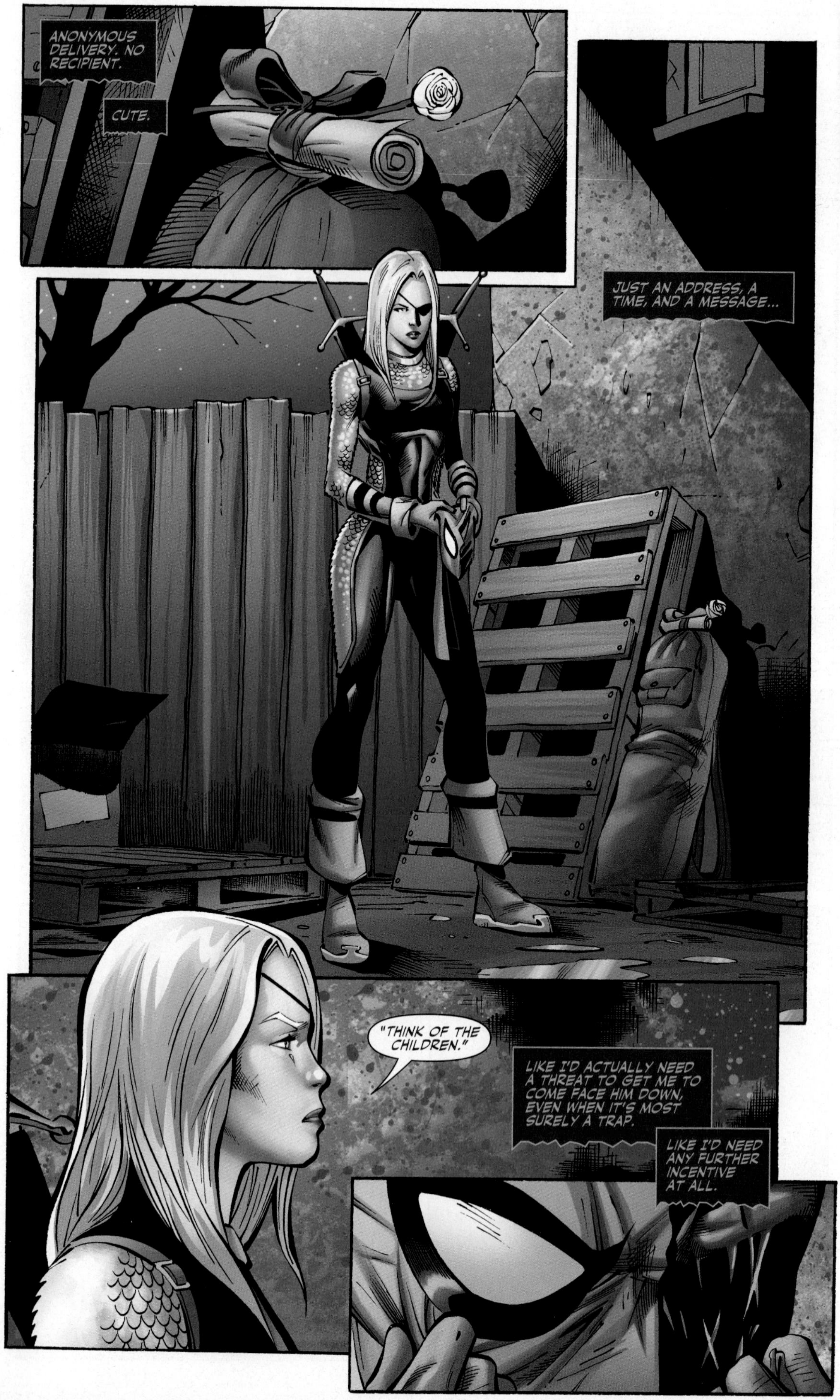
ANONYMOUS DELIVERY. NO RECIPIENT.
CUTE.
JUST AN ADDRESS, A TIME, AND A MESSAGE...
"THINK OF THE CHILDREN."
LIKE I'D ACTUALLY NEED A THREAT TO GET ME TO COME FACE HIM DOWN, EVEN WHEN IT'S MOST SURELY A TRAP.
LIKE I'D NEED ANY FURTHER INCENTIVE AT ALL.

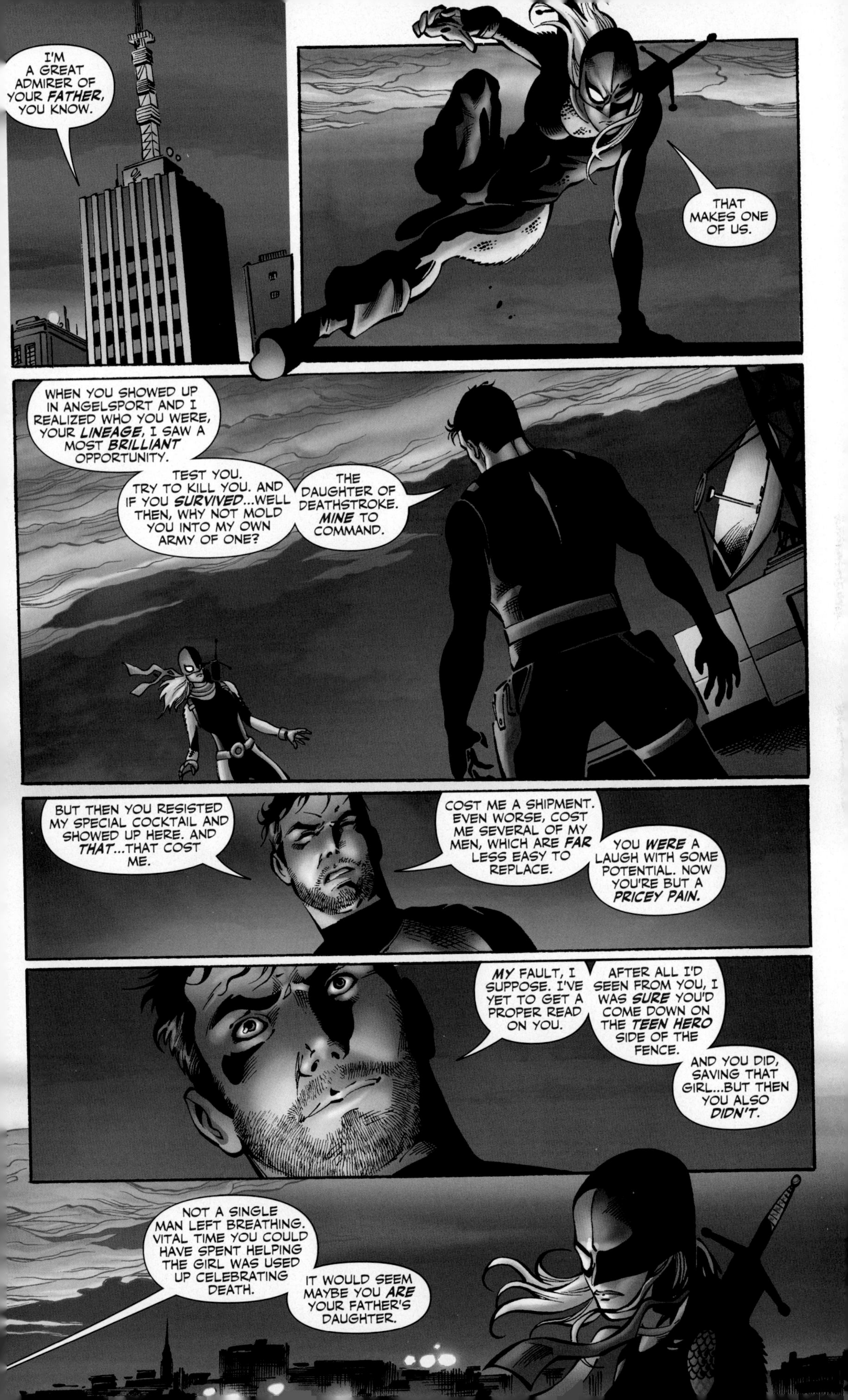
I'M A GREAT ADMIRER OF YOUR FATHER, YOU KNOW.
THAT MAKES ONE OF US.
WHEN YOU SHOWED UP IN ANGELSPORT AND I REALIZED WHO YOU WERE, YOUR LINEAGE, I SAW A MOST BRILLIANT OPPORTUNITY.
TEST YOU. TRY TO KILL YOU. AND IF YOU SURVIVED...WELL THEN, WHY NOT MOLD YOU INTO MY OWN ARMY OF ONE?
THE DAUGHTER OF DEATHSTROKE. MINE TO COMMAND.
BUT THEN YOU RESISTED MY SPECIAL COCKTAIL AND SHOWED UP HERE. AND THAT...THAT COST ME.
COST ME A SHIPMENT. EVEN WORSE, COST ME SEVERAL OF MY MEN, WHICH ARE FAR LESS EASY TO REPLACE.
YOU WERE A LAUGH WITH SOME POTENTIAL. NOW YOU'RE BUT A PRICEY PAIN.
MY FAULT, I SUPPOSE. I'VE YET TO GET A PROPER READ ON YOU.
AFTER ALL I'D SEEN FROM YOU, I WAS SURE YOU'D COME DOWN ON THE TEEN HERO SIDE OF THE FENCE.
AND YOU DID, SAVING THAT GIRL...BUT THEN YOU ALSO DIDN'T.
NOT A SINGLE MAN LEFT BREATHING. VITAL TIME YOU COULD HAVE SPENT HELPING THE GIRL WAS USED UP CELEBRATING DEATH.
IT WOULD SEEM MAYBE YOU ARE YOUR FATHER'S DAUGHTER.

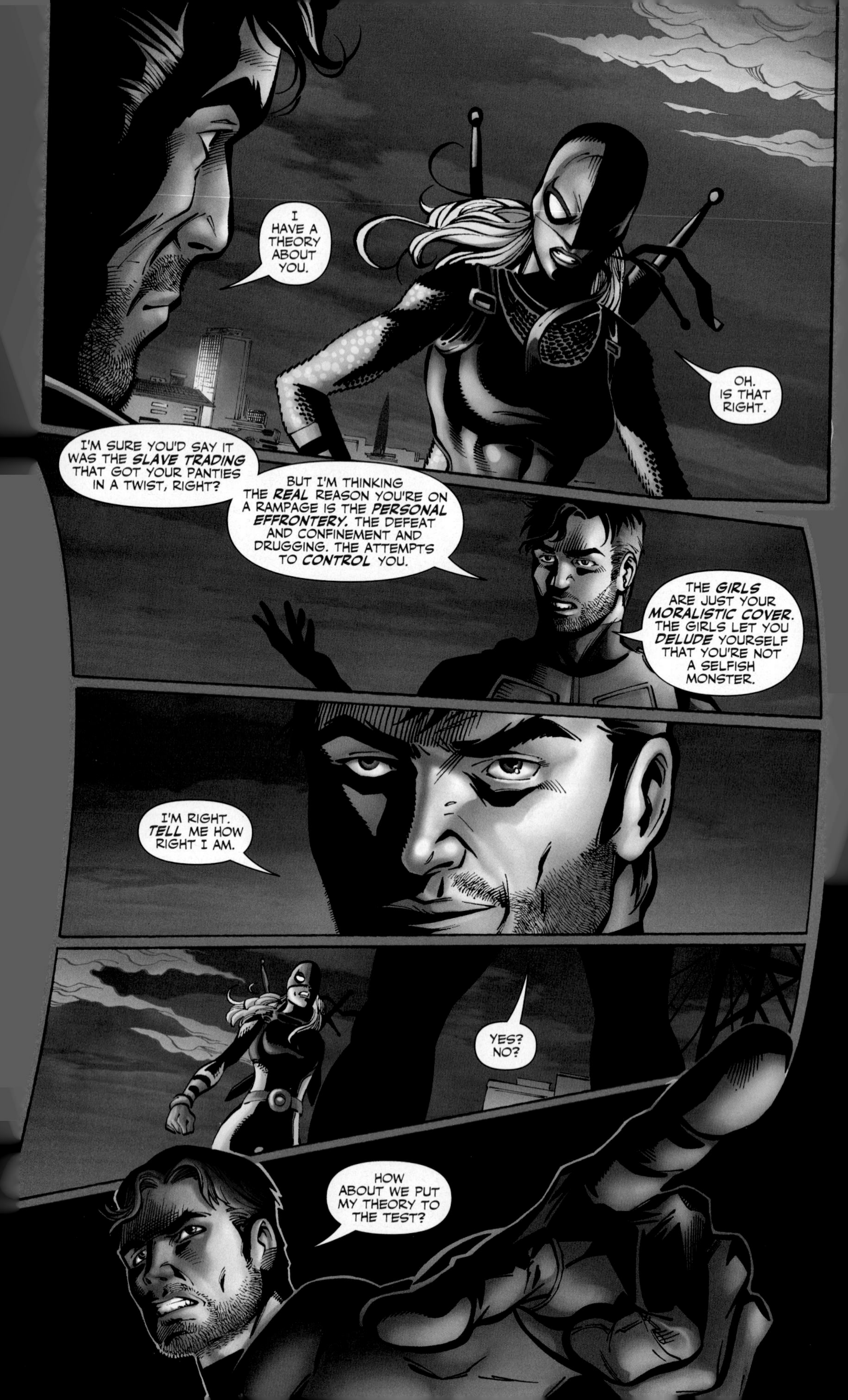
I HAVE A THEORY ABOUT YOU.
OH. IS THAT RIGHT.
I'M SURE YOU'D SAY IT WAS THE SLAVE TRADING THAT GOT YOUR PANTIES IN A TWIST, RIGHT?
BUT I'M THINKING THE REAL REASON YOU'RE ON A RAMPAGE IS THE PERSONAL EFFRONTERY. THE DEFEAT AND CONFINEMENT AND DRUGGING. THE ATTEMPTS TO CONTROL YOU.
THE GIRLS ARE JUST YOUR MORALISTIC COVER. THE GIRLS LET YOU DELUDE YOURSELF THAT YOU'RE NOT A SELFISH MONSTER.
I'M RIGHT. TELL ME HOW RIGHT I AM.
YES? NO?
HOW ABOUT WE PUT MY THEORY TO THE TEST?

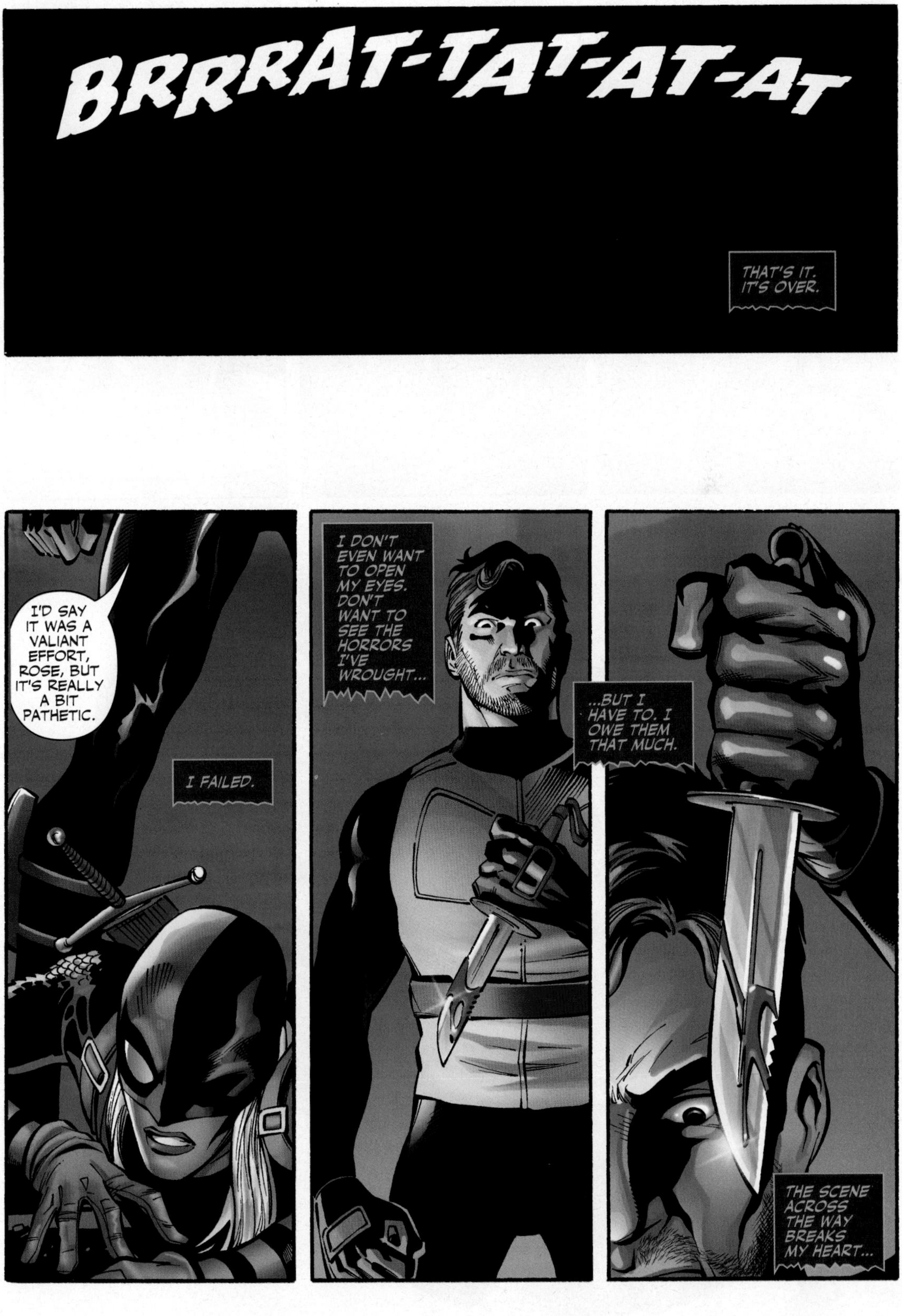
BRRRAT-TAT-AT-AT-AT
THAT'S IT. IT'S OVER.
I'D SAY IT WAS A VALIANT EFFORT, ROSE, BUT IT'S REALLY A BIT PATHETIC.
I FAILED.
I DON'T EVEN WANT TO OPEN MY EYES. DON'T WANT TO SEE THE HORRORS I'VE WROUGHT...
...BUT I HAVE TO. I OWE THEM THAT MUCH.
THE SCENE ACROSS THE WAY BREAKS MY HEART...

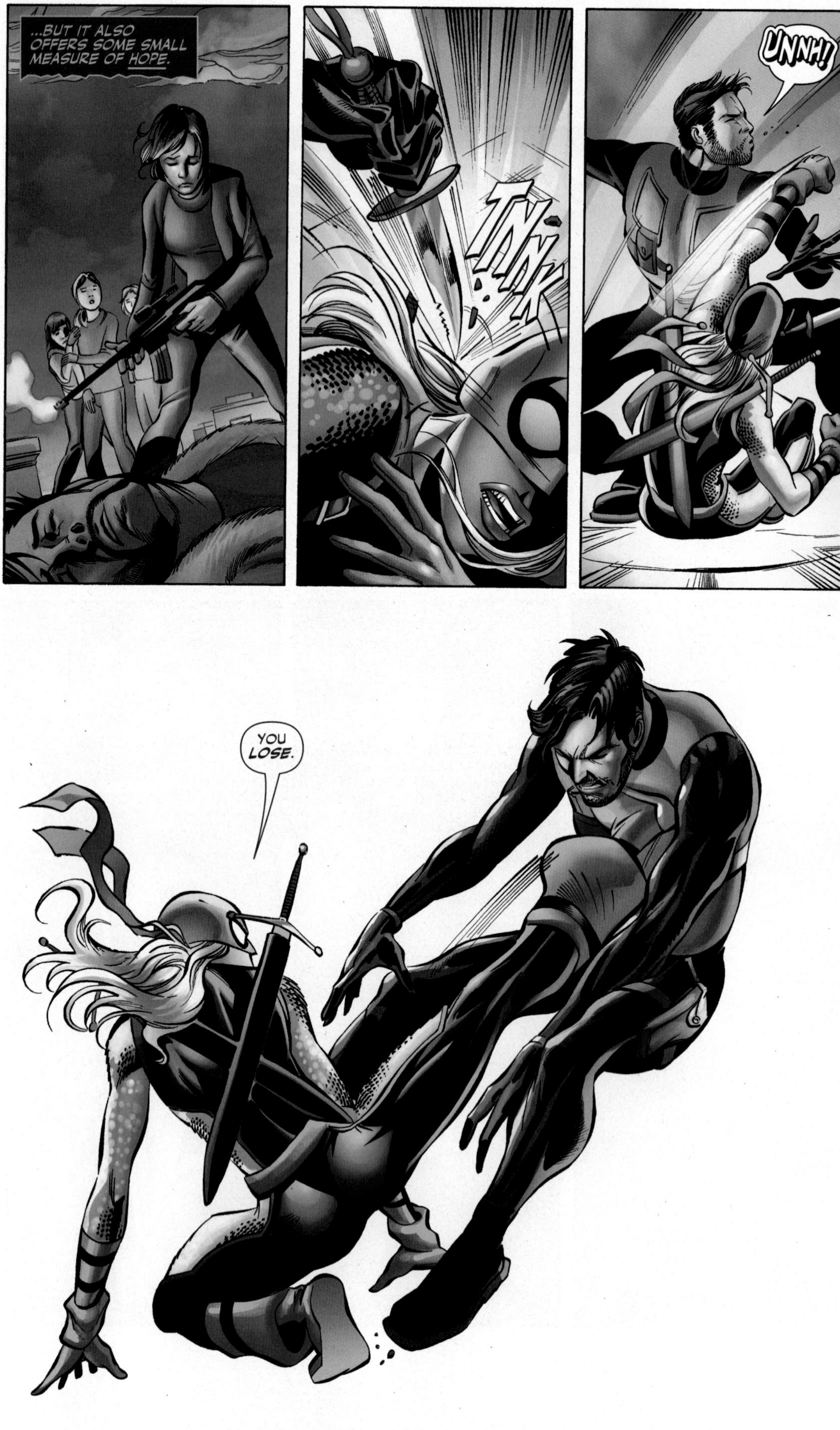
...BUT IT ALSO OFFERS SOME SMALL MEASURE OF HOPE.
TINK
UNNH!
YOU LOSE.

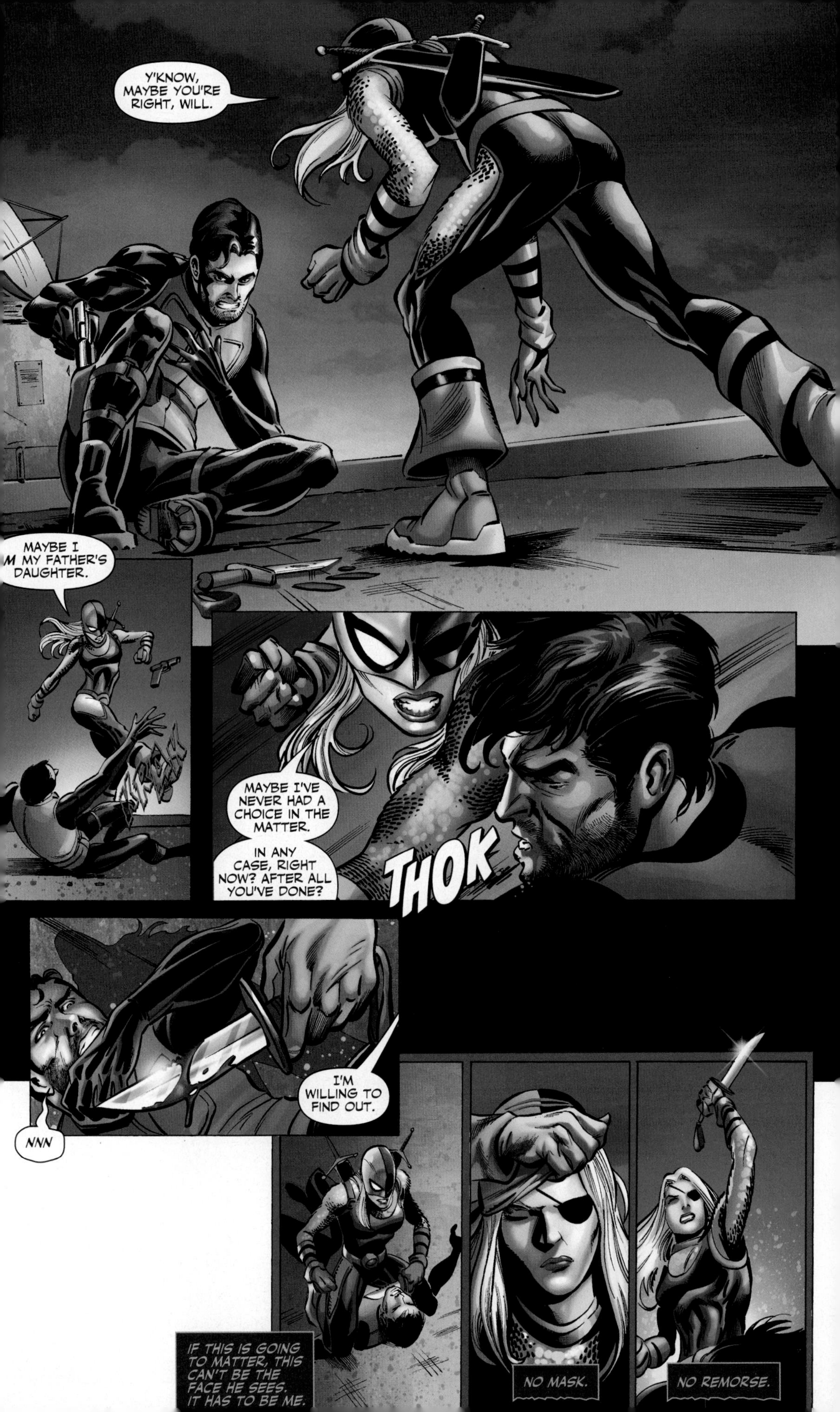

Y'KNOW, MAYBE YOU'RE RIGHT, WILL.
M MY FATHER'S DAUGHTER.
MAYBE I'VE NEVER HAD A CHOICE IN THE MATTER.
IN ANY CASE, RIGHT NOW? AFTER ALL YOU'VE DONE?
THOK
I'M WILLING TO FIND OUT.
NNN
IF THIS IS GOING TO MATTER, THIS CAN'T BE THE FACE HE SEES. IT HAS TO BE ME.
NO MASK.
NO REMORSE.

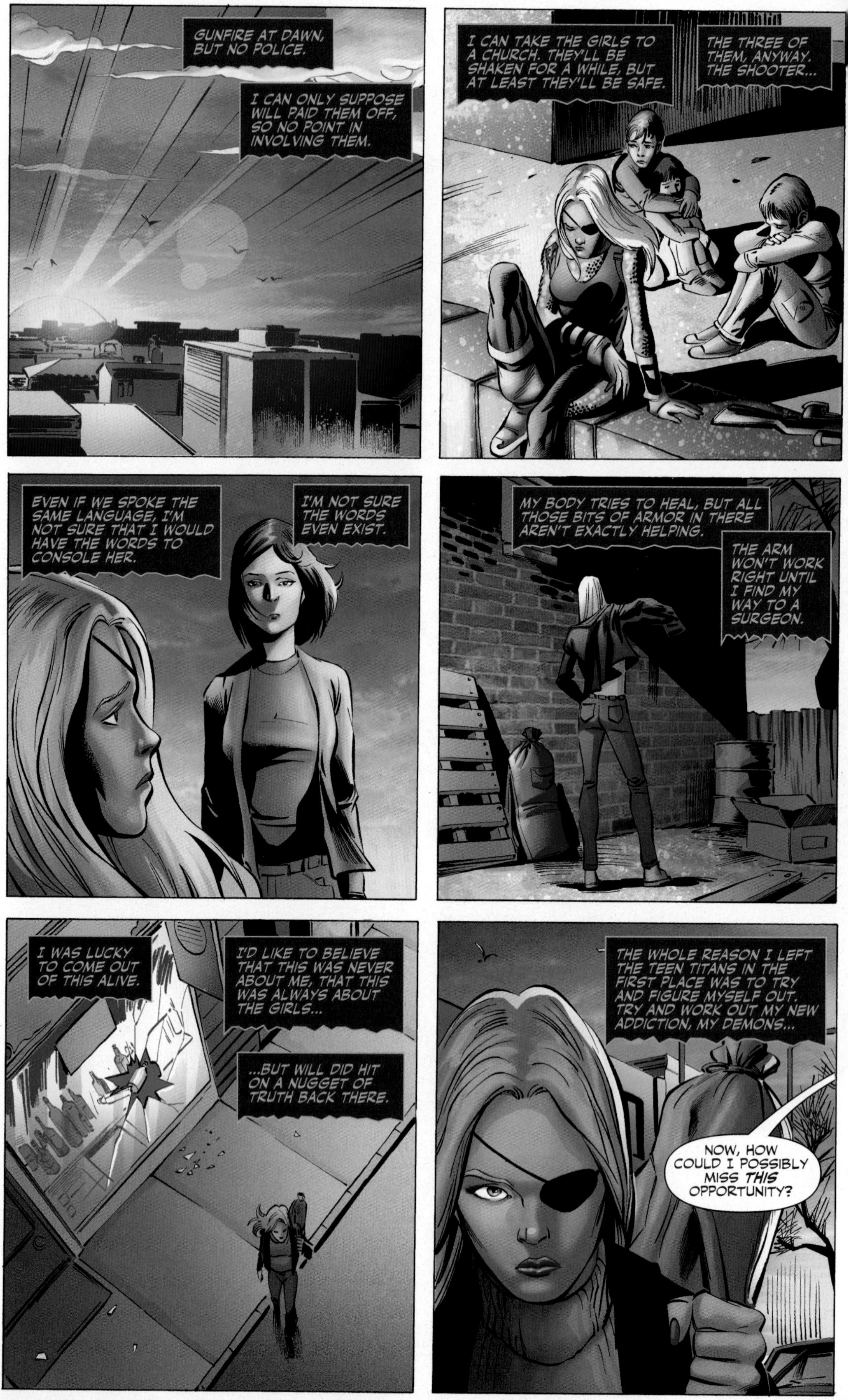
GUNFIRE AT DAWN, BUT NO POLICE.
I CAN ONLY SUPPOSE WILL PAID THEM OFF, SO NO POINT IN INVOLVING THEM.
I CAN TAKE THE GIRLS TO A CHURCH. THEY'LL BE SHAKEN FOR A WHILE, BUT AT LEAST THEY'LL BE SAFE.
THE THREE OF THEM, ANYWAY. THE SHOOTER...
EVEN IF WE SPOKE THE SAME LANGUAGE, I'M NOT SURE THAT I WOULD HAVE THE WORDS TO CONSOLE HER.
I'M NOT SURE THE WORDS EVEN EXIST.
MY BODY TRIES TO HEAL, BUT ALL THOSE BITS OF ARMOR IN THERE AREN'T EXACTLY HELPING.
THE ARM WON'T WORK RIGHT UNTIL I FIND MY WAY TO A SURGEON.
I WAS LUCKY TO COME OUT OF THIS ALIVE.
I'D LIKE TO BELIEVE THAT THIS WAS NEVER ABOUT ME, THAT THIS WAS ALWAYS ABOUT THE GIRLS...
...BUT WILL DID HIT ON A NUGGET OF TRUTH BACK THERE.
THE WHOLE REASON I LEFT THE TEEN TITANS IN THE FIRST PLACE WAS TO TRY AND FIGURE MYSELF OUT. TRY AND WORK OUT MY NEW ADDICTION, MY DEMONS...
NOW, HOW COULD I POSSIBLY MISS *THIS* OPPORTUNITY?

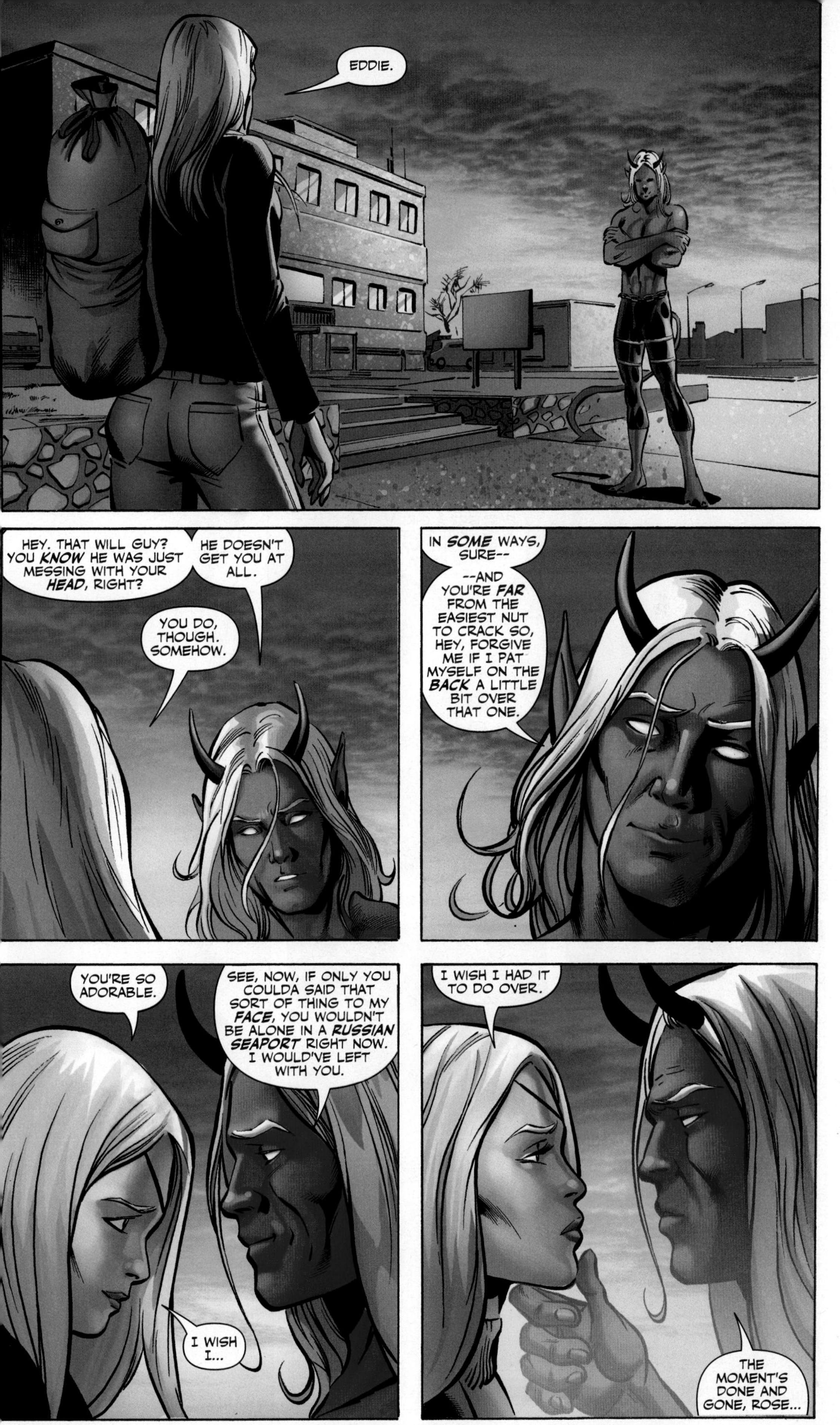

EDDIE.
HEY. THAT WILL GUY? YOU KNOW HE WAS JUST MESSING WITH YOUR HEAD, RIGHT?
HE DOESN'T GET YOU AT ALL.
YOU DO, THOUGH. SOMEHOW.
IN SOME WAYS, SURE--
--AND YOU'RE FAR FROM THE EASIEST NUT TO CRACK SO, HEY, FORGIVE ME IF I PAT MYSELF ON THE BACK A LITTLE BIT OVER THAT ONE.
YOU'RE SO ADORABLE.
SEE, NOW, IF ONLY YOU COULDA SAID THAT SORT OF THING TO MY FACE, YOU WOULDN'T BE ALONE IN A RUSSIAN SEAPORT RIGHT NOW. I WOULD'VE LEFT WITH YOU.
I WISH I...
I WISH I HAD IT TO DO OVER.
THE MOMENT'S DONE AND GONE, ROSE...

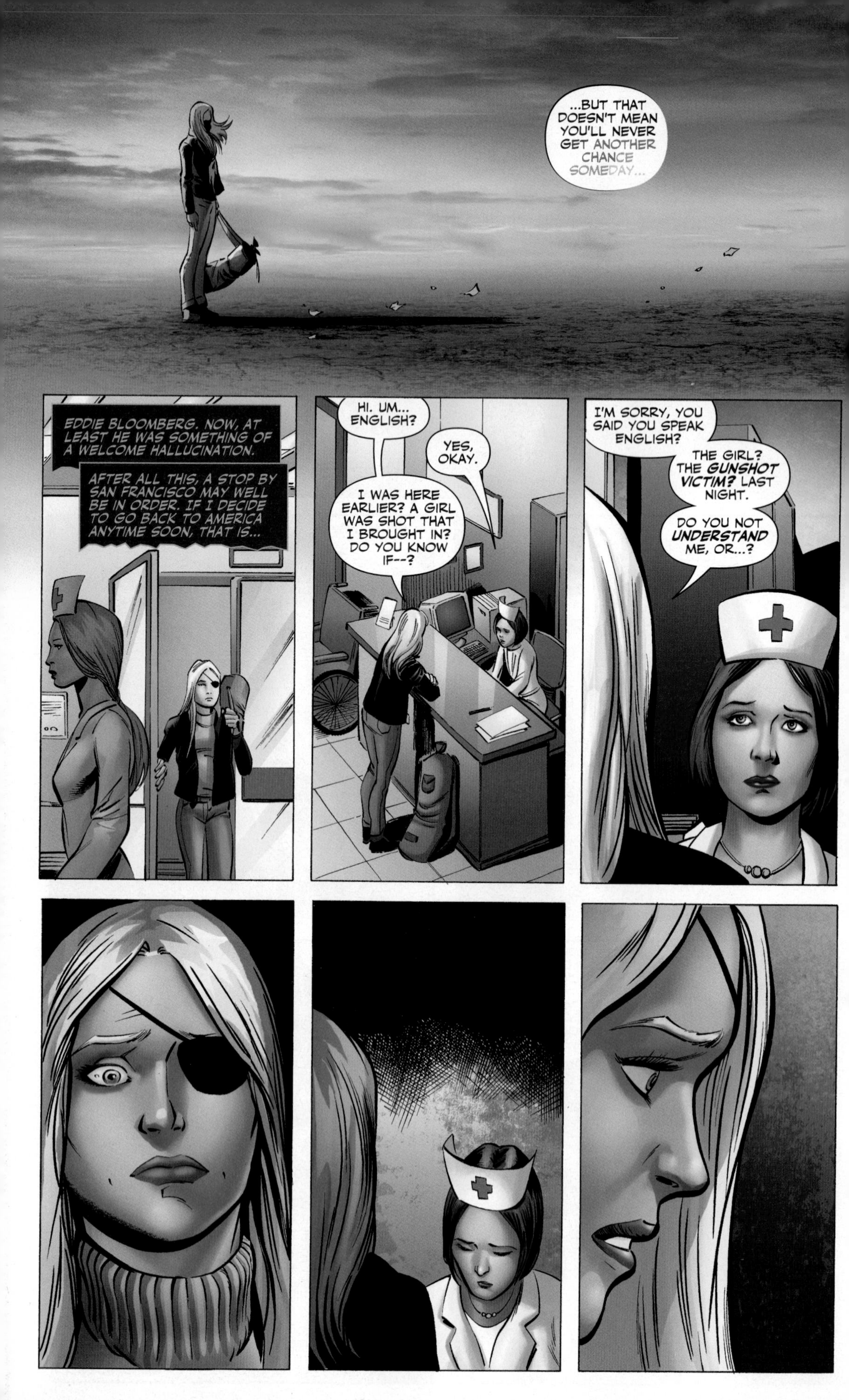
...BUT THAT DOESN'T MEAN YOU'LL NEVER GET ANOTHER CHANCE SOMEDAY...
EDDIE BLOOMBERG. NOW, AT LEAST HE WAS SOMETHING OF A WELCOME HALLUCINATION.
AFTER ALL THIS, A STOP BY SAN FRANCISCO MAY WELL BE IN ORDER. IF I DECIDE TO GO BACK TO AMERICA ANYTIME SOON, THAT IS...
HI. UM... ENGLISH?
YES, OKAY.
I WAS HERE EARLIER? A GIRL WAS SHOT THAT I BROUGHT IN? DO YOU KNOW IF--?
I'M SORRY, YOU SAID YOU SPEAK ENGLISH?
THE GIRL? THE GUNSHOT VICTIM? LAST NIGHT.
DO YOU NOT UNDERSTAND ME, OR...?

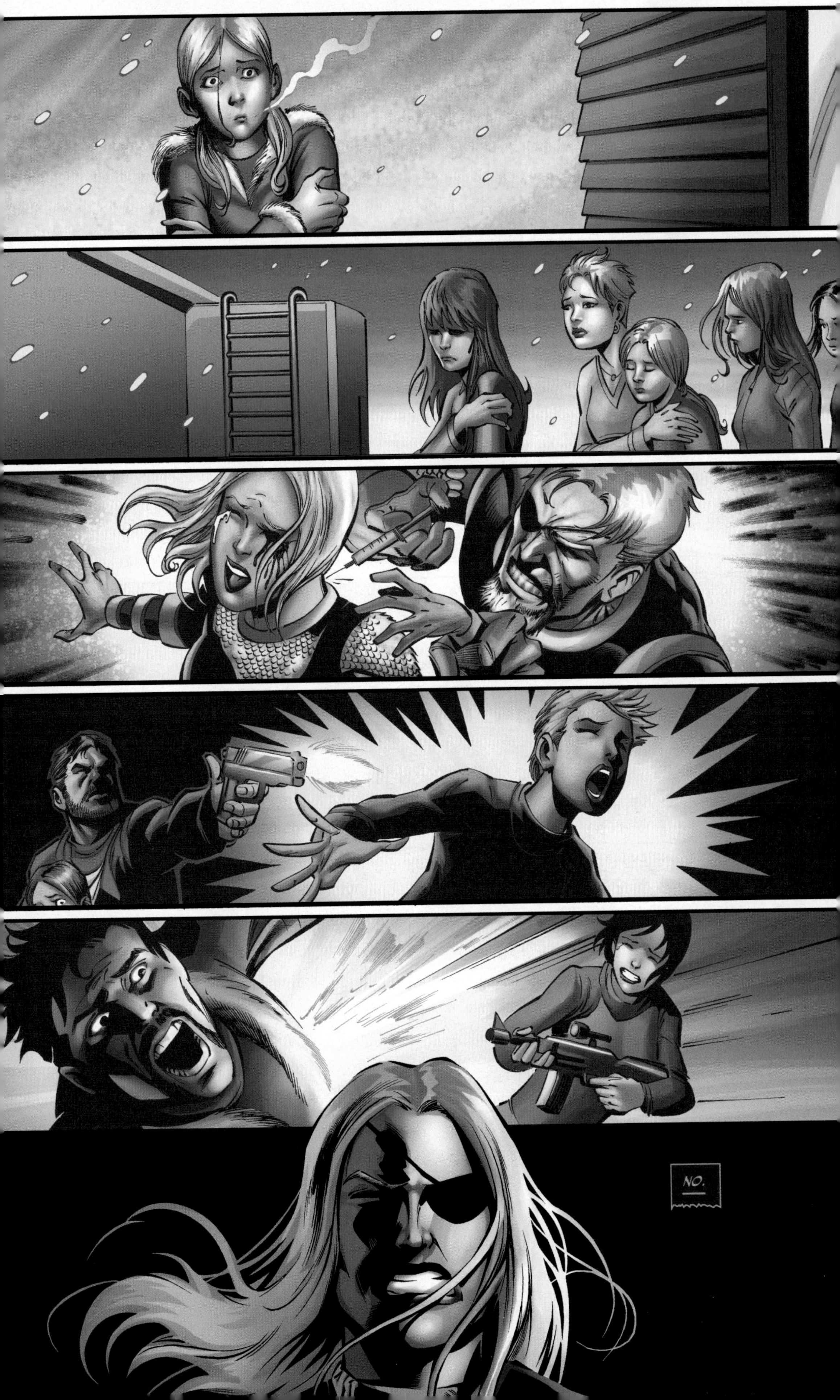
NO.

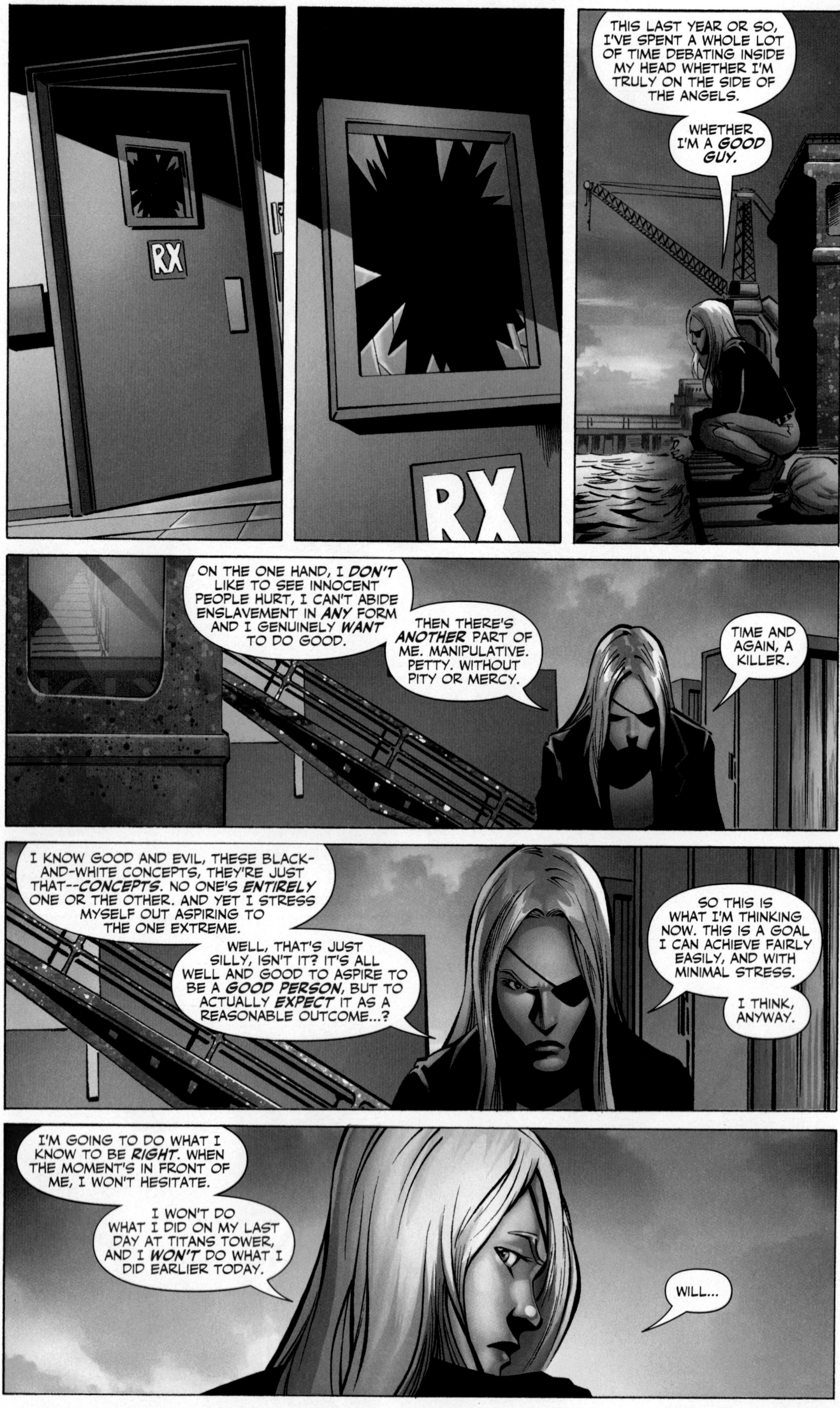
RX
RX
THIS LAST YEAR OR SO, I'VE SPENT A WHOLE LOT OF TIME DEBATING INSIDE MY HEAD WHETHER I'M TRULY ON THE SIDE OF THE ANGELS.
WHETHER I'M A GOOD GUY.
ON THE ONE HAND, I DON'T LIKE TO SEE INNOCENT PEOPLE HURT, I CAN'T ABIDE ENSLAVEMENT IN ANY FORM AND I GENUINELY WANT TO DO GOOD.
THEN THERE'S ANOTHER PART OF ME. MANIPULATIVE. PETTY. WITHOUT PITY OR MERCY.
TIME AND AGAIN, A KILLER.
I KNOW GOOD AND EVIL, THESE BLACK-AND-WHITE CONCEPTS, THEY'RE JUST THAT--CONCEPTS. NO ONE'S ENTIRELY ONE OR THE OTHER. AND YET I STRESS MYSELF OUT ASPIRING TO THE ONE EXTREME.
WELL, THAT'S JUST SILLY, ISN'T IT? IT'S ALL WELL AND GOOD TO ASPIRE TO BE A GOOD PERSON, BUT TO ACTUALLY EXPECT IT AS A REASONABLE OUTCOME...?
SO THIS IS WHAT I'M THINKING NOW. THIS IS A GOAL I CAN ACHIEVE FAIRLY EASILY, AND WITH MINIMAL STRESS.
I THINK, ANYWAY.
I'M GOING TO DO WHAT I KNOW TO BE RIGHT. WHEN THE MOMENT'S IN FRONT OF ME, I WON'T HESITATE.
I WON'T DO WHAT I DID ON MY LAST DAY AT TITANS TOWER, AND I WON'T DO WHAT I DID EARLIER TODAY.
WILL...

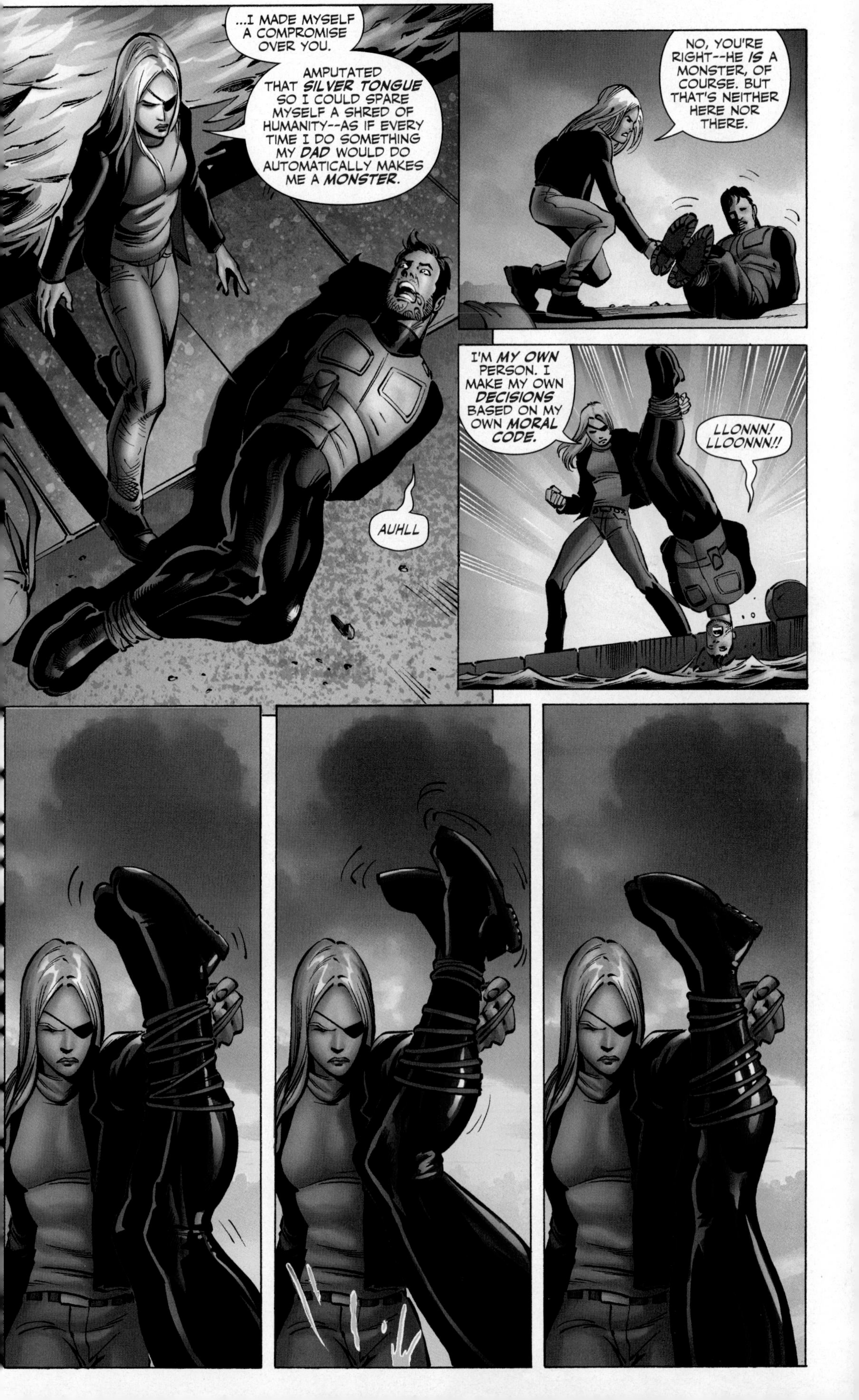
...I MADE MYSELF A COMPROMISE OVER YOU.
AMPUTATED THAT SILVER TONGUE SO I COULD SPARE MYSELF A SHRED OF HUMANITY--AS IF EVERY TIME I DO SOMETHING MY DAD WOULD DO AUTOMATICALLY MAKES ME A MONSTER.
AUHLL
NO, YOU'RE RIGHT--HE IS A MONSTER, OF COURSE. BUT THAT'S NEITHER HERE NOR THERE.
I'M MY OWN PERSON. I MAKE MY OWN DECISIONS BASED ON MY OWN MORAL CODE.
LLONNN! LLOONNN!!

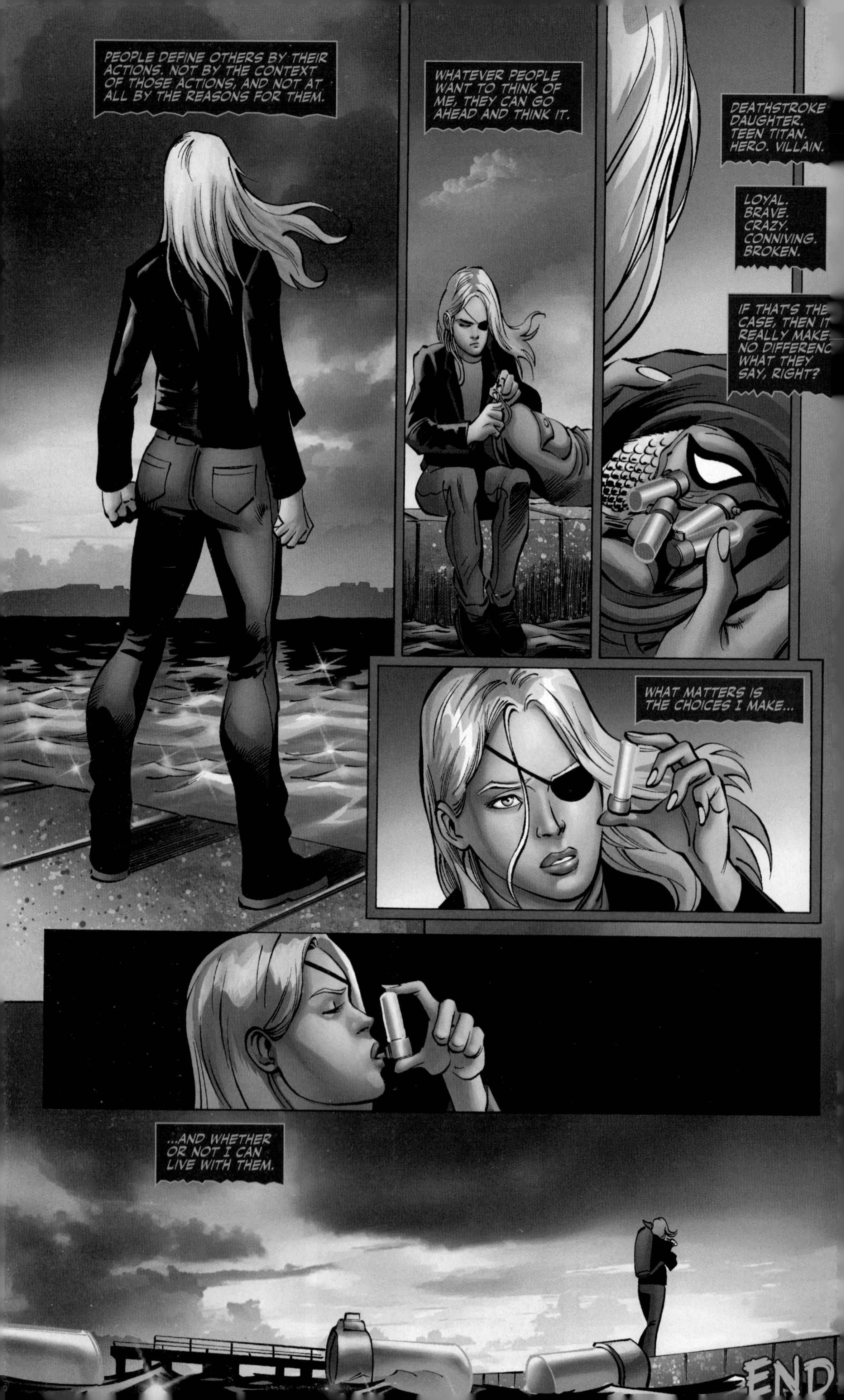
PEOPLE DEFINE OTHERS BY THEIR ACTIONS. NOT BY THE CONTEXT OF THOSE ACTIONS, AND NOT AT ALL BY THE REASONS FOR THEM.
WHATEVER PEOPLE WANT TO THINK OF ME, THEY CAN GO AHEAD AND THINK IT.
DEATHSTROKE DAUGHTER. TEEN TITAN. HERO. VILLAIN.
LOYAL. BRAVE. CRAZY. CONNIVING. BROKEN.
WHAT MATTERS IS THE CHOICES I MAKE...
...AND WHETHER OR NOT I CAN LIVE WITH THEM.
END